The Enlightened Mind

Education in the Long Eighteenth Century

Edited by

Amanda Strasik
Eastern Kentucky University

Series on the History of Art
Vernon Press

www.vernonpress.com

In the Americas:
Vernon Press
1000 N West Street, Suite 1200,
Wilmington, Delaware 19801
United States

In the rest of the world:
Vernon Press
C/Sancti Espiritu 17,
Malaga, 29006
Spain

Series on the History of Art

Library of Congress Control Number: 2022941597

ISBN: 978-1-64889-699-6

Also available: 978-1-64889-514-2 [Hardback]; 978-1-64889-535-7 [PDF, E-Book]

Cover design by Vernon Press.

Cover image: Jeanne-Elisabeth Chaudet, *Little Girl Teaching her Dog to Read*, 1799. Oil on panel, Location unknown. Wikimedia Commons. Public Domain.

Table of Contents

List of Figures

About the Editor

Amanda Strasik is an Associate Professor of Art History at Eastern Kentucky University. She received her Ph.D. in eighteenth- and nineteenth-century European art history from the University of Iowa in 2016. Her research focuses on representations of royalty, childhood and family relationships, and issues of gender identity in French art during the long eighteenth century. Strasik has received numerous grants and fellowships to conduct research in France at the Musée du Louvre, the National Museum of the History of Education in Rouen, the Palace of Versailles, as well as The Frick Collection in New York City. She has presented her work at the Art Institute of Chicago, The Cedar Rapids Museum of Art, and conferences for the American Society for Eighteenth-Century Studies and the Historians of Eighteenth-Century Art and Architecture, where she served on the executive board as the organization's first secretary. Strasik's scholarly publications explore notions of female agency in eighteenth-century French genre painting and portraiture and have appeared in *Women and French Studies, New Perspectives on the Eighteenth Century, Art Inquiries,* and, most recently, *Eighteenth-Century Life* with Duke University Press.

About the Contributors

Dorothy Johnson

Roy J. Carver Professor of Art History
The University of Iowa

Dorothy Johnson is Roy J. Carver Professor of Art History at the University of Iowa. She received her Ph.D. from the University of California, Berkeley, where she later taught as visiting professor. Her area of specialization is eighteenth and nineteenth-century French and European art. She has published articles on Chardin, the Romantic child, Rousseau and landscape painting, myth in French art, David d'Angers, Delacroix, Géricault, Jacques-Louis David, and most recently, on art and anatomy in France. She is the author of *Jacques-Louis David: Art in Metamorphosis* (Princeton University Press, 1993), *Jacques-Louis David: the Farewell of Telemachus and Eucharis* (Getty Museum Monograph Series, 1997) and is editor and contributing author of *Jacques-Louis David: New Perspectives* (University of Delaware Press, 2006). Her book, *David to Delacroix: the Rise of Romantic Mythology* (UNC Press) appeared in 2011 and won the Choice Outstanding Academic Title Award. Her articles and essays have appeared in *The Art Bulletin, Art History, Gazette des Beaux-Arts, Eighteenth-Century Studies, Master Drawings, The Cambridge Companion to Delacroix, Studies in Voltaire and the Eighteenth Century,* among others. Recent essays in edited volumes include "The Body Speaks: Anatomical Narratives in French Enlightenment Sculpture" (in *Body Narratives. Motion and Emotion in the French Enlightenment,* Brepols Press, 2017), "Visceral Visions: Art, Pedagogy, and Politics in Revolutionary France", in *Bellies, bowels, and entrails in the Eighteenth Century* (Manchester University Press, 2018), "Food for Thought: Consuming and Digesting as Political Metaphor in French Satirical Prints", in *Gut Feeling and Digestive Health in Nineteenth-Century Literature, History and Culture*", (Palgrave, 2018) and "Fabulations of the Flesh: Géricault and the Praxis of Art and Anatomy", in *Visualizing the Body in Art, Anatomy and Medicine since 1800: Models, Modelling,* (Routledge, 2019). She is currently working on a book on art and anatomy in France from 1750-1850.

Amanda Strasik

Associate Professor of Art History
Eastern Kentucky University

Amanda Strasik is an Associate Professor of Art History at Eastern Kentucky University. She received her Ph.D. in eighteenth- and nineteenth-century

European art history from the University of Iowa in 2016. Her research focuses on representations of royalty, childhood and family relationships, and issues of gender identity in French art during the long eighteenth century. Strasik has received numerous grants and fellowships to conduct research in France at the Musée du Louvre, the National Museum of the History of Education in Rouen, the Palace of Versailles, as well as The Frick Collection in New York City. She has presented her work at the Art Institute of Chicago, The Cedar Rapids Museum of Art, and conferences for the American Society for Eighteenth-Century Studies and the Historians of Eighteenth-Century Art and Architecture, where she served on the executive board as the organization's first secretary. Strasik's scholarly publications explore notions of female agency in eighteenth-century French genre painting and portraiture and have appeared in *Women and French Studies*, *New Perspectives on the Eighteenth Century*, *Art Inquiries*, and, most recently, *Eighteenth-Century Life* with Duke University Press.

Rachel Harmeyer

Ph.D. Candidate
Rice University

Rachel Harmeyer is a Ph.D. Candidate in Art History at Rice University. She earned her BFA from The School of the Art Institute of Chicago (2008) and holds an MA in Art History from the University of Houston (2013). Her primary focus is on the transatlantic circulation of visual and material culture during the long eighteenth century between Britain and the United States. Her doctoral thesis, *After Angelica Kauffman*, explores the ways in which the work of Angelica Kauffman, RA (1741-1807) 'went viral' in global eighteenth- and nineteenth-century visual and material culture, inspiring decorative and amateur artists to employ a wide variety of media to reiterate her designs, from stipple engravings and mechanical paintings to handpainted fans, British and Chinese export porcelain, silk embroideries, and ephemeral confections. Harmeyer's investigation of the "angelicamad" world will contribute to an examination of the late eighteenth-century culture of copying, consumption, and Kauffman's celebrity and legacy within and beyond Georgian Britain.

Brigitte Weltman-Aron

Professor of French and Francophone Studies
The University of Florida

Brigitte Weltman-Aron is a Professor of French and Francophone studies at the University of Florida, and the author of several articles and book chapters in literature, history, and philosophy. She published *On Other Grounds: Landscape Gardening and Nationalism in Eighteenth-Century England and* France (SUNY Press, 2001), co-edited with Laurence Mall a special issue of *L'esprit créateur* on

Rousseau and Emotions. De l'émotion chez Rousseau (vol. 52, no. 4, Winter 2012). She also specializes in contemporary francophone literature, and among other publications in that field, she is the author of *Algerian Imprints: Ethical Space in the Works of Assia Djebar and Hélène Cixous* (Columbia University Press, 2015).

Franny Brock

Ph.D. Candidate
University of North Carolina, Chapel Hill

Franny Brock is a Ph.D. candidate at the University of North Carolina, Chapel Hill, specializing in eighteenth-century French art and works on paper. She was advised by Dr. Mary D. Sheriff until Dr. Sheriff's passing in fall 2016. Her dissertation, entitled "Drawing the Amateur," is now supervised by Dr. Melissa Hyde (The University of Florida). Franny's project examines drawings made by amateurs, particularly women, working outside of the Académie royale de peinture et de sculpture in eighteenth-century France. Before arriving at UNC, Franny completed her BA in Art History at Oberlin College and her MA in the History of Art at The Courtauld Institute of Art in London. She completed her master's degree in eighteenth-century French and British drawings, taught by Dr. Katie Scott and Professor David Solkin. Franny has held positions at the Allen Memorial Art Museum, The Frick Collection, the Dallas Museum of Art, and the Ackland Art Museum. She has curated and co-curated a number of exhibitions, including "Visions of Antiquity in the Eighteenth Century" at the Dallas Museum of Art and "Celebrations and Revelries in Seventeenth-Century Dutch art" at the Ackland Art Museum. She also has expertise in student and faculty support, through her work at the UNC Writing and Learning Center and the Center for Faculty Excellence.

Madeline Sutherland-Meier

Associate Professor
Department of Spanish and Portuguese, University of Texas at Austin

Madeline Sutherland-Meier is an Associate Professor in the Department of Spanish and Portuguese at the University of Texas at Austin. Her area of specialization is Spanish literature, with particular interests in the Spanish Ballad or *Romancero* and eighteenth-century Spanish literature and periodicals. She also works in Disability Studies. She has collected ballads in the *pueblos* of Spain and has published on the modern oral tradition, including the Judeo-Spanish tradition, and the *romance de ciego* or blindman's ballad. She has also written on the relationship between high culture and mass culture in early modern Spain. The eighteenth-century writer and editor Antonio Valladares de Sotomayor has been the focus of her most recent research as has the history of the blind in Spain. She is the author of *Mass Culture in the Age of Enlightenment: The Blindman's Ballads of Eighteenth-Century Spain* and co-editor of *Leo Spitzer: Representative Essays.*

Karissa E. Bushman

Assistant Professor of Art History
Quinnipiac University

Karissa E. Bushman is an assistant professor of art history at Quinnipiac University. Her research focuses on the artwork of Francisco de Goya. Much of her research on Goya has dealt with his complex relationship with religion during the age of the Enlightenment and her dissertation was on his depictions of anticlericalism. She is also working on a monograph of Goya's various depictions of the human body.

Acknowledgements

This edited volume began as an interdisciplinary panel on education during the long eighteenth century that I co-organized with Karissa Bushman for the 2020 American Society for Eighteenth Century Studies (ASECS) conference in St. Louis, Missouri. My idea for this panel's inception grew from research on bourgeois girls' education in eighteenth-century Paris that I had conducted in 2019 at the Musée National de L'Éducation (MUNAÉ) in Rouen, France. This research was generously supported by a University Funded Scholarship Faculty Mini-Grant from Eastern Kentucky University.

While the COVID-19 global pandemic forced organizers to cancel the 2020 ASECS conference, our panel convened in 2021 at the virtual ASECS meeting and was a sweeping success. I wish to thank panel participants Franny Brock, Dorothy Johnson, Madeline Sutherland-Meier, and Brigitte Weltman-Aron for their flexibility and good spirits, both at the conference during a time of worldwide uncertainty and throughout the development of this project. Expanded versions of their original presentations can be found within this volume. I am also grateful for Rachel Harmeyer and Karissa Bushman, whose essays here have sparked new and lively discourses. Indeed, I am deeply indebted to all of the contributors to this collection, who not only joined me in rethinking meanings and implications of "education" during the Enlightenment era but demonstrated great understanding, insight, and patience at every turn. To Vernon Press, namely Blanca Caro Duran, Argiris Legatos, and Rosario Batana, I am forever appreciative of your counsel, support, and unwavering professionalism throughout the duration of this project. I also want to express my sincerest gratitude to the anonymous readers at Vernon Press for their invaluable feedback. And finally, I thank Christopher Richards, Elizabeth Spear, Ilona Szekely, and Patrick and Leslie Strasik for teaching me something new along the way.

The Enlightened Mind: Introduction

Amanda Strasik

Eastern Kentucky University

The rise of Enlightenment philosophical and scientific thought during the long eighteenth century in Europe and North America (c. 1688-1815) sparked artistic and political revolutions, reframed social, gender, and race relations, reshaped attitudes toward children and animals, and reconceptualized womanhood, marriage, and the family.[1] This movement also instituted new approaches to knowledge that emphasized rationality and empiricism over superstition, myth, and many religious traditions. As the period expanded global trade and commerce, introduced rapid technological changes, and fostered greater political freedoms (albeit to privileged population subsets), Enlightenment culture became synonymous with modernity in the West.[2]

The meaning of "education" at this time was wide-ranging and access to it was divided along the lines of gender, class, and race. As authors in this volume attest, learning happened in diverse environments under the tutelage of various teachers, ranging from bourgeois mothers at home, to Spanish clergy, to the outdoors and nature itself. For bourgeois and elite classes, approaches to education included instruction in specific academic, professional, and practical skillsets, as well as the advancement of physical health and mental wellness. For the female sex, the inculcation of virtue, along with the acquisition of manners and politeness, prevailed.[3] By 1750, new efforts to educate large swaths of the population were underway. Literacy rates climbed in urban areas and Paris became the center of intellectual exchange. French writings on the value of education emerged in different formats, namely Denis Diderot and Jean le Rond d'Alembert's authoritative *Encyclopédie*, with its lofty aim to systematize and make knowledge widely available, and pedagogical texts like Jean-Jacques Rousseau's *Emile, or On Education* (1762), which numerous contributors to this volume analyze. An explosion of printed materials on the natural and biological sciences, political treatises and memoirs, travel guides, novels and domestic advice pamphlets (many targeted at women), and more would have profound effects on artists, who engaged with these new ideas through dynamic visual imagery. French genre paintings of conjugal love and familial affection by artists like Jean-Baptiste Greuze, Marguerite Gérard, Etienne Aubry, and Jean-Honoré Fragonard were part of a visual campaign to educate elite and bourgeois audiences about the positive effects of these new social and cultural ideals.[4] The confluence of art and science became salient as artists and critics questioned the validity of anatomical instruction in art education at the Académie royale de peinture et de sculpture in Paris.

While ideologues advocated for unspoken access to knowledge and education, women, together with people of color and other socially vulnerable groups, faced barriers in their pursuits of institutionalized study. In the case of women, the Enlightenment's redefinition of bourgeois feminine identity led to fiery debates about what constituted womanhood (according to physiological, philosophical, and social concepts), women's roles in society, and how women were to participate in Enlightenment culture.[5] Middle- and upper-class women were not denied educational opportunities outright, but there were concerns about what subjects to teach girls, whether girls should learn in convents or privately at home, who was best suited to instruct girls, and for what purpose education served the female population.[6] In the first half of the eighteenth century in Paris, women helped to develop social and intellectual networks and created serious, collaborative working spaces for the French Republic of Letters. Career *salonnières* and friends of the Encyclopedists like Louise d'Epinay—who Brigitte Weltman-Aron and Amanda Strasik will address further in this volume—were educated in their own right. Through their organization and management of regular gatherings in private salons, these women became commanding facilitators of civil discourse that furthered the Enlightenment agenda.[7]

By the 1760s, some moralizing philosophes opposed women's powerful hand in guiding social reforms and called for them to return to the domestic sphere to serve as loving wives and devoted mothers. Children were now considered to be inherently innocent and women alone faced the unprecedented responsibility of shaping society's moral future by caring for and educating their young ones at home. This sweeping appeal for women to fulfill their "natural destinies"—however marginalized—also functioned politically to exclude women from public life, due to the looming fear of uncontrolled female authority, sexual unruliness, and the overt feminization of French social and intellectual life.[8] In his 1758 *Lettre à M. D'Alembert*, Rousseau warned against the social corruption that resulted from immodest women who pursued ambitions beyond the household. He wrote:

> There are no good morals for women outside of a withdrawn and domestic life; if I saw that the peaceful care of the family and the home are their lot, that the dignity of their Sex consists in modesty, that shame and chasteness are inseparable from decency for them, that when they seek for men's looks they are already letting themselves be corrupted by them, and that any woman who shows herself off disgraces herself.[9]

With strong allusions to the act of prostitution, such commentary complicated the identity of women and their place in society. Excessive ambition, exposure to institutionalized learning, or engagements with subjects beyond those required for the cultivation of feminine traits could endanger women's modesty. Rousseau's critique of public women especially relates to professional women artists that solicited clients and publicly displayed and sold their artworks, which doubled as extensions of themselves.[10]

The contributors to this cross-disciplinary volume weave together methods in art history, women and gender studies, and literary analysis to reexamine "education" in different contexts during the age of Enlightenment. They explore the implications of redesigned curricula, educational categorizations and spaces, pedagogical aids and games, the role of religion, and new prospects for visual artists, parents, children, and society at large. Collectively, the authors demonstrate – many for the first time in their fields – how learning reforms transformed not just familial structures and the socio-political conditions of major European cities, but redefined traditional artistic practices and women's roles as creators. The volume begins with Dorothy Johnson's overview of eighteenth-century debates about the teaching of anatomy to aspirant artists of the French Academy in Paris. Some feared that knowledge of the human body's interior, obtained through dissection and direct observation of cadavers, would corrupt notions of ideal beauty that artists were expected to attain. By midcentury, rising interests in natural science, the intellectual and social cachet of medical study, and the revival of classicism, once again led audiences to reflect upon the necessity of anatomical lessons to create ideal beauty. Johnson points to the French sculptor Jean Antoine Houdon who, together with a surgeon in 1767, created a life-size *Ecorché* figure to function as a pedagogical tool, demonstrating that naturalism, mimesis, and ideal beauty could co-exist in artistic creation.

Several authors consider how women intervened in Enlightenment culture as artists, pedagogical writers, teachers, activists, and consumers of enlightened textual and visual materials. Amanda Strasik and Rachel Harmeyer's analyses of women artists and their works in this volume, including French genre painter Jeanne-Elisabeth Chaudet (1761-1832) and embroiderers Caroline Williams (1789-1825), Lucy Coit Huntington (1794-1818), and Maria Crowninshield (1789-1870) from Britain and the United States, demonstrate how the Enlightenment paradox of progress and restriction affected women's lives. Against the backdrop of widespread misogyny, along with serious legal and social obstacles ushered in by the French Revolution (1789-1799), women found ways to navigate patriarchal systems and gendered rules to exercise personal agency. In Chapter Two, Strasik establishes that modern-day feminist art historians have not paid much attention to Chaudet's artistic identity, despite the artist's connection to Empress Joséphine Bonaparte, one of the most important patrons that supported women artists in late eighteenth- and early nineteenth-century France. Chaudet's subjects feature meaningful dialogues with Enlightenment discourses on girlhood, female sexuality and education, dolls as pedagogical toys, and the rise of petkeeping. At the 1799 French Salon—distinct for its record number of female exhibitors—Chaudet's *Little Girl Teaching her Dog to Read* captured critics' attention. One observer regarded the depicted girl's lapdog as her "doll and victim" while another doubted her virtue. These comments call attention to viewers' deep concerns over corrupted innocence in the education of girls, thus revealing the social magnitude of Chaudet's seemingly lighthearted genre painting—a subject that was historically more accessible to women artists but disparaged for its lack of intellectual and technical rigor. Strasik argues that as a genre painter of children and small animals, Chaudet inserts herself into Enlightenment discourse without transgressing the bounds of feminine propriety. Moreover, Chaudet's subject matter in *Little Girl Teaching* parallels her real-life experience as a women artist in post-revolutionary Paris, where Chaudet paradoxically faced new professional opportunities and severe limitations and prejudices at the same time.

Harmeyer's essay further contributes to this volume's discussions of women's education, challenges to the hierarchy of genres, and female artistic agency. She examines how British feminist writers like Catherine Macaulay (1731–1791), Hannah More (1745-1833), and Mary Wollstonecraft (1759-1797), in their demands for women's educational reforms, cited the superficiality of needlework and other feminine accomplishment arts as the flaw in women's education. Harmeyer contends that women's embroideries did not have to be viewed as purely ornamental and derivative. Women embroiderers' techniques and interpretations of existing subjects indicate their ambitious approaches to artmaking and a negotiation of gender expectations. Harmeyer identifies a subset of women embroiderers in Britain and the United States that re-presented Angelica Kauffman's *Hector and Andromache*, a neoclassical history painting shown publicly at the British Royal Academy's 1769 exhibition. By adapting elements of Kauffman's didactic and moralizing narrative as their needleworks' subjects, the aforementioned Caroline Williams, Lucy Coit Huntington, and Maria Crowninshield created a cross-continental fellowship of women artists. Their works highlighted strong heroines while functioning as models of eighteenth-century ideal femininity. Harmeyer believes that these women helped to elevate what was customarily a denigrated artform to a more serious endeavor, thus expressing their erudition and virtue from within an appropriately feminine framework.

Macaulay, More, and Wollstonecraft were part of a cohort of British and French women writers, whose publications on education vehemently denounced current pedagogical practices that were steeped in prejudice and outmoded traditions. These women reformers wrote to communicate with and help other women; to improve women's education, they proposed more progressive programs, bolder teaching methods, and new learning resources like game play, visual aids, and the development of children's books.[11] In France, by the end of the century, the general opinion on female pedagogy promoted the domestic education of girls and the crucial roles of women as domestic educators.[12] Stéphanie-Félicité, the Comtesse de Genlis, was a prolific writer whose novels and treatises on childhood education circulated widely throughout France and Britain. Franny Brock analyzes Genlis's 1800 treatise, *A New Method of Instruction for Children from Five to Ten Years Old*, alongside visual representations of children's drawing lessons, especially those for girls. While Genlis had no formal artistic training herself, she designed new processes for teaching children how to draw that emphasized amusement and entertainment to create a refined sense of judgment in her students. Brock explores how Genlis's techniques in *A New Method* engage with the Enlightenment reconceptualization of childhood and the development of children's pedagogy. Brock also mentions draftsmanship training for both boys and girls as a professional endeavor, or as a way to generate income for themselves and their families. Newly founded free drawing schools in Paris publicized drawing as a practical skill instead of one that cultivated personal refinement. Like Strasik and Harmeyer, Brock draws attention to the paradox of girls' education, access to art training, and the purpose of what girls could hope to achieve with their art.

Brigitte Weltman-Aron follows this investigative thread as she examines children's pedagogy and the upbringing of girls in Louise d'Epinay's (1726-1783) *Conversations d'Emilie* (1774), which won the prix Montyon in 1783 shortly before her death. Specifically, Weltman-Aron observes the author's response to Rousseau's recommendations of gendered outdoor activities for children in his treatise *Emile.* Weltman-Aron emphasizes D'Epinay's focus on girls' need to openly play, exercise, and develop physical strength in nature just as Rousseau's Sophie—Emile's female counterpart introduced to readers in Book V of *Emile*—while addressing to self-control during gameplay, beginning at an early age. In fact, Rousseau mostly examines outdoor activity in boys' "natural education." By contrast, in *Conversations,* D'Epinay recommends a series of outings that are educationally beneficial to little girls, revealing that "outside" has different meanings, particularly for upper-class French girls who lived in urban landscapes.

This volume's final two essays discuss key artists and pedagogical theorists of Enlightenment Spain.[13] Ideas on shifting perceptions of childhood, childcare, and the role of the family in early phases of children's education circulated against the backdrop of Catholicism. Given the Spanish crown's French roots, the Bourbon king Charles III (r.1759-1788) ruled Spain as an enlightened monarch. Charles III was sympathetic to change and employed ministers like José Moñino, the Count of Floridablanca, that supported progressive economic, industrial, and agricultural reforms. The renowned eighteenth-century Spanish artist Francisco de Goya (1746-1828), who Karissa Bushman will discuss in greater detail, came of age during this era of Enlightenment.

Significantly, during his childhood, Goya was likely enrolled in Spain's Pious Schools – one of the first free public schools in Europe that José de Calasanz, a Spanish Catholic priest and later venerated saint, originally founded in Rome in 1597. Calasanz strongly believed in free education for the poor across religions, and his initiative radically challenged class privileges that had long favored the wealthy. Curriculum at the Pious Schools featured instruction in religion alongside general subjects like reading, writing, and mathematics. Bushman suggests that Goya's attendance at this institution as a boy influenced his strong Catholic beliefs and approaches to religious painting. Later in life, once his artistic career was underway, Goya painted José de Calasanz, thereby suggesting an ideological kinship between the two.

Meanwhile, Madeline Sutherland-Meier's essay focuses on Spanish scholar and Benedictine monk Martín Sarmiento (1695-1772) and his thoughts on education from his publication *Discurso sobre el método que debia guardarse en la primera educación de la juventud* (1768). Sarmiento asserted that education should be a happy, fulfilling experience, where young students embraced and studied even the most difficult subjects to become lifelong learners. Sutherland-Meier notes that families, particularly mothers, fathers, and possibly an uncle in the clergy, played a significant role in children's early educations. Parents' duties included instilling the fear of God and respectful behaviors in their young ones, in addition to overseeing their physical health. Similar to the French pedagogical writers addressed in this volume, Sarmiento stresses the importance of maternal attachment and breastfeeding, thereby granting women an essential duty based on their sex.

As I have briefly outlined here, the seven contributors to this volume express ideas that frequently echo one another; at other times, they diverge entirely. Themes on children's pedagogy, artistic instruction, girlhood, and the plight of women artists and writers continuously surface, thus establishing a clear foundation for understanding the complexity of education for various populations during the period of Enlightenment in Western culture.

Notes

[1] Literature on the Enlightenment is vast and cannot be fully listed in this space. Two comprehensive sources are Dena Goodman and Kathleen Anne Wellman, eds., *The Enlightenment* (Boston: Wadsworth, Cengage Learning, 2004) and Dorinda Outram, *Enlightenment*, 4th ed. (Cambridge University Press, 2019). On women during the Enlightenment, see Margaret R. Hunt, *Women in Eighteenth-Century Europe* (London: Routledge, 2014). For a more global approach to Enlightenment studies, consult Lauren

R. Cannady and Jennifer Ferng, eds., *Crafting Enlightenment: Artisanal Histories and Transnational Networks* (Liverpool: Voltaire Foundation in Association with Liverpool University Press, 2021).

[2] We must recognize that the atrocities of eighteenth-century colonialism and the barbarity of the slave trade contradicted this idea of an enlightened, civilized, and modern European identity. See Dena Goodman, "Women and the Enlightenment," in *Becoming Visible: Women in European History*, eds. Renate Bridenthal, Susan Mosher Stuard, and Merry E. Wiesner (Boston: Houghton Mifflin, 1998), 239-242.

[3] Michèle Cohen, "Introduction," in *Journal for Eighteenth-Century Studies, Special Virtual Issue: Education in the Eighteenth Century* (2008): 1-4. Also see Dena Goodman, *The Republic of Letters: A Cultural History of the French Enlightenment* (Ithaca: Cornell University, 1996) and Adrian O'Connor, *In Pursuit of Politics: Education and Revolution in Eighteenth-Century France* (Manchester: Manchester University Press, 2019). A study of the education of members of lower social classes (e.g. urban laborers and rural peasantry) is mostly beyond the scope of this volume; however, educational opportunities for the Spanish poor are briefly addressed. Franny Brock, in Chapter Four of this volume, mentions free drawing schools in Paris. For more information on this topic in Enlightenment France, see Harvey Chisick, *The Limits of Reform in the Enlightenment: Attitudes Toward the Education of the Lower Classes in Eighteenth-Century France*, rev. ed. (Princeton: Princeton University Press, 2014).

[4] Carol Duncan, "Happy Mothers and Other New Ideas in French Art," *The Art Bulletin* 55, no. 4 (Dec 1973): 570-583.

[5] Goodman, "Women and the Enlightenment," 233-262. Also refer to Melissa Hyde, "Questions about the 'Woman Question': Déjà-Vu All over Again?," in *Becoming a Woman in the Age of Enlightenment: French Art from the Horvitz Collection*, eds. Melissa Hyde and Mary Sheriff. (The Horvitz Collection, 2017), 13-17 and Barbara Taylor and Sarah Knott, eds. *Women, Gender and Enlightenment* (Basingstoke: Palgrave Macmillan, 2007).

[6] Samia Spencer, "Women and Education," in *French Women and the Age of Enlightenment*, ed. Samia Spencer (Bloomington: Indiana University Press, 1984), 83-96.

[7] The London bluestocking circles of women also carried out a similar function. For more on these powerful women and their prominent roles in the Enlightenment Republic of Letters in France and England, see Goodman, "Women and the Enlightenment," 234-237. Also, Dena Goodman, "Enlightenment Salons: The Convergence of Female and Philosophic Ambitions," *Eighteenth-Century Studies* 22, no. 3 (1989): 329-50.

[8] In Europe, thinkers like Jean-Jacques Rousseau, Diderot, Antoine Léonard Thomas, and numerous women writers weighed in on the Woman Question. For further reading, refer to Melissa Hyde and Jennifer Milam, "Introduction: Art, Cultural Politics, and The Woman Question," in *Women, Art, and the Politics of Identity in Eighteenth-Century Europe*, eds. Melissa Hyde and Jennifer Milam (Ashgate, 2003), 1-19.

[9] Jean-Jacques Rousseau, "Letter to D'Alembert and writings for the theater," in *The Collected Writings of Rousseau*, eds. Roger D. Masters and Christopher Kelly (Hanover: University Press of New England, 1990), 311-312.

[10] In her study of Elisabeth Vigée-Lebrun, Mary Sheriff discusses the reconciliation of the public and private identities of female artists. See Mary Sheriff, *The Exceptional Woman: Elisabeth Vigée-Lebrun and the Cultural Politics of Art* (Chicago, 1996), 39-71.

[11] Spencer, "Women and Education," 88.

[12] Samia Spencer, "Introduction," in *French Women and the Age of Enlightenment,* ed. Samia Spencer (Bloomington: Indiana University Press, 1984), 14-16.

[13] For more context on Enlightenment discourse in Spain, see Jesús Astigarraga, *The Spanish Enlightenment Revisited* (Oxford: Voltaire Foundation, 2015). Also consult Francisco Sanchez-Blanco, *La Ilustración goyesca: La cultura en España durante el reinado de Carlos IV (1788-1808)* (Madrid): Consejo Superior de Investigaciones Científicas, 2007) and Francisco Aguilar Piñal, *La España del Absolutismo Ilustrado* (Madrid: Colección Austral, 2005). I thank Karissa Bushman for recommending Sanchez-Blanco and Aguilar Piñal's texts.

Bibliography

Aguilar Piñal, Francisco. *La España del Absolutismo Ilustrado.* Madrid: Colección Austral, 2005.

Astigarraga, Jesús. *The Spanish Enlightenment Revisited.* Oxford: Voltaire Foundation, 2015.

Cannady, Lauren R. and Jennifer Ferng, eds. *Crafting Enlightenment: Artisanal Histories and Transnational Networks.* Liverpool: Voltaire Foundation in Association with Liverpool University Press, 2021.

Chisick, Harvey. *The Limits of Reform in the Enlightenment: Attitudes Toward the Education of the Lower Classes in Eighteenth-Century France.* Rev. ed. Princeton: Princeton University Press, 2014.

Cohen, Michèle. "Introduction." In *Journal for Eighteenth-Century Studies, Special Virtual Issue: Education in the Eighteenth Century* (2008): 1-6.

Duncan, Carol. "Happy Mothers and Other New Ideas in French Art." *The Art Bulletin* 55, no. 4 (Dec 1973): 570-583.

Goodman, Dena. "Enlightenment Salons: The Convergence of Female and Philosophic Ambitions." *Eighteenth-Century Studies* 22, no. 3 (1989): 329-50.

________. *The Republic of Letters: A Cultural History of the French Enlightenment.* Ithaca: Cornell University, 1996.

________. "Women and the Enlightenment." In *Becoming Visible: Women in European History,* edited by Renate Bridenthal, Susan Mosher Stuard, and Merry E. Wiesner, 233-262. Boston: Houghton Mifflin, 1998.

________. and Kathleen Anne Wellman, eds., *The Enlightenment.* Boston: Wadsworth, Cengage Learning, 2004.

Hunt, Margaret R. *Women in Eighteenth-Century Europe.* London: Routledge, 2014.

Hyde, Melissa and Jennifer Milam. "Introduction: Art, Cultural Politics, and The Woman Question." In *Women, Art, and the Politics of Identity in Eighteenth-Century Europe,* edited by Melissa Hyde and Jennifer Milam, 1-19. Ashgate, 2003.

________. and Mary Sheriff, eds. *Becoming a Woman in the Age of Enlightenment: French Art from the Horvitz Collection.* The Horvitz Collection, 2017.

O'Connor, Adrian. *In Pursuit of Politics: Education and Revolution in Eighteenth-Century France.* Manchester: Manchester University Press, 2019.

Outram, Dorinda. *Enlightenment.* 4th ed. Cambridge University Press, 2019.

Rousseau, Jean-Jacques, "Letter to D'Alembert and writings for the theater." In *The Collected Writings of Rousseau,* edited by Roger D. Masters and Christopher Kelly, Volume 10. Hanover: University Press of New England, 1990.

Sanchez-Blanco, Francisco. *La Ilustración goyesca: La cultura en España durante el reinado de Carlos IV (1788-1808).* Madrid: Consejo Superior de Investigaciones Científicas, 2007.

Sheriff, Mary. *The Exceptional Woman: Elisabeth Vigée-Lebrun and the Cultural Politics of Art.* Chicago, 1996.

Spencer, Samia, ed. *French Women and the Age of Enlightenment.* Bloomington: Indiana University Press, 1984.

Taylor, Barbara and Sarah Knott, eds. *Women, Gender and Enlightenment.* Basingstoke: Palgrave Macmillan, 2007.

Chapter 1

Anatomy Lessons: Teaching Anatomy to Artists in Eighteenth-Century France

Dorothy Johnson

The University of Iowa

Abstract

This article addresses the fluctuating fortunes of the teaching of anatomy at the Académie royale de peinture et de sculpture in eighteenth-century France from its suppression in 1737 to its re-establishment in the curriculum after mid-century. Important sculptors, such as Bouchardon and Houdon, created écorchés as pedagogical tools and promulgated anatomical study at a time when critics of its teaching, including the leading *philosophe* of the time, Diderot, warned against the aesthetic dangers of visualizing what lies beneath the skin which could detract from the prevailing goals of ideal beauty in the representation of the human figure. After mid-century, however, books of anatomical plates began to proliferate and surgeons taught dissection to art students in new ways. During this period, when the prestige of medicine and the natural sciences was ascendant, the conundrum confronting pedagogy was how to make visible and re-animate the "dead subject" in a way that was useful to the arts.

Keywords: Anatomical plate, Bouchardon, Dissection, Ecorché, Houdon

***

The complex and contested history of teaching anatomy to artists at the Académie royale de peinture et de sculpture in eighteenth-century France is a subject that has inspired recent attention amid a general resurgence of interest in the visual culture of anatomy from the Renaissance to the present day.[1] Eighteenth-century France, in particular, which witnessed continual changes in art, culture, politics, and the natural sciences, offers a fertile ground for exploring anatomical propadeutics in the visual arts. The fluctuating history of the teaching of anatomy at the Académie is characterized by key moments of transformation effected through the interventions of a small number of artists, theorists, thinkers, critics, and even surgeons. The ideas governing the pedagogical merits of anatomy as integral to the art curriculum were based on beliefs concerning the best methods of achieving the goals of naturalism combined with ideal beauty in the depiction of the human figure, seen throughout much of the Enlightenment period in France as a foundational principal in painting and sculpture. These ideas that informed the curriculum changed over time and were influenced by many factors – aesthetic, cultural, and ideological. This essay addresses a few salient episodes in this fascinating development that reveal beliefs about the representation of the human figure and how best to teach student artists the conventions governing corporal form.

A pivotal moment in this history, one that has not been given requisite attention, occurred in 1737 when the Académie royale de peinture et de sculpture suppressed the teaching of anatomy in its curriculum.[2] Two years later, at the Salon of 1739, the King's sculptor, Edme Bouchardon, who famously created the monumental bronze equestrian of his patron, Louis XV, exhibited a terra cotta version of *Amor Carving his Bow from the Club of Hercules* (Fig. 1.1).[3]

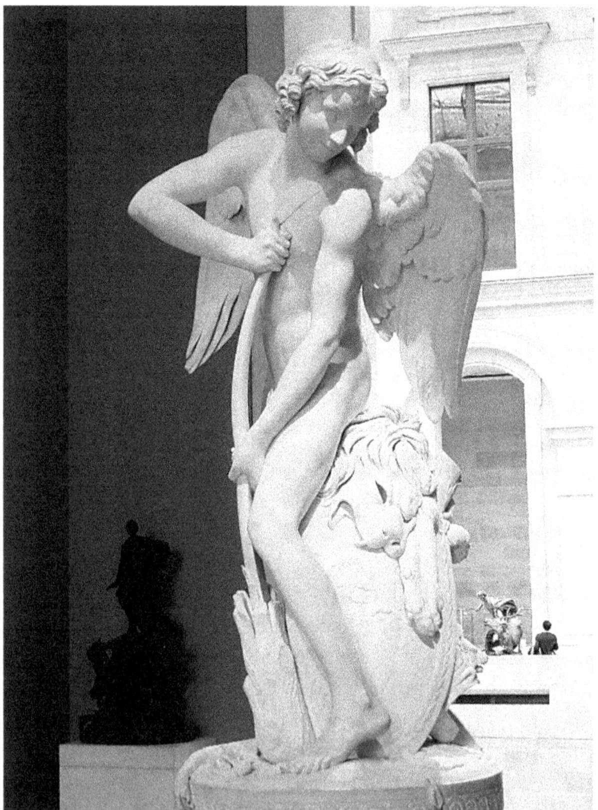

Figure 1.1: Edme Bouchardon, *Amor Carving his Bow from the Club of Hercules*, 1739-1750. Musée du Louvre. Wikimedia Commons. Public Domain

In 1740 he received the royal commission for a marble version, but work was delayed until 1745 due to his other ongoing projects. In 1741, Bouchardon's

L'Anatomie nécessaire pour les arts du dessein appeared, a publication that I believe constituted an effort to counter the Académie's decision about anatomical teaching and to reinstate the teaching of anatomy to artists.[4] What does *Amor Carving his Bow*, begun in 1739 and completed in 1750, destined to be seen as Bouchardon's most exquisite work, have in common with his anatomy manual for artists, a manual accompanied by a small-scale replica of his sculpted *Ecorché* (Fig. 1.2)? In looking at *Amor* and the *Ecorché* side by side, it is hard to imagine that they were made by the same artist. But I believe it is important to look at these works together, for they reveal Bouchardon's profound engagement with anatomy and its importance in the creation of ideal beauty in the human form.

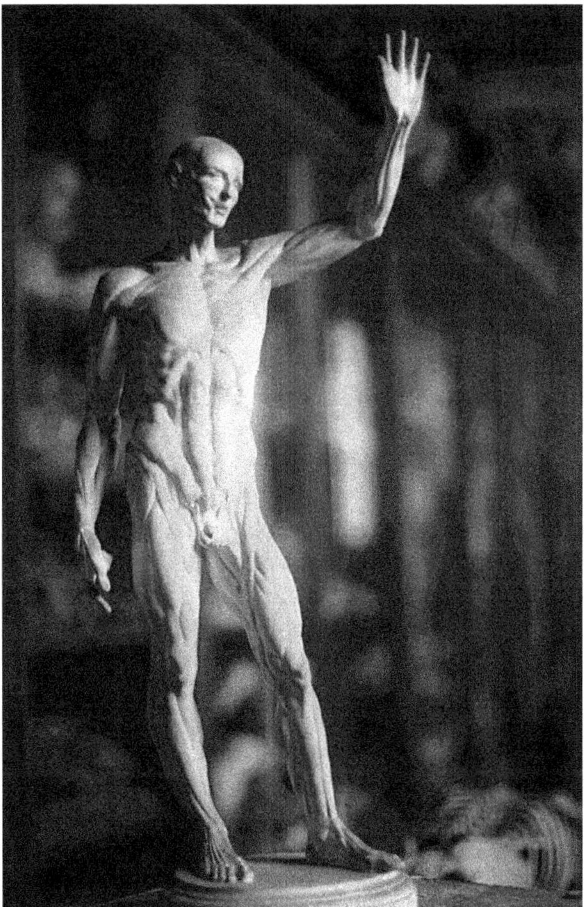

Figure 1.2: Edme Bouchardon, *Ecorché*, ca. 1740. Ecole Nationale Supérieure des Beaux Arts, Paris. Photo: Jacques de Caso

Bouchardon lavished an enormous amount of time on *Amor Carving his Bow*. He created many magnificent large-scale preparatory drawings in red chalk based on a series of adolescent models, had casts made of the arms, legs, and other body parts of live models to serve as additional studies, and completed two preliminary sculpted versions (one in terra cotta and one in plaster).[5] These multiple two and three-dimensional instantiations informed the final marble which was presented publicly at Versailles in 1750. The finished work was immediately hailed by artists for its beauty, grace, and elegance and was destined to achieve great fame and recognition over the centuries.[6] The exquisitely rendered *Amor Carving his Bow* (actually, Amor is leaning on his bow, testing its tensile strength) reveals a confluence of naturalism and idealism that demonstrates Bouchardon's mastery of the aesthetics of antique sculpture that he studied and assiduously copied while a Prix de Rome student in the eternal city (he famously carved a marble replica of the Hellenistic *Barberini Faun* for the King that was hailed as superior to the original).[7]

A number of critics of the time, however, including Voltaire and Diderot, expressed reservations. In a letter to the Comte de Caylus in 1739, Voltaire expressed concern that Bouchardon intended to represent the god of love in a banausic role as carpenter and sculptor.[8] Diderot wrote in 1763 that the idea of Cupid as carpenter "shocks my imagination. I do not like to see Cupid spend such a long time on manual labor."[9] Others, such as the art critic, La Font de Saint-Yenne, were unhappy with what they perceived as the complexity of the subject—Amor's omnipotent triumph over Mars and Hercules whose weapons he has stolen and used to carve his bow—in a seemingly simple single figure that some found too naturalistic.[10] Bouchardon, in fact, does represent the god of love as a sculptor engaged in manual labor, fashioning the tool he deems necessary for his assigned task of assuring that the force of Eros, however destructive, will ensure the continuity of regeneration on earth.

In 1750, Bouchardon's close friend, Pierre-Jean Mariette, in order to deflect criticism from the court as well as early observers, published a long defense of the work in the *Mercure de France.*[11] Mariette described in detail Bouchardon's figure as well as the process in making the *Amor.* He emphasized the modernity of the work by pointing out that it had no precedent in ancient art in either subject or style. He discussed the artist's studies of multiple adolescent models in his quest to perfectly capture the naturalism of the youthful god, first in drawing, and then in his sculpted version. He affirmed that Bouchardon sought to represent in an accurate, corporeal manner an adolescent Amor who, although somewhat ungainly and not fully developed physically, was nonetheless old enough and strong enough to be Psyche's lover. In one passage, he described the anatomical accuracy of *Amor* in the following terms: "As far as the workmanship is concerned, it is flesh itself rendered without affectation, allowing all the characteristics of the skin to be seen as well as the correctness of the muscles and the parts to which the muscles are attached."[12]

In several passages of his essay, Mariette underscores the anatomical underpinnings of Bouchardon's figure. In fact, *Amor Carving his Bow* is a type of artistic manifesto about the art of sculpture powered by passion, but it is also a demonstration of the outcome of the artist's education—the forging of the human figure through the study of drawings, antique sculpted examples, the live model, and also, very significantly, anatomy. For at the very time that Bouchardon was undertaking the commission for the marble version of Amor he was also in the process of providing drawings for his illustrated anatomy manual for artists that was accompanied by the figure of an *Ecorché*, as mentioned above. *L'Anatomie nécessaire pour les arts du dessein*, with plates engraved by Gabriel Huquier, was published in 1741 and sold by Huquier in his shop in Paris with the recommendation that clients also purchase Bouchardon's accompanying *Ecorché* (Fig. 1.2).[13] The title alone that insists on the necessity of anatomy to the arts of *dessein*, indicates that Bouchardon was defying the 1737 proscription of the teaching of anatomy at the Académie royale de peinture et de sculpture. It is telling that Bouchardon's manual was the first anatomy book for artists since the 1668 publication of François Tortebat's *Abrégé de l'anatomie accomodé aux arts de peinture* (reprinted in 1733), a work used in the teaching of anatomy since the late seventeenth century.[14] The fact that no new anatomy book was adapted for use at the Académie Royale for sixty-nine years reveals the extent to which the centrality of anatomy to the art curriculum had lapsed at the Académie in the early decades of the eighteenth century in France, a fact lamented by some critics of the period who thought that art education overall had become too lax. The early eighteenth century, of course, witnessed the rise of the Rococo style at court, a style that de-emphasized classical models and focused on stylized conventions in the depiction of the human form. Bouchardon resisted these trends in favor of classicism combined with empirical observation of nature. He hoped to re-establish some earlier principles in teaching the representation of the human figure, including the important role of anatomy. In this, he presaged the neoclassical movement in the second half of the eighteenth century that witnessed a renewed and vigorous emphasis on the teaching of anatomy at the Académie. In order to understand better the importance of Bouchardon's role in anatomical propaedutics and the new developments in anatomical education that followed, it will be important to review briefly some of the main aspects of the teaching of anatomy at the Académie Royale.

Since the founding of the Académie royale de peinture et de sculpture in 1648, the study of anatomy had been an important part of the curriculum. This was also true of its sister institution, the Académie de France à Rome.[15] An important factor to keep in mind is that the focus of anatomical study was on the male skeleton, écorché, and cadaver subject (similarly, académie drawings were based on the male nude model). In the seventeenth century, anatomy courses for art students were given by surgeons, beginning with François Quatroulx, who taught between 1648 and 1672. Quatroulx used casts of cadaver parts as one means of instruction (students thus studied fragments of the dead body) but students also studied plates engraved after Vesalius's 1543 ur-text, *De humani corporis fabrica* as well as replicas of sculpted écorché figures, including the very expressive flayed figure then attributed to Michelangelo and Cicogli's famous sixteenth-century *Ecorché.*[16] After 1670, the Académie presented conferences on the essential role of anatomy for the arts.[17] In the late seventeenth century, concerns regarding the study of anatomy arose, however, and had to do with two principal issues. One was that students who were required to learn how to make idealized human figures through the study of academy drawings of the nude male figure as well as from the live model might understandably be repulsed by the two-dimensional plates and three-dimensional écorchés of the anatomized body to say nothing of the impact of attending dissections.[18] The goal of academic art was to create convincing, idealized figures, and the fear was that the study of cadavers through dissection and cadaver casts, would thwart these objectives. The famous art theorist Roger de Piles, who wrote the preface to Tortébat's 1668 *Abrégé de l'anatomie*, expressed concerns that student artists might experience revulsion at the sight of the dissected cadaver and its instantiations in images of the skeleton and especially the flayed figure.[19] Other concerns were related to the fact that surgeons, with no expertise in the aesthetics of the human form, were teaching anatomy to art students (in 1672 the Académie decided that a painter capable of teaching anatomy would be preferable to a surgeon).[20] The mid-eighteenth-century artist Jacques-Fabien Gautier d'Agoty, who specialized in colored anatomical plates (addressed later in this essay), reiterated these concerns in his 1753 *Observations sur la peinture et les tableaux anciens et modernes:*

> The demonstrator is a surgeon, he does not know the gracefulness of the antique, noble proportion, beautiful form, the action of the muscles, the effects in all of the poses, the suppleness of contours. He cannot show what he does not know.[21]

These concerns and reservations reveal a divergence in underlying pedagogical philosophies. Art students were supposed to learn from the most beautifully rendered representations of the human figure from antiquity and the Renaissance in order to emulate their great predecessors. Study of the dissected cadaver and its facsimiles in casts, sculpted écorchés or anatomical plates, stood in direct conflict with this educational objective. A question continuously posed in the late seventeenth and first half of the eighteenth century relates to the significance of knowledge of the interior of the body. Many considered this to be the domain of medicine and the natural sciences, not the visual arts. Do artists need to understand anatomy in order to create ideal beauty? Famous artists such as Leonardo da Vinci and Michelangelo could serve as important precedents because they believed anatomy to be foundational to their art.[22] And there was another persuasive argument for the artistic study of anatomy—namely, the belief promulgated by many theorists and academicians that classical Greek sculptors had studied anatomy via dissection and used this as the basis of their art. Plates of famous works of antique sculpture anatomized abound during this period and debates for and against the idea continued throughout the eighteenth century.[23] At the very end of the eighteenth century, a French surgeon and would-be artist, Jean-Galbert Salvage, sought to prove definitively that the ancients studied dissection and that anatomical study formed the basis of their ideally beautiful sculpted figures. For his pedagogical treatise, *Anatomie du Gladiateur Combatant* (begun in 1802), Salvage dissected cadavers of muscular young soldiers and made casts from others to use as the basis of detailed plates of the anatomized *Borghese Gladiator*.[24]

An argument against the study of dissection as the basis of anatomical verism in painting and sculpture had to do with the profound differences between a live figure and a dead one. The Vitalist School of Medicine in Montpellier during the eighteenth century studied the changes that occurred in the human body in muscle and tissue when the vital element that animates life ceased.[25] What could the cadaver teach that the study of the live model and great precedents in art could not? This became another essential aesthetic debate during the second half of the eighteenth century, one we will return to later in this essay. It was often deemed more useful and appropriate for art students to learn about the interior of the body from anatomical plates. These two-dimensional renditions of osteology and myology were typically picturesque and took their inspiration from the illustrations to Vesalius that established a typology and led to conventions that formed the basis of subsequent iterations. A principal convention had to do with the use of narrative fictions. Skeletons and flayed figures were typically depicted in activities or at rest in pictorial settings such as a landscape. The figures appeared alive and unselfconscious of their condition, often even ebullient. Albinus's famous and influential 1747 manual on osteology and myology provides a wonderful example of how anatomical illustrations can succeed by creating narratives in compelling settings.[26] These conventions were visually pleasing and served as a means for artists to learn about the interior structures of the body without having to experience revulsion or disgust.

Although Bouchardon knew well these pictorial conventions (he owned copies of Vesalius and Tortebat), in his *Anatomie nécessaire* he completely rejected them to focus instead on a simple flayed or skeletal figure.[27] The manual consists of a preface by the engraver/publisher Huquier and a one-page table that identifies by number or letter the bones and muscles that correspond to those inscribed on the figures. The fourteen plates appear without any text and include eight flayed figures and six skeletons (Edme's brother Jacques-Philippe, a sculptor who worked with him in his studio, contributed these).[28] The figures are seen in a variety of poses—frontal, back, three-quarter, and profile views—but with no picturesque setting. In fact, all appear as though they were live models posing on small bases (abstract and indicated by hatching in the case of the skeletons) or platforms (as in the case of the écorchés) without any other details and all against the neutral background of the page. Hatching used for light and shade creates the illusion of three-dimensional figures. The écorché figures are particularly striking because they give the impression of the live model posing for an academy drawing with the difference that we can see through the skin and flesh as though the figure was transparent in order to have us observe the muscle layers beneath (Fig. 1.3).

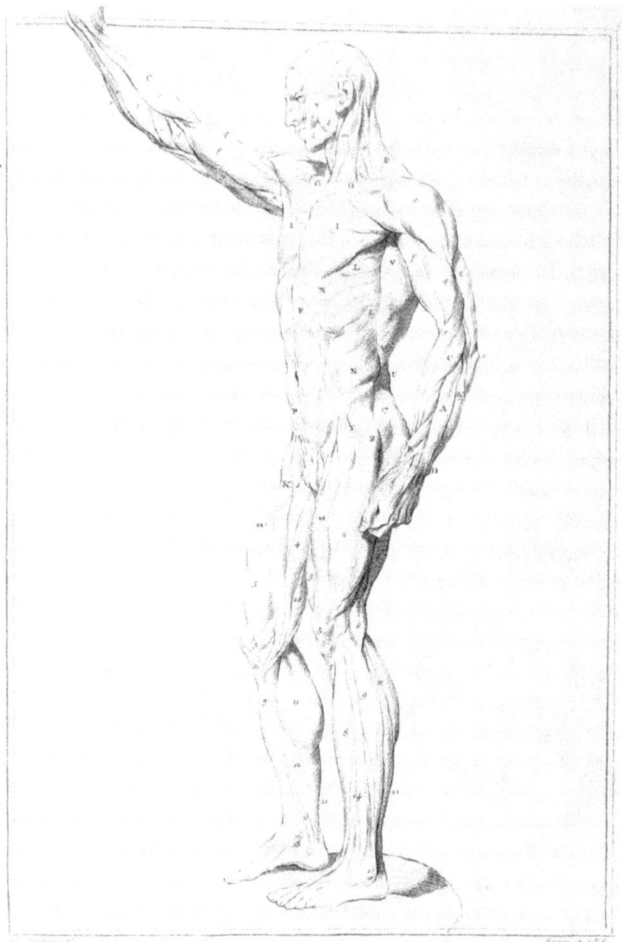

Figure 1.3: Edme Bouchardon, *Ecorché*, from *L'anatomie nécessaire pour les arts du dessein par Edme Bouchardon, sculpteur du Roy*. Paris: Huquier, 1741. Public Domain

The figures stand in contrapposto to indicate movement and the muscles whether shown tensed or relaxed, are instinct with vitality. The elegance and grace of the drawing style, the suppleness and fluidity of the contours, call to mind Bouchardon's beautiful academy nudes and contribute to the overall effect of a model posing in the studio. This is further emphasized by the vivid individualized faces and features of the flayed figures with opened eyes and mouths, distinctive noses and lips, etc. Their expressions are serious and thoughtful. The faces are summarily flayed, the skull is not opened and the hands and feet are not flayed at all but beautifully drawn in fine detail. Thus, Bouchardon has retained those features and elements that convey that these figures are depictions of individual human beings. The quiddity of the human being is made visible in spite of the fact that the figures are displaying an interior layer of the body—its myology. Thus, artists could visualize what the muscles looked like beneath the skin and how they were attached to one another without losing sight of the integrity of the figure. Bouchardon demonstrates how a skilled artist can teach anatomy to artists without causing revulsion or disgust at seeing the interior of the body. Similarly, in three of the skeleton plates drawn by his brother, an outer envelope seems to cover the skeletons, outlined by fluid yet firm contours, transforming the figures into "transparent men."[29]

Scholars have suggested that Bouchardon and his brother were inspired to a certain extent by two anatomical plates by the late seventeenth-century Spanish anatomical engraver, Chrysóstome Martínez.[30] Martínez, who worked in Paris, initially published the plates in 1689. They were republished in Paris in 1740 at the very time Bouchardon was working on his manual. Plate 2, the osteology plate, shows a crowd of skeletons in a picturesque setting with the unusual feature of having firm outlines that serve as envelopes for the bones and that turn them into renditions of "transparent men." The ones in the foreground are standing on small, raised platforms that resemble those seen in the Bouchardon manual. Martínez's first plate depicts a youthful male figure partially flayed and depicted from the front, back, and in profile with arms in different positions (accompanied by the frontal skeleton of a small child). The views combine osteology with myology, unlike the figures of Bouchardon. The heads and faces, however, are intact and this conveys to the viewer that the figure is based on a live model. There is no background, but intersecting concentric circles indicate the proportions of the human form. Edme and his brother do seem to have been inspired by certain elements of the Martínez plates. In making his flayed figures for the manual, Bouchardon emulated the features of the Martínez figures that conveyed a sense of the live model posing. His images could resonate with student artists because of their referents to models posing in the studio.

Bouchardon's manual with its emphasis on the unitary figure without any pictorial context, provides a simple and direct way to study anatomy in the two-dimensional format. As an instructional anatomy manual for artists, it is unique in its simplicity and its modest and direct educational objectives which differ from immediate successors in almost every way. It may have served as an inspiration for the painter Charles Monnet's *Etudes d'anatomie pour l'usage des peintres* (ca. 1770-1774), a work that was frequently reprinted in the eighteenth century and which inspired Géricault's drawings of anatomical fragments.[31] Monnet depicts anatomized parts of the body, such as the limbs and extremities against a blank page as a means of helping students focus on specific areas when making the human figure. It serves as a type of handbook with detailed information about each fragment that accompanies the figure on the page itself but does not put the fragments together into an integral figure. The limbs and extremities seen in this manner recall the many drawing manuals of the time that serve as pattern books that reproduce stereotypes of noses, lips, ears, hands, feet, etc. that artists could study and insert into their paintings. These images also resonate with the popularity in eighteenth-century France of the drawing and painting of disarticulated limbs, seen in the works of academic artists of the period.[32]

Bouchardon's contemporary, Jacques-Fabien Gautier d'Agoty, mentioned earlier, would go in another direction altogether.[33] In his 1746 *Myologie complette en couleur et grandeur naturelle*, for example, he sought to appeal not only to artists but an expanded market of surgeons, artists, and anatomy aficionados who collected anatomical illustrations, three-dimensional models in a variety of materials, and even preserved or mummified body parts. This appeal is evinced in his plate that depicts a woman with a flayed back (Fig. 1.4), rediscovered by the Surrealists and dubbed, "The Flayed Angel."[34]

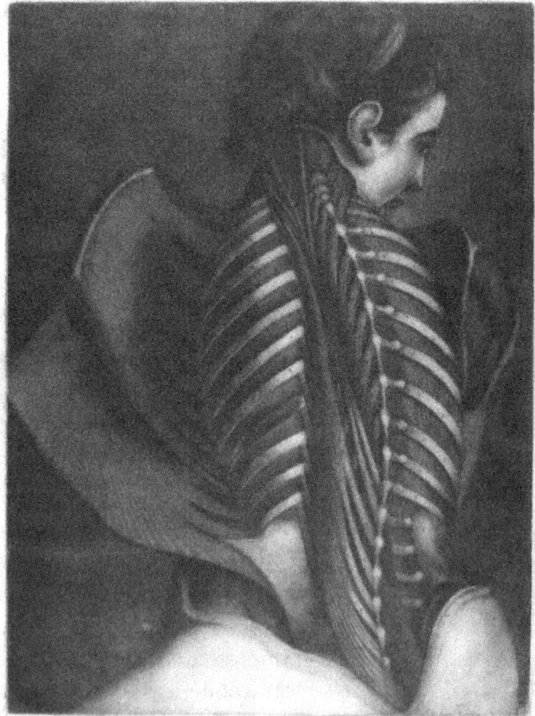

Figure 1.4: Jacques-Fabien Gautier d'Agoty, *Muscles of the Back*, from *Myologie complette en couleur et grandeur naturelle*, Paris: Gautier, 1746. Public Domain

Amateur anatomy enthusiasts were growing in number by midcentury, responding to the new fashion for the natural sciences. Having a "cabinet d'anatomie" to exhibit one's collection contributed to the prestige of the wealthy who had pretense to knowledge and expertise in this domain. Unlike Bouchardon, Gautier d'Agoty wanted to shock and astound with his large-scale plates that claimed anatomical accuracy and were also in color, a great innovation in anatomical plates of the time. His illustrated anatomy books with life-size anatomized figures, were monumental in format and were made to appeal to those who could afford these deluxe editions. Gautier d'Agoty created a new kind of picturesque anatomy, one that presented an attractive, youthful figure, whether male or female, and emphasized, through dramatic color, form, and composition, the picturesque aspects of the interior of the body, indulging in the growing fascination with what lies beneath the envelope of skin and tissue. Many figures seem to pose seductively, offering a view of their insides to the viewer. Gautier d'Agoty replaces the pictorial settings and narratives seen in picturesque anatomies with compelling picturesque views of muscles and viscera. The *Myologie complette* was the first in a series of anatomy books that Gautier d'Agoty produced in a similar format. He was so successful that he established a kind of industry and contributed to the popularization of anatomical plates of this nature. Like so many others, he was sharply criticized by surgeons of the time for the inaccuracy of his anatomical representations.

It is important to consider why representations of the inside of the body—osteology, myology, organs, etc. from the eighteenth century are so denigrated, then as now, by medical specialists for their gross inaccuracies. This has to do, in part, with the fictional aspect of the depictions, whether in two-dimensional or three-dimensional formats. The envisaging of the interior of the body is always an effort of the imagination. Prior to modern imaging technologies from the x-ray to the MRI, it was imperative to have this kind of interior corporal mapping to help artists and surgeons visualize more clearly where muscles, tendons, nerves, blood vessels, bones, organs, etc. are located, but such images were always imaginary reconstructions. As Alfred Korzybski eloquently stated: "A map is not the territory it represents but, if correct, it has a similar structure to the territory, which accounts for its usefulness."[35] Mapping of the corporal interior was useful as a representation that served to stand in for the thing itself. But a requisite transposition takes place from the dissected cadaver to anatomized figures that serves as a type of resurrection of the dead. The conundrum confronting pedagogy in the arts and medicine in the eighteenth century was how to make visible and re-animate the "dead subject" in a way that was useful to these arts. Even cadaver casts of the period placed the dead subject in the pose of famous works of art, typically antique sculpture.[36] This confluence of the arts and sciences would be of utmost importance in the second half of the eighteenth century. Those who represented the skeletal structure and myology for the purpose of art or medical propaedeutics, were tasked with bringing the dead back to life, for medicine and the visual arts needed to understand how the body functioned and appeared in its vitality.

The issue of how best to teach anatomy specifically to art students became increasingly urgent after midcentury. In 1746 Jean-Joseph Sue was hired as an adjunct professor of anatomy.[37] He gave lessons on dissection that included demonstrations with the live model, an important innovation that acknowledged continuing concerns about the pitfalls of teaching anatomy to art students via dissection and its representations (I will return to Sue's precepts and especially those of his son who followed in his footsteps later in this essay). While the teaching of anatomy was re-introduced into the curriculum, a number of academicians and critics continued to resist the teaching of anatomy to artists, even when its importance had been reaffirmed. The academician and professor of drawing, Charles Jombert, asserted in his 1755 *Méthode pour apprendre le dessin*, that "It is not necessary that students of drawing take an anatomy course, or that they assist in the dissection of a cadaver."[38] This precept was expanded upon by Diderot in his 1765 *Notes on Painting*:

> Study of the *écorché* doubtless has its advantages; but is it not to be feared that this *écorché* might remain in the imagination forever; that this might encourage the artist to become enamored of his knowledge and show it off; that his vision might be corrupted, precluding attentive scrutiny of surface appearance; that despite the presence of skin and fat he might come to perceive nothing but the muscles, their beginnings, attachments, and insertions; that he might overemphasize them, that he might become hard and dry…Since only the exterior is exposed to view, I would prefer to be trained to see it fully, and spared treacherous knowledge I would only have to forget. It is sad that the *écorché* is studied only to learn to observe nature, but experience suggests that after such study it is very difficult to see her any other way.[39]

For Diderot, the study of anatomy held many dangers for artists whom he feared would not be able to "unsee" their observations of the dissected cadaver and their studies of anatomical plates. These visualizations would inflect and infect their figures with cadaver imagery and the écorché. The article on "Anatomie" in the *Encyclopédie*, co-authored by Diderot, contains the asseveration that anatomy belongs to the realm of medicine.[40] It is interesting to note that many of the accompanying plates are based on examples of picturesque images of the skeleton and écorché figures inspired by Vesalius. Thus, although Bouchardon introduced an anti-picturesque method of presenting the skeleton and the flayed man, picturesque versions would continue to be produced throughout the eighteenth century in manuals that were pedagogical in nature. Some were innovative and odd such as Jacques Gamelin's remarkable work, *Nouveau recueil d'ostéologie et de myologie* of 1779, which was sui generis in its presentation of macabre painterly compositions, vignettes characterized by gallows humor, detailed anatomical graphs, and expressive skeletons and écorché figures.[41] Gamelin stated that his goal was to make an anatomy book that would have great visual appeal to artists who were always so attentive to what they observed before them.

Charles-Nicolas Cochin's revelatory illustration to the *Encyclopédie* article on "Dessein" of 1763, depicts the pedagogical stages of student artists in a drawing school (likely based on the Academy drawing class).[42] Students begin by copying the human figure from drawings of the masters, proceed to draw from the sculpted figure in the round, and finally advance to drawing from the live model. The sculpted écorché, skeleton, or anatomy plates of any kind are nowhere to be seen in this classroom. Casts made from live models of limbs and so forth hang on the wall, but no cadaver casts. This illustration reveals that the study of anatomy for art students was still not part of learning to draw in 1763, at least according to the *Encyclopédie.*

Just a few years later, however, in 1769, this would change dramatically, when the study of the sculpted écorché becomes an integral part of the study of art, mandated for art students. The écorché will re-enter art education in a very dramatic way. In order to understand the significance of this development, it is necessary to return to Bouchardon's *Ecorché* that accompanied his art manual in 1741 (Fig. 1.2). Bouchardon's *Ecorché* represents a strong, muscular, animated figure, standing in contrapposto, raising his left arm and opened hand in a rhetorical gesture. His opened mouth, tilted head and opened eyes suggest that the figure is speaking. The muscles and tendons of the flayed figure reveal an elasticity and vitality. The hands and feet are not flayed. This is a three-dimensional version of the resurrected cadaver, a transparent man who walks forward, seemingly unaware of his flayed status. This sculpted figure stands in dramatic contradistinction to the cadaver cast attributed to Bouchardon.[43] Although positioned as an upright walking man, also with an arm raised as if speaking, the thinness of the corpse and the lack of elasticity and vitality in the desiccated muscles and tendons provoke a visceral reaction to the macabre nature of this disturbing figure. For these reasons, it fails as a pedagogical demonstration. The idealized version was successful because it was removed from visual references to the actual "dead subject." Bouchardon's pedagogical *Ecorché* was not adopted by the Academy in its curriculum, but it was known during the second half of the eighteenth century. Its appearance in a 1795 ink drawing by François Maurice Granet, *Séance autour de l'Ecorché dit de Bouchardon,* reveals that even at that date, it was admired and esteemed as a pedagogical demonstration.[44]

Although Bouchardon's *Ecorché* was not adopted for pedagogical use at the Academy, it did serve as an important precedent in its form and function as a teaching tool. His idea for the *Ecorché* as a model for teaching anatomy would be realized by Houdon. Scholars have often noted the filiations between Bouchardon and Houdon for both artists embraced the ideals of classicism combined with an idealized naturalism as embodied in antique sculpture, this during a period in which the conventions of Rococo aesthetics still held sway. The neoclassical movement with its self-conscious purging of rococo formulas coincided with Houdon's emergence as one of the greatest sculptors of the second half of the eighteenth century. What is far less remarked upon is that Houdon followed in the footsteps of Bouchardon by embracing anatomy as the foundational basis of naturalism in the creation of ideal beauty in sculpture.

After winning the Prix de Rome in 1761, Houdon spent four years at the Académie de France à Rome and while there, studied anatomy independently. He wrote that he believed anatomy to be foundational to art: "I used the four years of my sojourn in Rome in the profound study of anatomy considered as the basis of composition."[45] He studied dissection in Rome with the surgeon Séquier who gave demonstrations on the cadaver at the Hôpital de Saint-Louis-des Français. While still a student, he received a commission in 1766 to sculpt a figure of *St. John the Baptist Preaching* for Santa Maria degli Angeli. In order to achieve naturalism as well as idealized beauty in this figure, he decided to make a life-sized anatomized version of St. John, an *Ecorché*, that would serve as its first-born anatomical twin (Fig. 1.5).[46] Houdon's friend and fellow student in Rome, Christian Mannlich, described Houdon's decision to make the écorché of St. John first and how its accuracy was approved by Séquier who oversaw the process. He writes that artists and amateurs encouraged Houdon to cast his figure in plaster for they considered it to be the "best anatomical statue ever made."[47] Mannlich asserts that Houdon's *Ecorché* was based on careful anatomical study via dissection. It is important to keep in mind, however, that Houdon, in fashioning his *Ecorché* figure, would also have had in mind earlier artistic precedents that he encountered as an art student in Paris, including the version by Bouchardon. Based on his avid interest in anatomy, he likely also knew Bouchardon's manual. If we compare the sculpted flayed figures of the two artists, we notice many affinities—the contrapposto stance, the tilt of the cranium, the partially flayed face, the opened mouth and rhetorical gestures (Houdon's figure has an extended horizontal arm like his *St. John the Baptist Preaching* but a later version of his figure conceived as an independent work of art and cast in bronze, has a raised arm like that of Bouchardon).

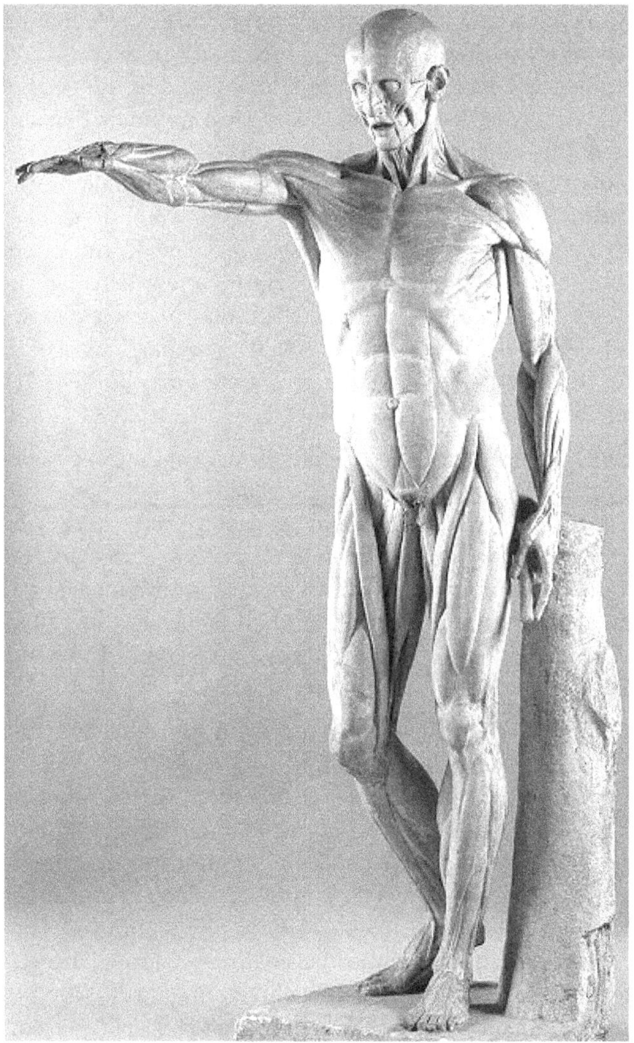

Figure 1.5: Jean-Antoine Houdon. *Ecorché*. Plaster, 1766-67. French Academy in Rome, Villa Medici. Photo: Jacques de Caso

Houdon's figure, however, unlike that of Bouchardon, would become immensely successful as a pedagogical tool. The Académie was much more receptive in 1769 than it had been in 1741. Houdon offered his *Ecorché* as a gift to the Académie de France à Rome in 1769 where it was greatly admired and very influential.[48] In 1775, when Joseph-Marie Vien served as the director of that institution, a new regulation was put into effect stipulating that all students must study anatomy and "must learn anatomy from the *Ecorché* of Houdon."[49] This was the beginning of the pedagogical life of Houdon's *Ecorché* that became so popular that it was replicated in life-size and smaller versions and adopted immediately as an anatomical teaching tool in art academies in France and throughout Europe. The figure remains admired and in use even today. As a life-size mimetic figure asseverating anatomical accuracy that appeared to have a vibrant life in spite of its flayed condition it did not inspire revulsion in art students of the period but admiration instead. Houdon represents an idealized instantiation of the flayed man with generalized geometries in its myological reconstructions and broad planes that defined form. It demonstrated the location and placement of the muscular structure which made it useful for artists to absorb if they sought to understand how to create a figure that was anatomically approximate while eschewing the rebarbative, visceral impact of the dissected cadaver. It was striking in appearance and aesthetically pleasing. It was a work of art.

By the late 1770s and 80s, teaching anatomy to artists had once again become foundational to the curriculum at the Académie royale de peinture et de sculpture. In 1772 the Comte de Caylus proposed a prize in osteology and in 1776 Maurice Quentin de La Tour established a *prix de torse* (torso prize).[50] For this competition, students had to paint a torso of the live model first and then, in a second version, anatomize the torso with the stipulation that all the muscles had to be identified. By 1776 art students were expected to have a deeper understanding of anatomy than in earlier periods.

During this later period, the famous surgeon, Jean-Joseph Sue (who bore the same name as his father, whom he succeeded as a teacher of anatomy at the Académie royale), taught art students via dissection, but following the precepts of his father, he also demonstrated on the live model.[51] In his 1788 *Elémens d'anatomie,* Sue wrote that for art students the study of the cadaver was not sufficient; it must be accompanied by study of the live model so that the live and dead versions can serve each other reciprocally, as a form of commentary.[52] The plates, however, employ picturesque anatomy, revealing the perseverance of this conventional form in the late eighteenth century. When Sue taught anatomy to art students in the 1790s, he added a full-scale replica of Houdon's *Ecorché* to his dissection classes as a means of demonstrating to students the resurrected form of the dead model as a work of art.[53] After the French Revolution, anatomy was considered such a prepotent aspect of art education that Sue received permission to set up a dissection theater in the Louvre itself, where artists still had their studios.[54] The triumph of anatomical teaching at the end of the eighteenth century would exert an indelible impact on French Romantic art. This is evinced in the 1805 pedagogical treatise for sculptors by the theorist Emeric-David, who instructed artists to bring cadavers into their studios and dissect them, to the works of the sculptor David d'Angers, who was a dissection enthusiast, and the paintings of Géricault, who brought cadaver parts into his studio for inspiration while working on *The Raft of the Medusa*.[55]

*Translations are mine unless otherwise noted.

Notes

[1] The essential modern historical survey and reference book for the teaching of anatomy to artists in France from the Renaissance to 2021 is Philippe Comar, editor and contributing author, *Figures du corps. Une leçon d'anatomie à l'École des Beaux-Arts* (Paris: Beaux-Arts de Paris, les Éditions, 2008). The basic early source is Mathis Duval and Edouard Cuyer, *Histoire de l'anatomie plastique: les maîtres, les livres, et les écorchés* (Paris: Picard & Kann, 1898). For seventeenth to nineteenth-century issues concerning dissection see Martial Guédron, "L'enseignement de l'anatomie artistique en France et la question de la dissection (XVIIIe-XIXe siècles)," *Les cahiers d'histoire de l'art* 2 (2004), 33-40.

[2] Comar, *Figures du corps*, 21.

[3] Anne-Lise Desmas, Edouard Kopp, Guilhem Scherf, *Bouchardon. Royal Artist of the Enlightenment* (Los Angeles: J. Paul Getty Museum, 2017), 350-352.

[4] Edme Bouchardon, *L'anatomie necessaire pour les arts du dessein par Edme Bouchardon, sculpteur du Roy* (Paris: Huquier, 1741). See Henry Ronot, "Le traité d'anatomie d'Edmé Bouchardon," *Bulletin de la Société de l'histoire de l'art français*, 1968, 93-100 and Monique Kornell, "Bouchardon's Anatomy Book for Artists," *Getty Research Journal* 8 (2016), 39-54.

[5] Desmas, Kopp, Scherf, *Bouchardon. Royal Artist of the Enlightenment*, 350-352.

[6] Ibid., 350-352.

[7] Ibid., 20.

[8] Voltaire, *Correspondence littéraire*, ed. Théodore Besterman, 13 vols (Paris: Gallimard, 1963-1993), vol. 2, 18-19. Translated in Desmas, Kopp, Scherf, *Bouchardon. Royal Artist of the Enlightenment*, 351.

[9] Denis Diderot, "Sur Bouchardon et la sculpture," in *Correspondence littéraire, philosophique et critique*..., 16 vols. (Nendeln: Kraus Reprint), vol. 5, 247-249. Cited in Desmas, Kopp, Scherf, *Bouchardon. Royal Artist of the Enlightenment*, 352.

[10] Etienne La Font de Saint-Yenne, *Réflexions sur quelques causes de l'Etat présent de la peinture en France, avec un examen des principaux ouvrages exposés au Louvre 1746*, in *La Font de Saint-Yenne, Oeuvres critiques*, ed. Etienne Jollet (Paris: ENSBA, 2001), 83-89. Translated in Desmas, Kopp, Scherf, *Bouchardon. Royal Artist of the Enlightenment*, 352.

[11] Discussed in Desmas, Kopp, Scherf, *Bouchardon. Royal Artist of the Enlightenment*, 352.

[12] Pierre-Jean Mariette, "Lettre à M***", *Mercure de France*, June, 1750, 111-116. "A l'égard du travail, c'est la chair même touchée: sans aucune manière, laissant voir toute: l'expression de la peau & toute la justesse des muscles & des attachemens."

[13] Kornell, "Bouchardon's Anatomy Book for Artists," 47-48.

[14] François Tortebat, *Abrégé de l'anatomie accommodé aux arts de peinture et de sculpture* (Paris: chez Tortebat, 1667-1668). Discussed in Comar, *Figures du corps*, 20-21.

[15] Comar, *Figures du corps*, 19-21.

[16] Ibid., 19-21.

[17] Ibid., 20.

[18] Discussed by Guédron, "L'enseignement de l'anatomie artistique en France et la question de la dissection (XVIIIe-XIXe siècles)".

[19] Ibid., 34.

[20] *Procès-verbaux de l'Académie royale de peinture et de sculpture 1648-1793* (Paris: Société de l'histoire de l'art français), 10 vols. 1875-1892, November, 1672 vol. I, 401. See Comar, *Figures du corps*, 20.

[21] Jacques-Fabien Gautier d'Agoty, *Observations sur la peinture et les tableaux anciens et modernes* (Geneva: Minkoff Reprints, 1972), 72-73. Discussed by Guédron, "L'enseignement de l'anatomie artistique en France et la question de la dissection (XVIIIe-XIXe siècles)," 35.

[22] Comar, *Figures du corps*, 146-147.

[23] See Aline Magnien, *La Nature et l'antique, le chair et le contour. Essai sur la sculpture française du XVIIIe siècle* (Oxford, Voltaire Foundation, 2004).

[24] Jean-Galbert Salvage, *Anatomie du Gladiateur combattant, applicable aux beaux-arts…* (Paris: chez l'auteur, 1812). See Raymond Lifchez, "Jean-Galbert Salvage and his *Anatomie du Gladiateur combattant*: Art and Patronage in Post-Revolutionary France," *Metropolitan Museum Journal*, v. 44 (2009): 163-184.

[25] See Elizabeth Williams, *A Cultural History of Medical Vitalism in Enlightenment Montpellier* (Burlington, Vermont: Ashgate, 2003) and *The Physical and the Moral: Anthropology, Physiology and Philosophical Medicine in France, 1750-1850* (Cambridge: Cambridge University Press, 1994).

[26] Bernhard Siegfried Albinus, *Tabulae sceleti et musculorum corporis humani…* (Leiden, 1747). See Comar, *Figures du corps*, 190-192.

[27] Ronot, "Le traité d'anatomie d'Edme Bouchardon."

[28] Kornell, "Bouchardon's Anatomy Book for Artists."

[29] Ronot, "Le traité d'anatomie d'Edme Bouchardon." See also Fabio Cafagna, "Images of Transparency and Resurrection from Leonardo da Vinci to Crisóstomo Martínez," *Nuncius*, vol. 32, # 1 (2017): 52-84.

[30] Ronot, "Le traité d'anatomie d'Edme Bouchardon," 96.

[31] Charles Monnet, *Etudes d'anatomie à l'usage des peintres* (Paris: 1774). For Géricault's copies see Comar, *Figures du corps*, 236-237.

[32] Susanna Caviglia, *History, painting, and the seriousness of pleasure in the age of Louis XV* (Liverpool: Liverpool University Press on behalf of the Voltaire Foundation, 2020), 141.

[33] Jacques-Fabien Gautier d'Agoty, *Myologie complette en couleur et grandeur naturelle…* (Paris: Gautier, 1746). See Comar, *Figures du corps*, 186-191 and, most recently, Patrick Mauriès, Corinne le Bitouzé, Anne-Marie Garcia, *Jacques-Fabien d'Agoty: Essais et traités anatomiques* (Paris: ENSBA, 2020).

[34] See Michel Lemire, *Artistes et mortels* (Paris, Raymond Chabaut, 1990).

[35] Alfred Korzybski, *Science and Sanity: An Introduction to Non Aristotelian Systems and General Semantics* (Brooklyn, NY: Institute of General Semantics, 5th ed., 1993), 58.

[36] Lifchez, "Jean-Galbert Salvage and his *Anatomie du Gladiateur combattant*: Art and Patronage in Post-Revolutionary France." See also Dorothy Johnson, "The Body Speaks: Anatomical Narratives in French Enlightenment Sculpture," in *Body Narratives. Motion and Emotion in the French Enlightenment*, ed. Susanna Caviglia (Turnhout: Brepols Publishers, 2017), 57-58.

[37] See Comar, *Figures du corps*, 22 and Guédron, "L'enseignement de l'anatomie artistique en France et la question de la dissection (XVIIIe-XIXe siècles)," 34-35.

[38] Charles Antoine Jombert, *Méthode pour apprendre le dessin....* (Paris: chez l'auteur, 1755).

[39] Denis Diderot, "Pensées détachées sur la peinture" in *Oeuvres esthétiques* (Paris: Garnier frères, 1968), 815. Translated by John Goodman, *Diderot on Art*, vol 1 (New Haven and London: Yale University Press, 1995), 193.

[40] Denis Diderot, "Anatomie", in Denis Diderot and Jean-Baptiste Le Rond d'Alembert, *Encyclopédie ou dictionnaire raisonné des sciences, des arts et des métiers, par une société des gens de lettres* (A. Lucques chez Vincent Giuntini, 1760), vol. I, 409.

[41] Jacques Gamelin, *Nouveau recueil d'ostéologie et de myologie dessiné d'après nature* (Toulouse: Desclassen, 1779). See Comar, *Figures du corps*, 182-183.

[42] Illustrated in Comar, *Figures du corps*, 168.

[43] Ibid., 200.

[44] Ibid., 201.

[45] Louis Réau, *Houdon, sa vie et son oeuvre*, 2 vols, (Paris: Nobele, 1964), I, 201 and Johnson, "The Body Speaks: Anatomical Narratives in French Enlightenment Sculpture," 32-34.

[46] Louis Réau, *Houdon, sa vie et son oeuvre*, I, 204-205.

[47] Ibid.

[48] Ibid., I, 208.

[49] Johnson, "The Body Speaks: Anatomical Narratives in French Enlightenment Sculpture," 34.

[50] Comar, *Figures du corps*, 24-25. For the *prix de torse* see *Procès-verbaux de l'Académie royale de peinture et de sculpture 1648-1793* (Paris: Société de l'histoire de l'art français), 10 vols. 1875-1892, March 30 and April 27, 1772, vol. VIII, 217-218.

[51] Comar, *Figures du corps*, 25-26.

[52] Jean-Joseph Sue, *Elémens d'anatomie à l'usage des peintres, des sculpteurs et des amateurs...* (Paris: chez l'auteur, 1788), iv-v.

[53] Comar, *Figures du corps*, 28-31.

[54] Johnson, "The Body Speaks: Anatomical Narratives in French Enlightenment Sculpture," 53-55.

[55] Dorothy Johnson, "Anatomie, réalité, idéalité dans l'art français autour de 1800," in *Ecrire les Sciences*, ed. Martial Guédron and Isabelle Laboulais, for *Etudes sur le 18e siècle*, vol 42, 2015, 177-192 and Dorothy Johnson, "Fabulations of the Flesh: Géricault and the Praxis of Art and Anatomy," in *Visualizing the Body in Art, Anatomy and Medicine since 1800: Models, Modelling*, ed. Andrew Graciano (Routledge. 2019), 39-60.

Bibliography

Albinus, Bernhard Siegfried. *Tabulae sceleti et musculorum corporis humani.* Leiden, 1747.

Bouchardon, Edme. *L'anatomie nécessaire pour les arts du dessein par Edme Bouchardon, sculpteur du Roy.* Paris: Huquier, 1741.

Cafagna, Fabio. "Images of Transparency and Resurrection from Leonardo da Vinci to Crisóstomo Martínez." *Nuncius* 32, no. 1 (2017): 52-84.

Caviglia, Susanna. *History, Painting, and the Seriousness of Pleasure in the Age of Louis XV.* Liverpool: Liverpool University Press on behalf of the Voltaire Foundation, 2020.

Comar, Philippe. *Figures du corps. Une leçon d'anatomie à l'École des Beaux-Arts.* Paris: Beaux-Arts de Paris, les Éditions, 2008.

Desmas, Anne-Lise, Edouard Kopp and Guilhem Scherf. *Bouchardon. Royal Artist of the Enlightenment.* Los Angeles: J. Paul Getty Museum, 2017.

Diderot, Denis. "Anatomie." In Denis Diderot and Jean-Baptiste Le Rond d'Alembert, *Encyclopédie ou dictionnaire raisonné des sciences, des arts et des métiers, par une société des gens de lettres.* Vol. I. A. Lucques: Chez Vincent Giuntini, 1760.

________. "Pensées détachées sur la peinture." In *Oeuvres esthétiques.* Paris: Garnier frères, 1968.

________. "Sur Bouchardon et la sculpture." In *Correspondence littéraire, philosophique et critique.* Vol. 5. Nendeln: Kraus Reprint, 1829.

Duval, Mathis and Edouard Cuyer. *Histoire de l'anatomie plastique: les maîtres, les livres, et les écorchés.* Paris: Picard & Kann, 1898.

Gamelin, Jacques. *Nouveau recueil d'ostéologie et de myologie dessiné d'après nature.* Toulouse: Desclassen, 1779.

Gautier d'Agoty, Jacques-Fabien. *Myologie complette en couleur et grandeur naturelle.* Paris: Gautier, 1746.

________. *Observations sur la peinture et les tableaux anciens et modernes.* Geneva: Minkoff Reprint, 1972.

Goodman, John. *Diderot on Art.* Vol 1. New Haven and London: Yale University Press, 1995.

Guédron, Martial. "L'enseignement de l'anatomie artistique en France et la question de la dissection (XVIIIe-XIXe siècles)." *Les cahiers d'histoire de l'art,* no. 2 (2004): 33-40.

Johnson, Dorothy. "Anatomie, réalité, idéalité dans l'art français autour de 1800." In *Ecrire les Sciences,* edited by Martial Guédron and Isabelle Laboulais, for *Etudes sur le 18e siècle,* Vol. 42, 177-192, 2015.

________. "The Body Speaks: Anatomical Narratives in French Enlightenment Sculpture." In *Body Narratives. Motion and Emotion in the French Enlightenment,* edited by Susanna Caviglia, 57-58. Turnhout: Brepols Publishers, 2017.

________. "Fabulations of the Flesh: Géricault and the Praxis of Art and Anatomy." In *Visualizing the Body in Art, Anatomy and Medicine since 1800: Models, Modelling,* edited by Andrew Graciano, 39-60. Routledge, 2019.

Jombert, Charles Antoine. *Méthode pour apprendre le dessin.* Paris: Chez l'auteur, 1755.

Kornell, Monique. "Bouchardon's Anatomy Book for Artists." *Getty Research Journal*, no. 8 (2016): 39-54.

Korzybski, Alfred. *Science and Sanity: An Introduction to Non Aristotelian Systems and General Semantics.* 5th ed. Brooklyn: Institute of General Semantics, 1993.

La Font de Saint-Yenne, Etienne. "Réflexions sur quelques causes de l'Etat présent de la peinture en France, avec un examen des principaux ouvrages exposés au Louvre 1746." In *La Font de Saint-Yenne, Oeuvres critiques*, edited by Etienne Jollet, 83-89. Paris: ENSBA, 2001.

Lemire, Michel. *Artistes et mortels.* Paris: Raymond Chabaut, 1990.

Lifchez, Raymond. "Jean-Galbert Salvage and his *Anatomie du Gladiateur combattant*: Art and Patronage in Post-Revolutionary France." *Metropolitan Museum Journal*, 44 (2009): 163-184.

Magnien, Aline. *La Nature et l'antique, le chair et le contour. Essai sur la sculpture française du XVIIIe siècle.* Oxford: Voltaire Foundation, 2004.

Mauriès, Patrick, Corinne le Bitouzé and Anne-Marie Garcia. *Jacques-Fabien d'Agoty: Essais et traités anatomiques.* Paris: ENSBA, 2020.

Monnet, Charles. *Etudes d'anatomie à l'usage des peintres.* Paris, 1774.

Procès-verbaux de l'Académie royale de peinture et de sculpture 1648-1793. Vol. I, *November 1672* and Vol. VIII, *March 30 and April 27, 1772.* Paris: Société de l'histoire de l'art français, 1875-1892.

Réau, Louis. *Houdon, sa vie et son oeuvre.* 2 vols. Paris: Nobele, 1964.

Ronot, Henry. "Le traité d'anatomie d'Edmé Bouchardon." *Bulletin de la Société de l'histoire de l'art français* (1968): 93-100.

Salvage, Jean-Galbert. *Anatomie Du Gladiateur Combattant, Applicable Aux Beaux Arts, Ou Traité des os, des muscles, du mécanisme des mouvements, des proportions et des caractères du corps humain.* Paris: Chez l'auteur, 1812.

Sue, Jean-Joseph. *Elémens d'anatomie à l'usage des peintres, des sculpteurs et des amateurs.* Paris: Chez l'auteur, 1788.

Tortebat, François. *Abrégé de l'anatomie accommodé aux arts de peinture et de sculpture.* Paris: Chez Tortebat, 1667-1668.

Voltaire, *Correspondence littéraire*, edited by Théodore Besterman. Vol. 2, 18-19. Paris: Gallimard, 1963-1993.

Williams, Elizabeth. *A Cultural History of Medical Vitalism in Enlightenment Montpellier.* Burlington, Vermont: Ashgate, 2003.

________. *The Physical and the Moral: Anthropology, Physiology and Philosophical Medicine in France, 1750-1850.* Cambridge: Cambridge University Press, 1994.

Chapter 2

Painting Paradoxes: Jeanne-Elisabeth Chaudet's *Little Girl Teaching her Dog to Read*

Amanda Strasik

Eastern Kentucky University

Abstract

At the 1799 Paris Salon—distinct for its record number of female exhibitors—Jeanne-Elisabeth Chaudet's breakout painting *Little Girl Teaching her Dog to Read* captured critics' attention. One observer regarded the girl's lapdog as her "doll and victim" while another commented upon her fading innocence. These criticisms suggest that *Little Girl Teaching* displays visual details that oscillate between female virtue and corrupted innocence—a major paradox that shaped women's experiences in late eighteenth-century French society. New attitudes toward childhood and childrearing, women's social roles, female sexuality, human-animal relations, and girls' education informed how audiences judged representations of girls and their animal companions. This chapter argues that Chaudet's subject is paradoxical, presenting new learning opportunities for girls while limiting their ambitions. This subject matter is one that, despite new educational and professional possibilities for the female sex, paralleled Chaudet's own experience as a post-revolutionary woman artist.

Keywords: female education, Elisabeth Chaudet, childhood , dolls, pets

***

Introduction

From the French Revolution to the First Empire (c. 1789-1814), women artists in Paris experienced an age of relative openness and new artistic possibilities. In August 1791, the National Assembly issued a ruling that permitted all artists—from non-academicians to women—to exhibit freely at the Salon, one of the most significant and influential public art venues in France. During this time, creative and professional opportunities for women reached new heights, despite the regressive 1804 Napoleonic Code and moralists' outcries about "unnatural" women who sought a life beyond the home.

I do not mean to suggest that this radical decree granted women artists visibility for the first time. Before 1791, the Académie royale de peinture et de sculpture restricted its female membership to four; nevertheless, women artists successfully navigated alternative modes of instruction, exhibition sites, and obtained other opportunities that existed outside the bounds of academic officialdom.[1] In her groundbreaking research, Paris Spies-Gans demonstrated that contrary to former claims of the Revolution and its aftermath having silenced women with extensive legal and political restrictions, female artists were ever-present and increasingly recognized for their contributions.[2]

Jeanne-Elisabeth Chaudet (née Gabiou, 1767-1832) was part of this rising group of women artists who benefitted from the Salons' newfound accessibility. Her first husband was Antoine-Denis Chaudet—a fellow artist with whom she studied, as was typical studio practice for aspiring professional women artists at the time. Much of Chaudet's oeuvre belongs to a heretofore unexamined subgenre of eighteenth-century French artworks that depict images of children—mostly girls—who care for, instruct, or mother humanized dogs and cats. For one, these subjects were indebted to seventeenth-century Netherlandish motifs and painting traditions, which were increasingly popular with a wealthy subset of French private collectors who delighted in uncovering double meanings in ostensibly straightforward compositions.[3] Domestic genre scenes were also among the most favorable and lucrative genres for women artists, who, despite increasing artistic opportunities, continued to be excluded from painting historical subjects, which persisted as the Salon's most esteemed genre. History paintings reigned supreme because they centered on the heroic actions of great men and required a mastery of the male nude form, from which women were mostly denied study.[4] Still, audiences enthusiastically received Chaudet's genre representations of girls and animals, which she exhibited from 1798 to 1814.[5] Her work also reached Empress Joséphine, who had begun to support female exhibitors and became one of Chaudet's most notable patrons. The empress purchased Chaudet's *Young Girl Feeding Chickens* from the 1802 Salon and commissioned additional works for her private collection at Malmaison.

At the 1799 Salon—distinct for its record number of women artists—Chaudet's breakout painting *Little Girl Teaching her Dog to Read* captured critics' attention (Fig. 2.1).[6] Chaudet depicts a pre-adolescent girl who holds a stylishly adorned pug on her lap. Her hunched posture belies a lady's formal, upright comportment. Instead, her pose and focused expression indicate intimacy and determination as she teaches her lapdog how to read from an ABC primer page. As she guides her pet's paw to letters of the alphabet, the animal is neither distressed by its frilly collar nor inhibited by its owner's restrictive embrace.

Instead, it submits to this distinctly human activity and turns to look at its mistress. This teaching moment prompted one critic to regard the dog as the child's "doll and victim," a comment that demonstrates an understanding of this imagery in terms of eighteenth-century pedagogical practices for girls and new ideas about the emotionality of animals.

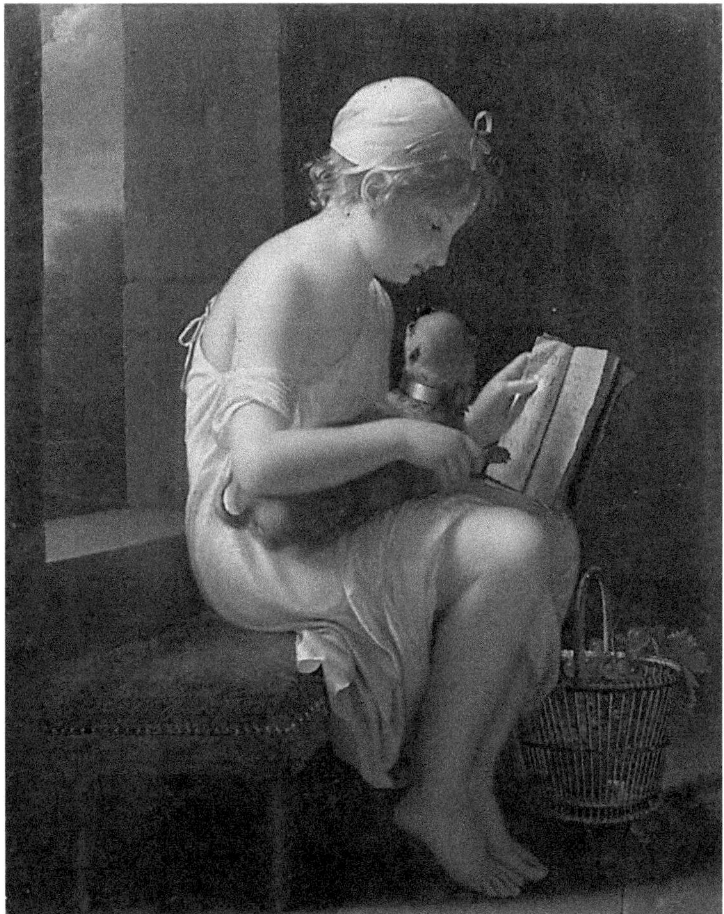

Figure 2.1: Jeanne-Elisabeth Chaudet, *Little Girl Teaching her Dog to Read*, 1799. Oil on panel, Location unknown. Wikimedia Commons. Public Domain

Another observer detected something more insidious. The Salon commentator remarked:

> I forgot to mention the pretty painting by la citoyenne Chaudet. Ah! Please look at this innocent little girl who wants to read the ABCs to her pug . . . What a happy age of simple pleasures! Why are you running so fast![7]

For this critic, the girl has grown up too quickly for her age and aspects of her fading innocence are undeniable. Her bonnet contains unkempt blonde curls—a possible reference to inner wildness or a slovenly appearance. She is barefoot and likely in a state of undress, wearing only a loose-fitting white chemise, a fashionable muslin dress associated with undergarments and boudoir culture. The girl's sleeve dips erotically to show her perfectly smooth back, shoulder, chest, and neck.

The girl's rumpled skirt is also raised to expose her leg, where Chaudet highlights the sumptuousness of the figure's bare knee. This representation recalls Jean-Baptiste Greuze's *Child Playing with a Dog* (1767, Private Collection), which juxtaposes a little girl and small dog to compel audiences to care for and protect the vulnerably innocent.[8] At the same time, other critics identified Greuze's girl as "half-naked" as her stocking slipped down to reveal her knee. Knobby knees were characteristic features of children's bodies and ones that Greuze emphasized to indicate the girl's charm and grace during childhood—a period when physical imperfections were acceptable since the body was still in formation. For a more nefarious subgroup of male viewers, however, exposure of girls' bodies unleashed erotic fantasies. These viewers found sexual pleasure in violating children's depicted innocence or paying for the virginity of child prostitutes.[9] From this standpoint, the partially unclad body of Chaudet's girl, with much of her flesh uncovered, may be seen as an object of sexual intrigue.

These criticisms reveal that *Little Girl Teaching* displays highly charged visual details that oscillate between female virtue and corrupted innocence—a paradox that defined women's experiences in late eighteenth-century French society. New, and at times contradictory, attitudes toward childhood and childrearing, women's social roles, female sexuality, and girls' education informed how audiences judged representations of little girls caring for their humanized animal companions. Evidence of shifts in petkeeping practices, new understandings of human-animal relations, and the symbolism of lapdogs also add to my discussion of society's fear of and desire to control animalistic impulses, especially in girls. From these perspectives, I contend that *Little Girl Teaching* communicates new opportunities for girls to learn and grow, but according to strict rules of feminine propriety that focused upon emotional and sexual restraint and relegation to domestic interiors.

This chapter also critically examines Chaudet's artistic prowess during a time of growing activity for French women artists at the turn of the century. I argue that *Little Girl Teaching*'s paradoxical subject matter parallels the experiences of women artists like Chaudet, who enjoyed new freedoms after the Revolution, but according to a prescribed set of gender expectations that imposed limitations. Archival data indeed confirms women's active participation in both public and private settings in the late eighteenth-century art world. Nonetheless, we must recognize that Chaudet and her female contemporaries largely spent their careers as painters of domesticity, fruits and flowers, pastels, miniatures, and portraiture because of biased conceptions of gender that persisted.[10] These subjects remained the most accessible, profitable, and professionally prudent; anything more ambitious by women could spark ruinous accusations of immodesty. Within Chaudet's corpus, *Little Girl Teaching* is one of many examples of paintings that depict socially "safe" subjects like young girls with baskets of fruit and small animals. Upon closer examination, I argue that *Little Girl Teaching* is distinct because of its far-reaching scope and ambition. In this genre painting, Chaudet asserts her artistic authority, plays with visual conventions, and engages with gender and class politics, but from within an appropriate "feminine" context that appeared unthreatening to the institutional artistic order. *Little Girl Teaching* teaches us that in spite of increasing pathways to equality, women still had a long way to go.

Redefining Childhood in Enlightenment France

By the middle of the eighteenth century, Enlightenment conceptions of children as naturally pure and innocent challenged long-standing Christian beliefs of children as born of Original Sin and inherently corrupt. Enlightenment thinkers and scientists came to view childhood, once thought to be insignificant, as a special phase of human development with distinct needs.[11] New ideas circulated in philosophy, biology, natural science, literary works, and the visual arts that changed how people understood children's relationships to nature, their parents, and the broader French society. Medical publications extoled the uniqueness of children's bodies and the specialized care they required for optimal survival. Naturalists like Georges-Louis Leclerc, the Comte de Buffon, admired the unaffected, imperfect beauty of children's bodies, which he discussed in *Histoire naturelle* (1749), an influential text from which Jean-Jacques Rousseau later borrowed for *Emile, or On Education* (1762). Buffon emphasized children's physical and emotional delicacy, particularly the fragility of their soft skin, skeletal structures, and sensitives to pain. He championed maternal affection, describing it as the most capable source for the vigilance of and minute attention toward "helpless innocents."[12] For Buffon, caring for innocent children was an outward expression of morality and humanity.

Later publications demonstrate sustained interests in children's developing bodies and malleable minds. Specialists reiterated Buffonian ideology as they analyzed children's anatomy in moral terms, emphasizing large heads, prominent cheeks, wide eyes, soft forms, and flushed skin as visible markers of physical health and spiritual virtue.[13] Physicians and moralists valued the natural grace of children's free-moving bodies instead of the artificial beauty that resulted from restrictive bodily devices like corsets and stilted behaviors. In visual culture, French artists interacted with Enlightenment approaches to children's forms to portray childhood innocence. Children now occupied a central place in the new bourgeois family order that emphasized affection and sentimentality, and images of childhood innocence functioned as powerful emblems of renewed morality and a hopeful future.[14]

Mother Knows Best

Eighteenth-century literature and philosophy discussed social reconstruction according to the newly refashioned family unit with the nurturing mother at its moral center. Rousseau most famously emphasized the necessity of children's moral education and the positive influence of a natural environment in *Emile*. According to his beliefs, children were not animalistic but naturally innocent. Rousseau believed that rational thought developed late during childhood, but only if children were liberated from civilization's constraints and learned freely from pedagogical tools, toys, and other methods that were useful and pleasing. When removed from the prison of social institutions steeped in tradition and artifice, children—gently guided by nurturing mothers during their formative years—naturally uncovered their true selves and flourished. Rousseau considered books, scientific study, and certain social practices that were hastily thrust upon children to be the blight of childhood.[15] To launch his social prescriptions, Rousseau advocated for children's physical and mental freedoms, lungs filled with fresh country air, and the restorative properties of maternal breastmilk as ways to raise strong children who would not only survive to adulthood, but positively contribute to society. Decades later, when the French Revolution officially reformed the meaning of family life, bourgeois domesticity with good mothers at the helm stood for republican virtue and honor.[16]

While revolutionaries framed maternal agency as the impetus for social change and moral regeneration, their encouragement of women's domestic lifestyles was politically motivated. Love marriages and one's enthusiastic embrace of motherhood were considered to be antidotes for women's excessive passions and sexual depravity. Although this rhetoric partly functioned to deny women political and economic equality outright, after the Revolution, it invested mothers with a degree of civic virtue and social purpose.[17] Moralizing calls to action placed women in unique positions to shape France's future by helping develop their children's minds and bodies; a new society would emerge from children's physical freedoms and emotional well-being.[18] This ideology framed the paradox of female educational programs in the late eighteenth century. Women were provided with opportunities for growth and instruction, as long as their authority was confined to the domestic interior, where it remained unthreatening to republican and later imperial patriarchal power structures.

An explosion of educational treatises in the late eighteenth century highlights *Emile*'s lasting impact and expanding interests in pedagogical practices for girls.[19] Authors debated what subjects to teach, education's effects on female virtue, and how much instruction was appropriate, hoping to strike a balance between advancing the Enlightenment's education agenda, on the one hand, and readying girls for domestic obligations, on the other. In 1774, writer Louise D'Epinay argued for a more comprehensive approach to girls' education and women's right to self-sufficiency, once they fulfilled their responsibilities as wives and mothers. Women first learned handiwork and housekeeping skills to pass on to their daughters. Only then could their curricula include male subjects to inspire expanded roles for future generations of educated girls. D'Epinay's ideas echo Fénelon's *De l'éducation des filles* (1687), which remained popular in the eighteenth century and attributed the deplorable state of girls' education to outmoded French customs and maternal indifference.[20] Fénelon saw households as small republics with women commanders; as such, women needed training in reading and writing to be able to accomplish their domestic duties and stave off immoral temptations.

Novelist and theorist Stéphanie-Félicité, the Comtesse de Genlis, not only adapted Fénelon's criticisms in her calls for educational reform, but her writings were motivated by and challenged Rousseau's pedagogy. Genlis's *Adèle et Théodore; ou Lettres sur l'éducation* (1782) declared that women must have access to diverse educational subjects to adequately prepare for and cope with the vicissitudes of marriage, motherhood, and domestic economy. Women should have talents, though female genius was a dangerous gift to cultivate since girls were ultimately destined for a "monotonous and dependent life" within domestic environments.[21] Similar to her contemporaries, Genlis preferred home education for the betterment of children's learning and women's sense of purpose.

For children to learn reading fundamentals at home, parents purchased ABC primers, like the one from Chaudet's painting. These small-scale books were plainly designed for clarity and helped girls and boys develop basic literacy skills through concrete examples and short fables.[22] Some ABC readers had a social angle and included brief moralizing stories about proper conduct alongside grammatical exercises. Other texts concentrated on simple lessons to teach classification, such as naming animals or famous French historical figures in alphabetical order.

Some ABC booklets were dedicated to "tender mothers" to emphasize women's centrality in early stages of learning. Jean-Siméon Chardin's *The Young Schoolmistress* (Fig. 2.2, c. 1737) represents an adolescent bourgeois girl, possibly a sister or cousin, privately teaching a young child the alphabet. The girl practices one of her primary responsibilities as a future mother—cultivating young minds and fostering an enthusiasm for education. She leans forward and points to a letter while patiently assessing her student's response. While Chaudet's girl may be too young for human pupils, that does not preclude her from domestic role play. The girl teaches her pug—a stand-in for a human charge—the alphabet and displays her morality and social value by nature of her budding maternal identity.

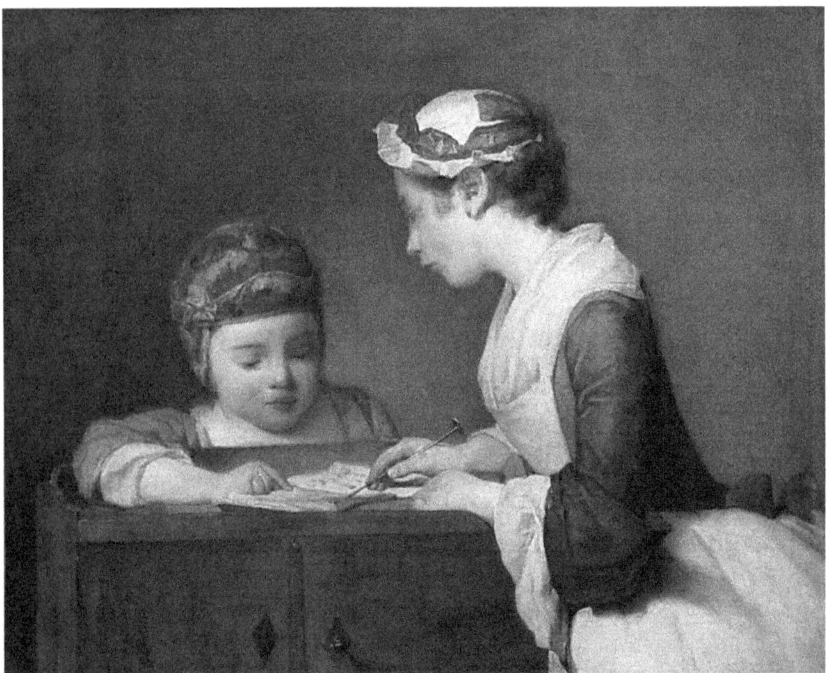

Figure 2.2: Jean-Siméon Chardin, *The Young Schoolmistress*, c. 1737. Oil on canvas, The National Gallery, London. Wikimedia Commons. Public Domain

All Dolled Up

Mothers could motivate their daughters to learn proper subjects and social behaviors by modeling examples themselves. Other forms of instruction included consistent affection, gentle encouragement, and play with new objects from the period's material culture. Eighteenth-century domestic advice manuals insisted that toys and games exhibit interesting aesthetic qualities while doubling as educational activities. Marionette dolls, for example, created hands-on sensory experiences to enrich children's learning processes. These slumped puppets became upright and alive when children moved their parts—a quality that might explain why boys, frequently associated with action toys like balls and drums, were often depicted with this doll variety. In Jean-Honoré Fragonard's *Monsieur FanFan* (Fig. 2.3, c. 1778), for example, a disheveled child runs across the foreground with a puppet draped over one arm and a fashion doll that slips out from under the other. Two spaniels chase FanFan and tug at the fashion doll's hair, pulling the toy further into their mouths. The dogs nip at the static plaything that doesn't do much to stimulate the child's senses or build his masculine character.

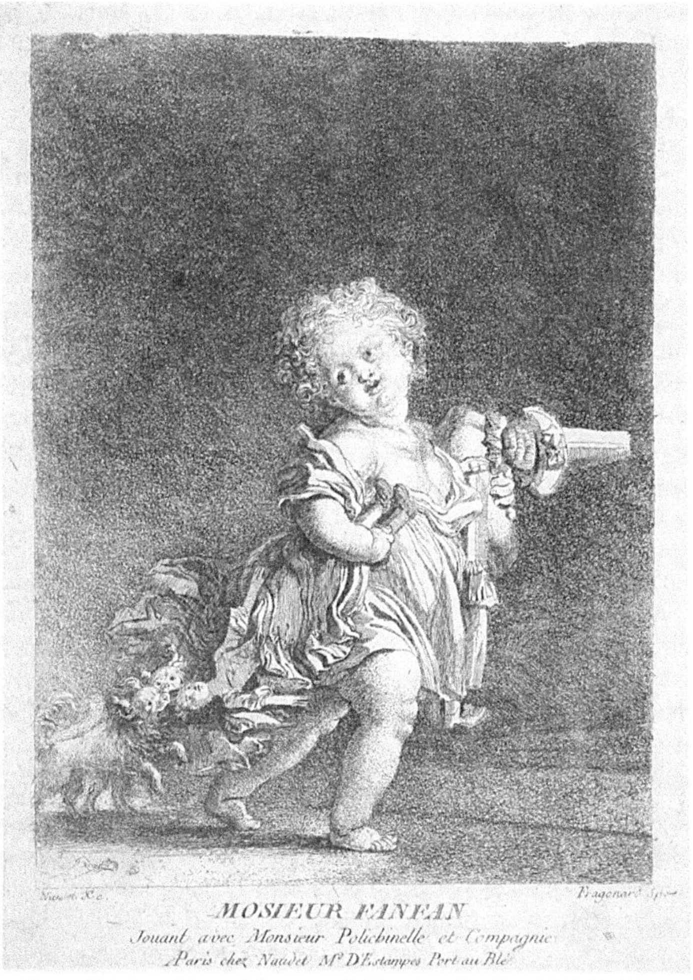

Figure 2.3: Jean-Honoré Fragonard, *Monsieur FanFan*, 1778. Etching, The Metropolitan Museum of Art, New York

The dogs' attack on the boy's fashion doll may be because doll play was mostly considered to be a female pastime; the objects were teaching instruments that prepared girls for feminine social behaviors.[23] I argue that when the Salon critic called the pug from Chaudet's painting a "doll," the girl transformed into a virtuous mother-teacher who, through pedagogical play, practices how to provide for and educate her future children. This action establishes the girl's agency as a burgeoning young woman, but paradoxically her influence is tied to her maternity and mostly limited to domestic contexts.

While dolls have not always been exclusive to children's play, they do have historic ties to girls, femininity, and maternity. Jaucourt's entry on "*poupée*" (doll) in the *Encyclopédie* identifies dolls' ritualistic origins in Ancient Rome. The scholar writes that dolls were well-known children's toys; however, young Roman girls most often carried dolls, which had provided simple amusement during childhood, to the altar of Venus. Jaucourt sees these dolls as votive offerings as girls prayed to the goddess of love for "pretty children" in their dolls' likenesses. Alternatively, this ritual may have been a symbolic sacrifice to signal the passage from childhood to adulthood. Girls left their dolls on Venus's altar to mark the end of frivolous girlhood games and their new embrace of more serious domestic pursuits.[24]

Jaucourt continues, informing readers that the Romans' use of dolls had been passed on to the French, though he believes that contemporary dolls, with their exquisite dresses and coiffures, are more beautiful than their ancient counterparts.[25] The encyclopedist may be referencing pandoras, which were doll types that modistes used to advertise and sell the latest ladies' styles in France and abroad. These dolls mostly represented adult women and were not for play; pandoras publicized eighteenth-century clothing trends before the advent of fashion plates. Until the late nineteenth century in France, many dolls continued to resemble scaled-down versions of elegant adult women to spread prevailing ideals about proper, modern bourgeois femininity.[26] For instance, in François Boucher's *The Luncheon* (1739, Musée du Louvre, Paris), a little girl holds a large doll at her side. Like the human figures in the painting, the doll is fashionably dressed as if it were an actual eighteenth-century French lady for the little girl to emulate.

Although dolls were prized for their educative capacities, critics advised that girls' interactions with dolls did not always promote exemplary moral lessons. By learning to sew for and dress their fashion dolls, some feared girls would go too far and become materialistic, immodest, and disobedient. D'Epinay, for one, viewed dolls as obstacles that distracted her grand-daughter Emilie from more serious pursuits. Jeanne-Marie Leprince de Beaumont was one of the first to bring dolls into children's literature; she recognized girls' affections for dolls, but also warned about the objects as symbols of female moral capriciousness. Leprince de Beaumont's moralizing *Magasin des enfants* (1758) includes a dialogue between three girls who wonder at what age they should renounce dolls. Twelve-year-old Lady Sensée wants to play with her new doll. Lady Spirituelle, also twelve, chastises her friend and says that at their age, Sensée should be more reasonable. Lady Babiole, the youngest of the group at age ten, reveals that she recently spied Spirituelle playing with dolls. Spirituelle confesses that may be true, but six months ago, she burned her dolls and asked her father to use the money spent on such trifles to pay for books and tutors.[27] Leprince de Beaumont's lesson cautions readers that doll play is not necessarily a positive influence as girls grow older. For more reasoned study, they should utilize learning tools less associated with girlhood frivolity.

Because of dolls' positive and negative associations as teaching aids for girls, it remained the responsibility of caretakers, like mothers or governesses, to monitor and manage their daughters' play. Careful surveillance of girls' interactions with dolls would help parents track educational progress, verifying the degree and effectiveness of children's moral training. Jaucourt advised readers that though dolls are silent, if they want to learn the happenings of a household, the tone of a family, to what extent the parents are prideful, and the foolishness of a housekeeper, people should study how girls reason with their doll.[28] Likewise, in *Adèle et Théodore*, Madame de Genlis wrote about how she saw Adèle teaching her doll the very lessons she had just learned herself.[29] By having observed the girl actively instructing her doll, Genlis was able to better assess Adèle's own aptitude and moral standing and implement change, if necessary. Returning to Chaudet's painting, the little girl plays with her fashionable "doll" without supervision. According to these pedagogical contexts, this behavior could have disastrous consequences if left unchecked.

A Girl's Best Friend: Lapdogs and Femininity

Although dolls proved to be effective educational tools during girlhood, the objects are inanimate. Domesticated creatures, however, are alive and respond to humans' actions. The Salon critic's secondary interpretation of the pug as a "victim" of the girl's reading lesson calls to mind numerous associations at once. "Victim" indicates the animal as a feeling subject. The dog is invested with human qualities and viewers may sympathize with it as it learns the alphabet, which is beyond its comprehension. The ability to use written and spoken language to transmit information and connect thoughts is human-specific since animals, in accordance with Buffonian theory, "can neither join nor separate ideas."[30] For Chaudet's dog to be worthy of serious critical attention demonstrates the period's widespread interest in psychology, sensation and sensibility, and concern for animal welfare, an activist movement that gained momentum in the eighteenth and nineteenth centuries.[31]

Eighteenth-century theorists on the sensitivity of animals argued that the soul manifested itself through animals' sensory perceptions of the world. Chaudet's pug, with its tail held high, conveys a fully sentient and alert awareness. Instead of a drooping tail that indicates distress or squirming to express suffering, the dog appears to be comfortable, obedient, and trusting as it looks up at its owner. The pug's calm demeanor in this game of make-believe rejects a representation of the dog as a victim of animal cruelty. Instead, the girl displays an appropriate sense of patience, maternal affection, and benevolence toward her pupil, aligning with Rousseau's belief that children's kindness toward animals would foster kindness toward human beings.[32] To further emphasize their loving bond, the girl wraps her arm around the pug and secures it on her lap. This emotional portrayal of animal sensibility encourages viewers to feel with the dog and shows Chaudet's understanding of the modern animal subject.

Additionally, in art and literature of the eighteenth century and earlier, dogs were symbolic attributes of human subjects. Canines' meanings shifted depending upon the depicted breed and context. Often, these animals communicated obedience, protection, and unbreakable loyalty. Dogs were also commodities that conveyed their owner's class and gender. At times, they represented various social and sexual anxieties. The female body and lapdog, for example, were associated with private spaces and conflated to illustrate the immoral convergence of consumption, luxury, leisure, and eroticism.[33] In *Little Girl Teaching*, the girl and lapdog inhabit the interior realm, turning their backs to the outside world that is visible through the open window. The pug's presence as a household pet becomes a marker of luxury and alludes to the moral dangers of female consumer culture.

"Pet" is defined as a subcategory of domesticated animals without practical function or economic worth. Throughout history, pets were given personal names, wore fashion accessories like collars, and mourned after their deaths. These actions show owners' deep financial and emotional investments in animals that lived in the home but did not work or supply milk, meat, or fur.[34] Pets occupied a liminal space and blurred the bounds between humans and animals as well as virtue and extravagance. From this perspective, I contend that Chaudet's depicted dog has paradoxical significance. Like doll play, the lapdog raises contradictory ideas about girls' cultivation of compassion and maternal tenderness, on the one hand, and immoral self-indulgence on the other.

Owning pets was once an aristocratic privilege, where one used animals, especially rare and exotic ones, as outward expressions of power and prestige.[35] Pugs' characteristic pushed-in heads indicated their East Asian origins, and they were imported into Western Europe along with tea and porcelain. Fashionable British and French women began to collect small dogs and china, which demonstrated rising colonialist attitudes and female-oriented consumer cultures.[36] In Oliver Goldsmith's *History of the Earth and Animated Nature* (1774), the naturalist wrote that the fetishization of "foreign useless dogs" as elite luxury items threatened middle-class virtue.[37] Lapdogs in England and

France came to embody the worst of fashionable consumption since these non-working animals were excessive consumers themselves. Moreover, women's supposed natural impulses to pamper lapdogs came to demonstrate their frivolity and general inability to understand what really mattered in life. In *Little Girl Teaching*, the critic's reference to the pug's victimhood may have been in the context of girls' susceptibilities to material pleasures and this particular girl's waning innocence, for which another critic had already expressed concern. Notice how the pug wears a lavish gold collar with red trim while the girl's skirt is hiked above her knee. This "dolled up" pug may point to the girl's superficiality and desire to be on display, which may worsen as she gets older and continues without proper moral guidance.

Conclusion

My close reading of *Little Girl Teaching* has shown how Chaudet and her audiences engaged with new discourses on girlhood, female sexuality and education, and empathy for animals, among other issues. Critics noticed tensions between female virtue, pursuits that could cross lines if left unchecked, and the looming threat of lost innocence. This paradoxical framework structured women's lives—Chaudet's included. In scholars' ongoing efforts to understand women and their experiences in the eighteenth-century French art world, they must critically consider the implications of what women artists exhibited and the persistent sociopolitical barriers that women navigated. While opportunities for education and professional art experiences expanded, they continued to be defined by societal constructs of femininity that emphasized modesty and domestic virtue. From this perspective, Chaudet's *Little Girl Teaching* points to inherent contradictions that not only shaped women's lives, but ones that undermined contemporary movements toward greater gender equality.

Notes

[1] Key sources on eighteenth-century French women artists include Eik Kahng, Marianne Roland Michel, et al., *Anne Vallayer-Coster: Painter to the Court of Marie-Antoinette* (Dallas: Dallas Museum of Art, 2002); Jordana Pomeroy, Laura Auricchio, et al., *Royalists to Romantics: Women Artists from the Louvre, Versailles and Other French National Collections* (London: Scala, 2012); Melissa Hyde and Mary D. Sheriff, *Becoming a Woman in the Age of Enlightenment: French Art from the Horvitz Collection* (The Horvitz Collection, 2017).

[2] Paris Amanda Spies-Gans, "Exceptional, but not Exceptions: Public Exhibitions and the Rise of the Woman Artist in London and Paris, 1760-1830," *Eighteenth-Century Studies* 51, no. 4 (Summer 2018): 404-410. Also see Spies-Gans's forthcoming book on women artists, *A Revolution on Canvas: The Rise of Women Artists in Britain and France*, 1760-1830 (Yale University Press, 2022).

[3] Amanda Strasik, "Going (Neo-) Dutch: Establishing Marguerite Gérard's Artistic Agency," *Art Inquiries* XVII, no. 4 (2019): 406.

[4] Melissa Hyde, "Some Autobiographical Reflections on 'Becoming a Woman,'" in *Becoming a Woman in the Age of Enlightenment: French Art from the Horvitz Collection*, ed. Melissa Hyde and Mary D. Sheriff (The Horvitz Collection, 2017), 104.

[5] No comprehensive critical study of Chaudet and the historical significance of her artistic identity and *oeuvre* exists. Two catalogue resources, however, provide a brief overview of her biography and identify some of her works. See Charlotte Foucher, *Vie et oeuvre de Jeanne-Elisabeth Chaudet, 1767-1832* (M.A. Thesis, Université François Rabelais à Tours, 2006), 19-21 and Geneviève Lacambre, "Jeanne-Elisabeth Chaudet," in *From David to Delacroix: French Painting 1774–1830: The Age of Revolution*, ed. Pierre Rosenberg and Robert Rosenblum (Paris; Detroit; New York City: Wayne Univ. Press, 1975), 347-348.

[6] Collection Deloynes, Tome 21 (1799–1800). «Coup d'oeil sur le Salon», *Mercure de France*, 1799, 3 pag. Ms. 269; «Exposition de tableaux au Salon du Louvre», *Journal d'indications*, 1799; «Exposition des ouvrages de peinture, sculpture, architecture, gravures, dessins, modèles composes par les artistes vivans et exposés dans le Salon du Musée central des Arts», *le Journal de la Décade*, par le. C. Chaussard, 1799; «Exposition des peintures, sculptures, dessins, architecture, et gravures exposés au Salon du Louvre», 1799, *Journal de Paris*.

[7] Collection Deloynes, Tome 21 (1799–1800). «Coup d'oeil sur le Salon», *Mercure de France*, 1799, 3 pag. Ms. 269.

[8] Emma Barker, "Imagining Childhood in Eighteenth-Century France: Greuze's Little Girl with a Dog," *The Art Bulletin* 91, no. 4 (December 2009): 426-445.

[9] Ibid., 436-438.

[10] Spies-Gans mentions two British artists, Angelica Kauffman and Mary Moser, who depicted history subjects. Moser studied the human figure, albeit the female nude. In France, some women were able to study the live nude model, but in private ateliers with chaperones. See Spies-Gans, "Exceptional, but not Exceptions," 396.

[11] Philippe Ariès, *Centuries of Childhood: A Social History of Family Life*, trans. Robert Baldick (New York: Vintage Books, 1965). Subsequent scholars have challenged and expanded upon Ariès's groundbreaking research on the "discovery" of modern childhood as a distinct period of human life in seventeenth-century Europe. Relevant studies on the cultural and historical redefinition of bourgeois children and the ideology of childhood in eighteenth-century France are Donald Geoffrey Charlton, "Happy Families: Age of Innocence," *New Images of the Natural in France: A Study in European Cultural History 1750-1800* (Cambridge: Cambridge University Press, 1984), 135-177; Colin Heywood, *Childhood in Modern Europe* (Cambridge: Cambridge University Press, 2018), 79-120; Hugh Cunningham, *Children and Childhood in Western Society Since 1500*, 2nd Edition (New York: Routledge, 2005), 41-80; Linda Pollock, *Forgotten Children: Parent-Child Relations from 1500-1900* (Cambridge: Cambridge University Press, 1983), 1-67.

[12] Georges Louis Leclerc Buffon, *De l'homme: Histoire naturelle*, (Paris: Vialetay, 1971), 27-28.

[13] Jacques Ballexserd, *Dissertation sur l'éducation physique des enfants, depuis leur naissance jusque'a l'age de puberté* (Paris: Chez la Veuve Vallat-La-Chapelle, 1762), 16–17; Jean-Louis Fourcroy, *Lettres sur l'education physique des enfants* (Amiens: Chez la Veuve

Godart, 1772); Riballier, *De l'éducation physique et morale des enfants des deux sexes* (Paris, 1785).

[14] Key studies on representations of children and the bourgeois family in eighteenth-century French art are Carol Duncan, "Happy Mothers and Other New Ideas in French Art," *The Art Bulletin* 55, no. 4 (Dec 1973): 570-583; Dorothy Johnson, "Engaging Identity: Portraits of Children in Late Eighteenth-Century European Art," in *Fashioning Childhood in the Eighteenth Century: Age and Identity*, ed. Anja Muller (Burlington: Ashgate, 2006), 101-116; Christine Kayser, ed., *L'enfant chéri au siècle des Lumières: après l'Émile* (Louveciennes: Musée-Promenade de Marly-le-Roi, 2003).

[15] Jean-Jacques Rousseau, *Emile, or On Education*, trans. Allan Bloom (Basic Books: New York, 1979), 116.

[16] Mary Jacobus, "Incorruptible Milk: Breast-Feeding and the French Revolution," in *Rebel Daughters: Women and the French Revolution*, ed. Sarah E. Melzer and Leslie W. Rabine (New York: Oxford University Press, 1992), 54-75.

[17] Joan Landes, *Women and the Public Sphere in the Age of the French Revolution* (Ithaca: Cornell University Press, 1988), 1-13.

[18] Jennifer Popiel, *Rousseau's Daughters: Domesticity, Education, and Autonomy in Modern France* (Durham: University of New Hampshire, 2008), 8-10; Lesley Walker, *A Mother's Love: Crafting Feminine Virtue in Enlightenment France* (Lewisburg: Bucknell University Press, 2008).

[19] Carol Strauss Sotiropoulos, *Early Feminists and the Education Debates: England, France, Germany 1760-1810* (Madison, Teaneck: Fairleigh Dickinson University Press, 2007), 76.

[20] Nadine Bérenguier, *Conduct Books for Girls in Enlightenment France* (Burlington: Ashgate, 2011), 1-2.

[21] Adrian O'Connor, "Nature, Nurture, and the Social Order: Imagining Lessons and Lives for Women in Ancien Régime France," *French Politics, Culture & Society* 30, no. 1 (2012): 1-22.

[22] Popiel, *Rousseau's Daughters*, 112-122.

[23] Ibid., 78. Also Ariane Fennetaux, "Transitional Pandoras: Dolls in the Long Eighteenth Century," in *Childhood by Design: Toys and the Material Culture of Childhood, 1700-Present*, ed. Megan Brandow-Faller (New York: Bloomsbury Visual Arts, 2018), 47-66.

[24] Jaucourt, "POUPÉE," in *Encyclopédie, ou dictionnaire raisonné des sciences, des arts et des métiers, etc.*, ed. Denis Diderot and Jean le Rond d'Alembert. University of Chicago: ARTFL Encyclopédie Project (Autumn 2017 Edition), Robert Morrissey and Glenn Roe (eds), http://artflsrv02.uchicago.edu/cgi-bin/philologic/getobject.pl?c.12:460.encyclopedie0513.

[25] Ibid.

[26] Anna Green, *French Paintings of Childhood and Adolescence, 1848-1886* (Burlington: Ashgate, 2007), 130-134; Greg M. Thomas, "Impressionist Dolls: On the Commodification of Girlhood in Impressionist Painting," in *Picturing Children: Constructions of Childhood between Rousseau and Freud*, ed. Miriam Brown (Burlington: Ashgate, 2007), 103-105.

[27] Michel Manson, *Jouets de toujours, de l'Antiqué à la Révolution* (Paris, Fayard, 2001), 231-250.

[28] Jaucourt, "POUPÉE," *Encyclopédie.*

[29] Genlis quoted in Jennifer Milam, *Fragonard's Playful Paintings: Visual Games in Rococo Art* (Manchester: Manchester University Press, 2006), 92.

[30] Buffon quoted in Joanna M. Gohmann, "Living together: Representations of Animals and the Performance of Elite Identities in French Spaces of Sociability, 1700-1789" (Ph.D. dissertation, UNC Chapel Hill, 2016), 135.

[31] Sarah Cohen, "Chardin's Fur: Painting, Materialism, and the Question of Animal Soul," *Eighteenth-Century Studies* 38, no. 1 (Fall 2004): 39-61; Cohen, "Thomas Gainsborough's Sensible Animals," in *Animals and Humans: Sensibility and Representation*, 1650-1820, ed. Katherine M. Quinsey (Oxford: Voltaire Foundation, 2017), 206-211; Hester Hastings, *Man and Beast in French Thought of the Eighteenth Century* (Baltimore: Johns Hopkins Press, 1936); Leonora Rosenfield, *From Beast-Machine to Man-Machine; The Theme of Animal Soul in French Letters from Descartes to La Mettrie* (New York: Oxford University Press, 1941).

[32] Rousseau, *Emile*, 203.

[33] Jodi L. Wyett, "The Lap of Luxury: Lapdogs, Literature, and Social Meaning in the 'Long' Eighteenth Century," *Literature, Interpretation, Theory* 10 (2000): 275-301.

[34] Erica Fudge, *Pets* (Routledge, 2016), 15-20; James Serpell, *In the Company of Animals: A Study of Human-Animal Relationships* (New York: Cambridge University Press, 1996), 169-170; Ingrid Tague, *Animal Companions: Pets and Social Change in Eighteenth-Century Britain* (University Park: Pennsylvania State University, 2015), 3-4.

[35] Kimberly Chrisman-Campbell, "Beauty and the Beast: Animals in the Visual and Material Culture of the Toilette," *Studies in Eighteenth-Century Culture* 42 (2013): 147-171.

[36] Chi-ming Yang, "Culture in Miniature: Toy Dogs and Object Life," *Eighteenth-Century Fiction* 25, no. 1 (Fall 2012): 144-150.

[37] Wyett, "The Lap of Luxury," 280-281.

Bibliography

Ariès, Philippe. *Centuries of Childhood: A Social History of Family Life.* Translated by Robert Baldick. New York: Vintage Books. 1965.

Ballexserd, Jacques. *Dissertation sur l'éducation physique des enfants, depuis leur naissance jusque'a l'age de puberté.* Paris: Chez la Veuve Vallat-La-Chapelle, 1762.

Barker, Emma. "Imagining Childhood in Eighteenth-Century France: Greuze's Little Girl with a Dog." *The Art Bulletin* 91, no. 4 (December 2009): 426-445.

Bérenguier, Nadine. *Conduct Books for Girls in Enlightenment France.* Burlington: Ashgate, 2011.

Buffon, Georges Louis Leclerc, le comte de. *De l'homme: Histoire naturelle.* Introduction by Jean Rostand. Paris: Vialetay, 1971.

Charlton, Donald Geoffrey. *New Images of the Natural in France: A Study in European Cultural History 1750-1800.* Cambridge: Cambridge University Press, 1984.

Chrisman-Campbell, Kimberly. "Beauty and the Beast: Animals in the Visual and Material Culture of the Toilette." *Studies in Eighteenth-Century Culture* 42 (2013): 147-171.

Cohen, Sarah. "Chardin's Fur: Painting, Materialism, and the Question of Animal Soul." *Eighteenth-Century Studies* 38, no. 1 (Fall 2004): 39-61.

———. "Thomas Gainsborough's Sensible Animals." In *Animals and Humans: Sensibility and Representation*, 1650-1820, edited by Katherine M. Quinsey, 191-218. Oxford: Voltaire Foundation, 2017.

Collection Deloynes, Tome 21 (1799–1800). «Coup d'oeil sur le Salon», *Mercure de France*, 1799, 3 pag. Ms. 269; «Exposition de tableaux au Salon du Louvre», *Journal d'indications*, 1799; «Exposition des ouvrages de peinture, sculpture, architecture, gravures, dessins, modèles composes par les artistes vivans et exposés dans le Salon du Musée central des Arts», *le Journal de la Décade*, par le. C. Chaussard, 1799; «Exposition des peintures, sculptures, dessins, architecture, et gravures exposés au Salon du Louvre», 1799, *Journal de Paris*.

Cunningham, Hugh. *Children and Childhood in Western Society Since 1500*, 2nd Edition. New York: Routledge, 2005.

Duncan, Carol. "Happy Mothers and Other New Ideas in French Art." *The Art Bulletin* 55, no. 4 (Dec 1973): 570-583.

Fennetaux, Ariane. "Transitional Pandoras: Dolls in the Long Eighteenth Century." In *Childhood by Design: Toys and the Material Culture of Childhood, 1700-Present*, edited by Megan Brandow-Faller, 47-66. New York: Bloomsbury Visual Arts, 2018.

Foucher, Charlotte. *Vie et oeuvre de Jeanne-Elisabeth Chaudet, 1767-1832.* M.A. Thesis, Université François Rabelais à Tours, 2006.

Fourcroy, Jean-Louis. *Lettres sur l'education physique des enfants.* Amiens: Chez la Veuve Godart, 1772.

Fudge, Erica. *Pets.* Routledge, 2016.

Gohmann, Joanna M. "Living together: Representations of Animals and the Performance of Elite Identities in French Spaces of Sociability, 1700-1789." Ph.D. dissertation, UNC Chapel Hill, 2016.

Green, Anna. *French Paintings of Childhood and Adolescence, 1848-1886.* Burlington: Ashgate, 2007.

Hastings, Hester. *Man and Beast in French Thought of the Eighteenth Century.* Baltimore: Johns Hopkins Press, 1936.

Heywood, Colin. *Childhood in Modern Europe.* Cambridge: Cambridge University Press, 2018.

Hyde, Melissa and Mary D. Sheriff, eds. *Becoming a Woman in the Age of Enlightenment: French Art from the Horvitz Collection.* The Horvitz Collection, 2017.

Jacobus, Mary. "Incorruptible Milk: Breast-Feeding and the French Revolution." In *Rebel Daughters: Women and the French Revolution*, edited by Sarah E. Melzer and Leslie W. Rabine, 54-75. New York: Oxford University Press, 1992.

Jaucourt. «POUPÉE.» In *Encyclopédie, ou dictionnaire raisonné des sciences, des arts et des métiers, etc.*, edited by Denis Diderot and Jean le Rond d'Alembert. University of Chicago: ARTFL Encyclopédie Project (Autumn 2017 Edition),

Robert Morrissey and Glenn Roe (eds), http://artflsrv02.uchicago.edu/cgi-bin/philologic/getobject.pl?c.12:460.encyclopedie0513.

Johnson, Dorothy. "Engaging Identity: Portraits of Children in Late Eighteenth-Century European Art." In *Fashioning Childhood in the Eighteenth Century: Age and Identity*, edited by Anja Muller, 101-116. Burlington: Ashgate, 2006.

Kahng, Eik, Marianne Roland Michel, et al. *Anne Vallayer-Coster: Painter to the Court of Marie-Antoinette.* Dallas: Dallas Museum of Art, 2002.

Kayser, Christine, ed., *L'enfant chéri au siècle des Lumières: après l'Émile.* Louveciennes: Musée-Promenade de Marly-le-Roi, 2003.

Lacambre, Geneviève. "Jeanne-Elisabeth Chaudet." In *From David to Delacroix: French Painting 1774–1830: The Age of Revolution*, edited by Pierre Rosenberg and Robert Rosenblum, 347–48. Paris; Detroit; New York City: Wayne University Press, 1975.

Landes, Joan B. *Women and the Public Sphere in the Age of the French Revolution.* Ithaca: Cornell University Press, 1988.

Manson, Michel. *Jouets de toujours, de l'Antiqué à la Révolution.* Paris, Fayard, 2001.

Milam, Jennifer. *Fragonard's Playful Paintings: Visual Games in Rococo Art.* Manchester: Manchester University Press, 2006.

O'Connor, Adrian. "Nature, Nurture, and the Social Order: Imagining Lessons and Lives for Women in Ancien Régime France." *French Politics, Culture & Society* 30, no. 1 (2012): 1-22.

Pollock, Linda. *Forgotten Children: Parent-Child Relations from 1500-1900.* Cambridge: Cambridge University Press, 1983.

Pomeroy, Jordana, Laura Auricchio, et al. *Royalists to Romantics: Women Artists from the Louvre, Versailles, and Other French National Collections.* London: Scala, 2012.

Popiel, Jennifer. *Rousseau's Daughters: Domesticity, Education, and Autonomy in Modern France.* Durham: University of New Hampshire Press, 2008.

Riballier, *De l'éducation physique et morale des enfants des deux sexes.* Paris, 1785.

Rosenfield, Leonora. *From Beast-Machine to Man-Machine; The Theme of Animal Soul in French Letters from Descartes to La Mettrie.* New York: Oxford University Press, 1941.

Rousseau, Jean-Jacques. *Emile, or On Education.* Translation and Introduction by Allan Bloom. New York: Basic Books, 1979.

Serpell, James. *In the Company of Animals: A Study of Human-Animal Relationships.* New York: Cambridge University Press, 1996.

Sotiropoulos, Carol Strauss. *Early Feminists and the Education Debates: England, France, Germany 1760-1810.* Madison, Teaneck: Fairleigh Dickinson University Press, 2007.

Spies-Gans, Paris Amanda. *A Revolution on Canvas: The Rise of Women Artists in Britain and France,* 1760-1830. Yale University Press, 2022.

———. "Exceptional, but not Exceptions: Public Exhibitions and the Rise of the Woman Artist in London and Paris, 1760–1830." *Eighteenth-Century Studies* 51, no. 4 (Summer 2018): 404-410.

Strasik, Amanda. “Going (Neo-) Dutch: Establishing Marguerite Gérard’s Artistic Agency.” *Art Inquiries* XVII, no. 4 (2019): 400-409.

Tague, Ingrid. *Animal Companions: Pets and Social Change in Eighteenth-Century Britain.* University Park: Pennsylvania State University, 2015.

Thomas, Greg M. “Impressionist Dolls: On the Commodification of Girlhood in Impressionist Painting,” In *Picturing Children: Constructions of Childhood between Rousseau and Freud,* edited by Miriam Brown, 103-125. Burlington: Ashgate, 2007.

Walker, Lesley. *A Mother's Love: Crafting Feminine Virtue in Enlightenment France.* Lewisburg: Bucknell University Press, 2008.

Wyett, Jodi L. “The Lap of Luxury: Lapdogs, Literature, and Social Meaning in the ‘Long’ Eighteenth Century.” *Literature, Interpretation, Theory* 10 (2000): 275-301.

Yang, Chi-ming. “Culture in Miniature: Toy Dogs and Object Life.” *Eighteenth-Century Fiction* 25, no. 1 (Fall 2012): 144-150.

Chapter 3
The Education of Daughters: Embroidered Pictures after Angelica Kauffman

Rachel Harmeyer

Rice University

Abstract

Pictorial embroideries made by young women in Britain and North America in the late eighteenth and early nineteenth centuries have historically been overlooked by art historical scholarship, though they have long been studied and appreciated by collectors. This chapter examines embroidered pictures after Angelica Kauffman, RA (1741–1807) by Caroline Williams (1789–1825), Lucy Coit Huntington (1794–1818), and Maria Crowninshield (1789–1870) and situates them within Enlightenment debates about female education.

Advice literature in the late eighteenth century often questioned the value of the system of accomplishments in women's schooling, and during this time, the term accomplishment itself accrued negative associations with the purely ornamental. However, by choosing moral and didactic subjects such as Kauffman's *Hector and Andromache*, young women employed the genre of history painting to demonstrate that their needlework was no empty accomplishment, but an encapsulation of their education as they sought to negotiate expectations of gender.

Keywords: embroidery, silkwork, Neoclassicism, Angelica Kauffman, women artists

***

> A wild wish has just flown from my heart to my head, and I will not stifle it though it may excite a horse-laugh.—I do earnestly wish to see the distinction of sex confounded in society… For this distinction is, I am firmly persuaded, the foundation of the weakness of character ascribed to woman; is the cause why the understanding is neglected, whilst accomplishments are acquired with sedulous care; and the same cause accounts for their preferring the graces before the heroic virtues.[1]

In *Vindication of the Rights of Woman*, Mary Wollstonecraft (1759–1797) censured socially prescribed gender differences in education because she believed they were detrimental to women. Wollstonecraft finds women to be overly focused on acquiring superficial "accomplishments" rather than improving their minds and laments at their "preferring the graces before the heroic virtues" due to the distinctions of sex placed on them by society. Inspired by the Enlightenment, women writing on education in the late eighteenth century questioned the value placed on accomplishments in women's schooling. Wollstonecraft, Catharine Macaulay (1731–1791), and Hannah More (1745–1833) discussed needlework, and accomplishments in general, within young women's education and arrived at different conclusions about the role they should play. Needlework was a key subject for young women and the creation of an embroidered picture was often a capstone project for female students.[2] Pictorial embroideries made by young women in Britain and North America in the late eighteenth and early nineteenth centuries as part of their education have historically been overlooked by art historical scholarship, though they have long been appreciated by collectors.[3] Often dismissed as ornamental and derivative rather than significant works of art in their own right, this chapter will show that these "schoolgirl embroideries" were serious endeavors that reproduced and reinterpreted works by eminent history painters of the British Royal Academy, notably Angelica Kauffman, RA (1741–1807). The making of this ambitious kind of needlework demonstrated their understanding of history, literature, and moral lessons. This chapter will provide a close study of amateur embroidered pictures made after Kauffman's *The Parting of Hector and Andromache*, 1768 (Saltram House, National Trust) and will argue that makers of embroidered pictures emulating history paintings responded to debates on women's education and sought to elevate the genre of needlework. Caroline Williams's *The Parting of Hector and Andromache*, c. 1800-10 and Lucy C. Huntington's *Hector Taking Leave of Andromache*, 1810, demonstrate how Kauffman's iconography took on new associations and resonances within the context of education, expanding the reception of her art to the United States. Further, they show how such disparate genres as history painting and silk embroidered pictures could be united in imagery, subject, and purpose.

This chapter contributes to scholarship on underrepresented women artists and outsider art by showing that amateur artists aspired for their needlework to be recognized as art within their own time and communicate meaningful ideals to the viewer. Shining a light on these works and recognizing their significance through their authors' adaptation of preexisting iconography provides a means to study objects made by anonymous or marginal artists outside of traditional methods of art production or exhibition, applying iconographic and object-based analysis to works typically excluded from art status. This is crucial work, because the changing categories of what constitutes legitimate art are necessarily informed by institutions of power that have been shaped by systemic sexism, classism, and racism. My focus on the work of amateur needleworkers contributes to this scholarship by showing that amateur embroidered pictures engaged with the visual language and principles of Neoclassical painting, even if the resulting works were meant to be exhibited privately. Despite their exclusion from artistic status by museums, embroidered pictures were typically made by middle- and upper-class white women out of expensive materials and kept as heirlooms or decoration. Though this places these works in a privileged category, I believe my iconographic and object-based approach, blending material, visual culture, and art historical methodologies can provide a model for scholars investigating works made by underrepresented artists outside of traditional categories of fine art.

While recent scholarship has led to a better understanding of women artists' significant participation in exhibition culture, my work focuses on embroidered pictures made by young women who did not typically show their work in formal exhibitions or seek professional careers as artists. Scholars like Heidi Strobel, who examines Mary Linwood (1755–1845), a needlework artist who successfully promoted and exhibited her work in London, and Paris Spies-Gans, in "Exceptional but not Exceptions," are rightly drawing attention to the work of women artists and their participation in exhibition culture in the eighteenth and nineteenth centuries in cultural hubs like London and Paris.[4] As Spies-Gans points out, the Royal Academy's exclusion of copies and "Needle-work, artificial Flowers, Shell-work, or anything of that Kind," were clearly meant to exclude women exhibitors.[5] My intervention focuses on embroidered pictures made by young women as amateur artists connected with their education, not necessarily intended for public display, and seeks to understand why women made needlework copies of paintings. Embroidered pictures largely functioned outside centers of exhibition and public recognition. Though the makers of the embroidered pictures may have had wealth or social status, most held an outsider status as artists. However, they were not merely creating naïve art in a vacuum, they engaged with fine art and exhibition culture by proxy, through their employment of the iconography and subjects by renowned academic artists whose works were familiar to them through reproductive prints.

Kauffman's careful negotiation of gender boundaries and morally instructive subjects in her oeuvre, a necessity in her position as an academic artist, made her designs an appealing choice for copying by women in particular. History painting traditionally centered on the heroic male figure, but Kauffman expanded on these conventions, sensitively portraying the female perspective in famous narratives. Her choice of subjects not only appealed to women but represented what was permissible to be portrayed by a woman: Kauffman typically eschewed nudity or themes that would be inappropriate for a general audience, making the propriety of her work notable. This choice, part of her own reputation management, can be linked to the widespread reproduction of her iconography in decorative art by professionals and amateurs alike: her designs were appropriate in every room of the house. Kauffman's iconography is frequently included in extant embroidered pictures dating across a number of decades, from the late eighteenth through early nineteenth centuries. Because subjects for embroidered pictures were typically connected to a narrative that presented a clear moral lesson, Kauffman's self-presentation and subjects held especial appeal for women using needlework as part of their self-fashioning.

One avenue pursued by some of the women educated in this manner was a career in education, as headmistresses or governesses. Their skills and curriculum had to be attractive to prospective students and their families, meaning they had to contend with the growing criticism of accomplishments as well as traditional expectations that they would be taught. Student work reflected on the teacher as well as the pupil, advertising a teacher's skills as an educator. Betty Ring, a pioneering researcher on the subject of American "schoolgirl embroideries," identified particular styles used in various academies in New England, showing the guidance the teacher could have on the look of their student's embroidery. Judith A. Tyner's 2015 volume *Stitching the World: Embroidered Maps and Women's Geographical Education* provides a model for what I seek to accomplish in my investigation of embroidered pictures.[6] Tyner focuses on a particular category of needlework, embroidered map samplers, and uses her expertise in the field of geography to analyze and interpret embroidered maps made by young women during the nineteenth century. This lays the groundwork for my analysis, in which I use my knowledge of Kauffman's history paintings, which saturated the print market as reproductive engravings, to investigate women artists' selection and adaptation of their imagery in embroidered pictures, a specific genre of silk-on-silk needlework that emulated paintings. Students and teachers demonstrated that needlework had a place in an enlightened women's education through their adaptation of history paintings into embroidered pictures. Just as Kauffman chose to align herself with history painting as a genre in order to elevate her artistic practice and gain recognition and respect within the Royal Academy, many women used the Neoclassical visual language promoted in history paintings to elevate their embroidery.

"This phrenzy of accomplishments"

How was a young woman to convey that she was educated at the beginning of the nineteenth century, in the wake of debates on the subject of women's education? During the eighteenth century, Macaulay, Wollstonecraft, and More each wrote in favor of improving women's education and criticized accomplishments as a flawed system due to their superficiality. Embroidered pictures fall under the general category of feminine accomplishments, and needlework was often part of this debate. In "Letters on Education," Macaulay writes,

> The art of needle-work, had formerly Minerva for its patroness; and though it has been too much depreciated in modern days, it has been in all ages highly instrumental to the preservation of female virtue and happiness. On these reasons I would rather see it resume all its former importance than be entirely left out of female education. Let us not give up one of the great privileges of female life, which is the consent of the world, that we may amuse ourselves with trifles. Let us not look with a supercilious contempt on an art so justly valued by our ancestors, and which, from its endless variety, affords an inexhaustible source of innocent enjoyment.[7]

Macaulay recommends that boys learn handicrafts as part of their education, though she does not go so far as to recommend needlework, which she seems to define as belonging solely to women: "Don't be frightened, Hortensia; I am not going to give the distaff into the hands of my male pupils."[8] For Macaulay, needlework is an innocent pastime and a traditional form of art, even if she regards it as merely a trifling amusement.

Authors writing from quite different perspectives ultimately make similar admonitory statements about accomplishments, as is the case with Mary Wollstonecraft, feminist philosopher, and Hannah More, Evangelical moralist. Both emphasize the essential falseness of accomplishments. In her first publication, *Thoughts on the education of daughters: with reflections on female conduct, in the more important duties of life* (1787), Wollstonecraft derides "Exterior Accomplishments." She writes, "Under this head may be ranked all those accomplishments which merely render the person attractive; and those half-learnt ones which do not improve the mind."[9] Wollstonecraft chiefly seems to object to surface-level accomplishments that fail to cultivate intellect or understanding: "Girls learn something of music, drawing, and geography; but they do not know enough to engage their attention and render it an employment of the mind. If they can play over a few tunes to their acquaintance and have a drawing or two (half done by the master) to hang up in their rooms, they imagine themselves artists for the rest of their lives."[10] Wollstonecraft emphasizes the necessity of solely authoring a work, as her "half done by the master" comment illustrates. In her *Vindication*, Wollstonecraft expands on Catharine Macaulay's rejection of Rousseau's misogyny. She repudiates a passage from Rousseau's *Emile*, where he states that works of genius are beyond the capacity of women.[11]

Wollstonecraft's emphasis on sole authorship seems connected with this, as she clearly believes women are capable of works of genius.

Wollstonecraft's criticism of accomplishments in women's education center on their superficiality and lack of intellectual rigor, and she sees needlework as part of the problem.[12] Particularly, she condemns the prominence of needlework not only in young women's education, but in women's lives in general. In her *Vindication of the Rights of Woman*, she sharply criticizes "the custom of confining girls to their needle, and shutting them out from all political and civil employments; for by thus narrowing their minds they are rendered unfit to fulfil the peculiar duties which nature has assigned them."[13] She views needlework as a restrictive task, a way to keep women out of the public sphere as passive rather than active citizens.

Hannah More, like Wollstonecraft an abolitionist and social reformer, was not a proponent of needlework or accomplishments in general. More especially decries false accomplishments:

> Not a few of the evils of the present day arise from a new and perverted application of terms; among these, perhaps, there is not one more abused, misunderstood, or misapplied, than the term accomplishments. This word in its original meaning signifies completeness, perfection. But I may safely appeal to the observation of mankind, whether they do not meet with swarms of youthful females, issuing from our boarding schools, as well as emerging from the more private scenes of domestic education, who are introduced into the world, under the broad and universal title of accomplished young ladies, of all of whom it cannot very truly and correctly be pronounced, that they illustrate the definition by a completeness which leaves nothing to be added, and a perfection which leaves nothing to be desired.[14]

More dismisses the frequent artifice of accomplishments, but unlike Wollstonecraft, sees them as disruptive of the social order.

> This phrenzy of accomplishments, unhappily, is no longer restricted within the usual limits of rank and fortune; the middle orders have caught the contagion, and it rages downward with increasing and destructive violence... is it not obvious, that as far as this epidemical mania has spread, this very valuable part of society is declining in usefulness, as it rises in its unlucky pretensions to elegance? till this rapid revolution of the manners of the middle class has so far altered the character of the age...Their new course of education, and the habits of life and elegance of dress connected with it, peculiarly unfits them for the active duties of their own very important condition; while, with

> frivolous eagerness, and second hand opportunities, they run to snatch a few of those showy acquirements which decorate the great. This is done apparently with one or other of these views either to make their fortune by marriage, or if that fail, to qualify them to become teachers of others: hence the abundant multiplication of superficial wives, and of incompetent and illiterate governesses.[15]

More's anti-revolutionary rhetoric is particularly vivid here and reveals where she diverges most sharply from Wollstonecraft. Wollstonecraft initially embraced the principles of the French Revolution and criticized needlework for preventing women from civic and political engagement. More, who is more conservative, reveals in the above passage an anxiety regarding upheaval in the social order. Contrarily, More perceives accomplishments as unfitting young women for their stations in life through mimicking the habits of the elite.

While both Wollstonecraft and More propose a more substantive course of women's education, it seem that accomplishments are especially distasteful to More when acquired by those of lesser rank. More sees accomplishments in relationship with a mercenary marriage market, with socially inferior women trying to lure men in possession of good fortunes. Another significant problem from More's perspective is that the accomplishment system creates as a by-product a surplus of teachers, who perpetuate this cycle of miseducation by passing on useless accomplishments to their pupils. Whether it is women selling themselves through the marriage market, or peddling their false accomplishments to prospective pupils, More condemns them as dangerous to the social order, and particularly degrading to the morals of the middle classes.

Embroidery and women's education

Macaulay, Wollstonecraft, and More show the strong opinions and contradictory advice young women and their teachers contended on the subject of women's education and needlework. The embroidered pictures produced by students under their teacher's supervision can be seen in conversation during these debates, a material response that seeks to reconcile multiple points of view. Embroidered pictures spoke to a student's ability to create elaborate stitches, a useful as well as decorative domestic skill. Through her inclusion of text and imagery, they indicated the lessons she had learned. As Ring shows in *Girlhood Embroidery*, embroidered pictures differed from samplers, which were often created by the very young as a means of improving embroidery technique.[16] Rather, embroidered pictures made by amateurs seem to have been largely produced by young women on the threshold of marriageable age. They were often designed or composed with sometimes significant collaboration on the part of their teachers. Ring has discussed the influence of English silk embroideries on young women's education in America, particularly in New England.[17] Often this education took place in a domestic space, where pupils might live as well as be educated. Headmistresses at these schools created an environment for living and learning for their students. In fact, the needlework produced by the student might be the sole production and the entire purpose of sending a young woman to school.[18] Jane Austen satirizes this practice in *Sense and Sensibility* when she describes the silk embroidery made by Mrs. Jennings's daughter: "over the mantelpiece still hung a landscape in colored silks of her performance, in proof of her having spent seven years at a great school in town to some effect."[19] This a jibe at the character of Charlotte, whose embroidered picture is portrayed as a feeble result. Austen's satirical example shows that teachers and pupils were at pains to prove the worth of their endeavors.

Pictorial silk embroidery could stand as the summation of what a young woman had learned during her education. The costly materials used in the making of embroidered pictures, and their exhibition of refined needlework techniques indicate the social importance of these objects: their scale and rectangular format have the impact of paintings, and they could include painted details. The destiny of these embroideries was display, typically within the private sphere, but it should be noted that some of these works were publicly exhibited. Young women learned needlework as part of their education because society expected them to spend much of the rest of their lives either sewing themselves or supervising the sewing of others. Whether it was practical needlework taught to young women destined to enter service or fancy and elevated needlework taught to women of a higher social status, sewing was an expected task for women to perform. Connected deeply with feminine identity as a social construct, it was an essential as well as decorative domestic skill. Learning to stitch letters, "marking," was only the beginning, and samplers made by girls frequently included epigrams that spoke to the sort of education they received. An embroidered sampler signed by "Lydia Pearson was born June/ 24th 1791 Aged 11 years 1802," now in the Metropolitan Museum of Art, includes the following embroidered inscription: "How blest the Maid whom circling years improve/ Her God the object of her warmest love/ Whose useful hours successive as they glide/ The book the needle and the pen divide."[20] Fancy and elevated forms of stitching were not only a marker of accomplishment and skillful needlework for the sewer, but were connected to social position, wealth, and gender roles.

The choice of subject for an embroidered picture reflected on the sewer who worked, or "wrought," it, and was not a matter to be taken lightly. Ring differentiates embroidered pictures from samplers as a category of needlework frequently done by young women as the last stage in their education.[21] Embroidered pictures were not merely Neoclassical in style and subject, they were often specifically derived from history paintings exhibited at the Royal Academy.[22] Pictures by Kauffman and other eminent academic painters were popular sources for these works. While embroidered pictures themselves were barred from Royal Academy and Royal Society of Artists exhibitions, British needlework artists, like Mary Linwood, found or created other avenues for their public exhibition.[23] Linwood led a private boarding school for young ladies (who no doubt learned needlework) and became renowned for her intricate embroideries after paintings by Gainsborough, Reynolds, Stubbs, and Morland which she exhibited to great acclaim.[24] Margaret Ansell (n. d.) exhibited embroidered pictures after West's *William Penn's Treaty with the Indians* and *The Death of General Wolfe* at the Society of Artists Exhibition in 1776, demonstrating that innovations in history painting were represented in needlework, not only the canonical classical and biblical subjects of history painting.[25] The morality of these subjects made them an appealing choice for both professional and amateur needleworkers who wished to display both their erudition and their virtue. The apex of the hierarchy of genres, the subject of history, resonated with the makers of embroidered pictures, even if they were only familiar with them through reproductive prints. Through the making of these pictorial embroideries, young women sought to accommodate new standards of what it meant for women to be truly educated while continuing to use needlework as a meaningful skill and expression of femininity.

Hector and Andromache

Kauffman's painting *Hector Taking Leave of Andromache*, displayed first at the Society of Artists exhibition in 1768 and later at the inaugural Royal Academy exhibition in 1769, had a rich and productive afterlife as a subject for embroidered pictures in Britain and America. Wendy Roworth has shown that these paintings were vital to cementing Kauffman's reputation in London and earned the artist praise for her pursuit of the elevated academic genre of history painting.[26] Kauffman's painting illustrates the affecting scene from *The Iliad* when Hector departs from his wife and son to lead the defense of Troy. Andromache grasps her husband Hector's hand as he departs for war. They share a poignant moment of connubial tenderness before they part forever. To the left of the composition, a nurse holds Andromache and Hector's baby. She gazes at him lovingly as the infant reaches up to touch her face. The rich, colorful attire of Hector and Andromache stands out against the somber, limited palette of the background. James Watson's 1772 mezzotint after Kauffman's painting faithfully reproduces most of its features (Fig. 3.1).

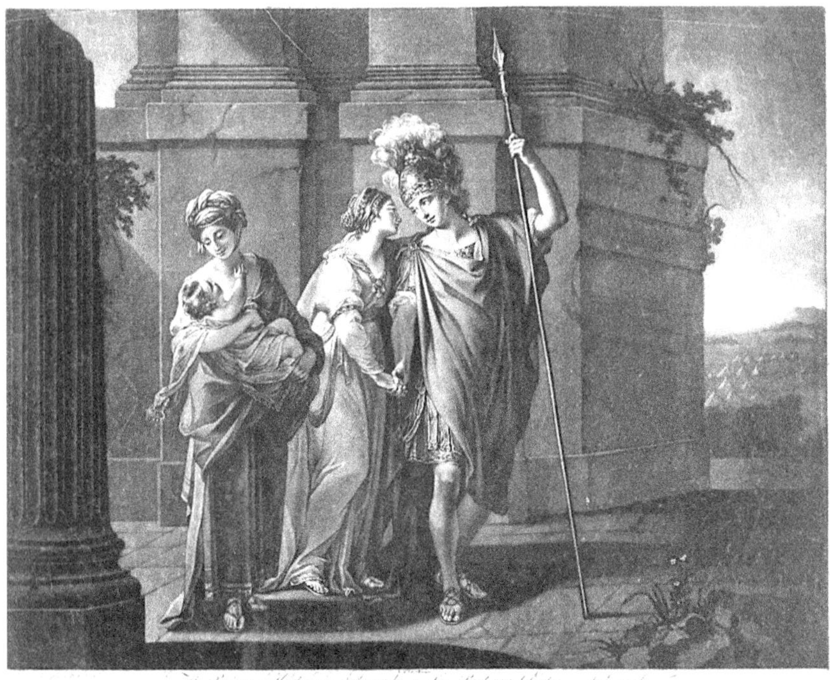

Figure 3.1: James Watson after Angelica Kauffman, *The parting of Hector and Andromache*, 1772. The British Museum, London

Watson added a few embellishments, including more cracks in the architecture and introduces plants creeping up the wall, as well discernible rows of military tents in the distance, a reference to Hector's fate as he prepares to go into battle. Watson's print circulated widely and was used as a visual resource by amateur artists on both sides of the Atlantic. By choosing moral and didactic subjects such as Kauffman's *Hector and Andromache*, young women employed the aesthetics of early Neoclassical history painting to indicate that their needlework was no empty accomplishment, but an encapsulation of their talents and education as they sought to negotiate expectations of social identity.

Kauffman's dramatization of the interaction between Hector and Andromache as a history painting illustrates the importance of civic duty and courage over personal gratification, while reifying gender roles. Alexander Pope's translation of *The Iliad*, popular in the late eighteenth century, summarizes the scene thus: "Hector, having performed the orders of Helenus, prevails upon Paris to return to the battle, and, taking a tender leave of his wife Andromache, hastens again to the field."[27] Hector does not find Andromache at home, as she is out searching for him at the gates of the city. She is accompanied by their infant son, Astyanax, who is held by his nurse.[28]Andromache is described as already in a state of mourning for her husband, foreshadowing his tragic destiny. She begs him to stay with her and not to make her a widow. Hector explains that he must do his heroic duty and go to the battlefield, even if it means he will never return. Hector reaches to take their son from the nurse. Astyanax is frightened by the helmet, which makes Hector and Andromache smile. Hector takes off his helmet and lifts up the boy, praying for his future. He then gives the baby to Andromache directly, who places him on her breast.[29]

Kauffman's painting concentrates on the heroic virtue of Hector, as he chooses to put his duty before his desire to remain with his wife and child, and Andromache's emotional response.[30] It seems to take place at the moment where Andromache and Hector greet each other, before Hector removes his helmet for Astyanax, likely during Andromache's plea for him to remain with her. Despite the fact that this is their tragic final moment together, it is also a scene of domestic happiness. While the scene takes place at the gates of the city, the print, painting, and original text directly engage with the domestic context. Hector first seeks his wife in their home but is told that she is waiting for him at the gates where they ultimately meet. In the poem, as Hector departs, he encourages Andromache to return to that domestic setting. She is expected to focus on their son, the hope of Troy, rather than Hector, who must return to the war and is prepared to die for the sake of the city. The strong implication here is that Andromache must perform her duty and return to the private sphere of the home, her proper station, according to socially prescribed gender roles.

Though Kauffman's painting and the reproductive print after it depict a scene set in public, as material objects they can be related to a domestic context, albeit a grand one: her patron John Parker, 1st Baron Boringdon and his second wife Theresa Parker of Saltram purchased *Hector Taking Leave of Andromache*, along with five other history paintings representing moments from classical literature and early British history, for Saltram House in Devon.[31] Watson's print after Kauffman's *Hector and Andromache* was used as a resource for multiple embroidered silk pictures made in the early part of the nineteenth century, two of which will be examined below. The subject's invocation of the domestic sphere and marital tenderness seems to have contributed to its popularity in embroidered pictures.

Caroline Williams, *The Parting of Hector and Andromache*, c. 1800-10

Caroline Williams (1789-1825), born in Boston more than a decade after Watson's reproduction after Kauffman's painting was first circulated in London, relied closely on the engraving as a model, so much so that her embroidered picture bears precisely the same title as the print: *The Parting of Hector and Andromache*, c. 1800-10 (Fig. 3.2).

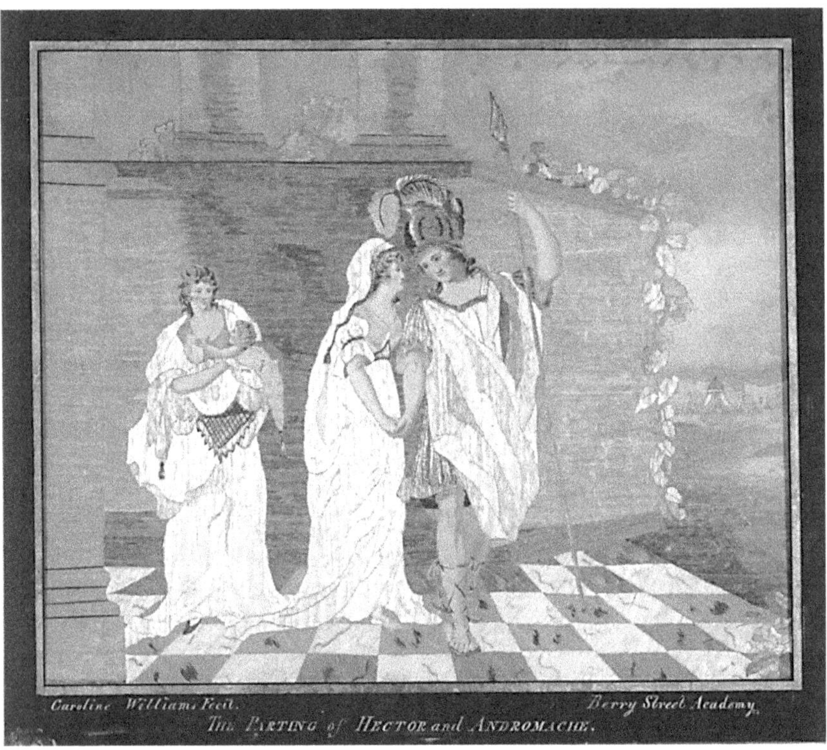

Figure 3.2: Caroline Williams, *The Parting of Hector and Andromache*, c. 1800-10. Peabody Essex Museum, Salem, MA

With silk and metallic threads on top of a watercolor on silk background, this embroidered picture both emulates and departs from its print source. The two key figures of Hector and Andromache appear much as they do in the print, with a few cosmetic alterations. The more surprising changes in Williams's embroidery appear in the figure of the nurse, whose head and upper body appear to derive from another print source entirely. Her position has been reversed from the print while those of Hector and Andromache have not. Her face bears little resemblance to the one in the original print, and a close examination of her garments and the baby she cradles reveal further departures. A wider gap appears between the nurse and the baby and Andromache: their figures are no longer overlapping. This may have been done to give the viewer a less occluded view of Andromache, but distances her further from her child. No longer looking at each other in this version, the child and the nurse seem to have a less intimate relationship, a departure from the tenderness Kauffman depicted in her original painting.

Differences in dress between print and embroidery speak to Williams's process of selection and adaptation. In the print Andromache has braids in her hair and is wearing a headdress, as is the nurse, who wears a kind of turban. In Williams's version, Andromache has more of a trailing veil with curls framing her face. The nurse's head, in addition to no longer wearing the turban, appears disproportionately small relative to the rest of her body. Her hair is in ringlets, and she does not wear a cap. Williams has updated Andromache's costume: in the print, Andromache's sleeves cover her arms, while in Williams's version, her arms are bare to just above her elbow, while her upper arms are covered by short, puffed sleeves. This may have been inspired by changing fashions for women by the early nineteenth century.

Through its inclusion of text, the frame brings up issues of authorship, subject, and social context. Williams's embroidered picture appears within its original eglomise frame – black with gold reverse-glass painting. Its golden lettering on the left reads, "Caroline Williams, fecit." On the right side, "Berry Street Academy." Below and in the center, mirroring the title of the print source, "The Parting of Hector and Andromache." Caroline Williams, the named maker of this silk embroidered picture, likely did not inscribe her own name on the frame. Rather, it would have been done by the professional framer of the picture, likely with the involvement of her teachers. The lettering on the frame aligns with print conventions, with the Latin "fecit," a printmakers' phrase meaning "made by" in Latin. Different phrases and abbreviations are commonly used to give credit to the individuals for their various roles in the collaborative printmaking process. "Caroline Williams, fecit." gives Williams the "made by" credit, but does not name Kauffman or her reproductive printmakers, only the title derived from the print, and the school where she made it, supplanting those other authors. Williams steps into the role of author. It would be easy to associate the use of Latin here as merely an imitation of printmaking conventions, or perhaps a framing device foisted on the work by more learned adults. However, unique details about the specific institution where Williams studied, Berry Street Academy, suggest other possibilities.

The curriculum at Berry Street Academy, where Caroline Williams made her embroidered picture, demonstrates the impact of reform on educational practices for young women. The institution was a small co-educational school in Boston run by William Payne and his wife Sarah Isaacs, who died in 1807. After her death, Payne closed the school and returned with his family to New York until his death in 1812. The relatively brief time the Berry Street Academy was open allows us to date this embroidery with more precision. Specific details about this particular school confront many assumptions attached to silk embroidered pictures, namely that they were the products of academies for girls alone. The

Paynes educated their own children along with other pupils who boarded with them. In his advertisement for his new English grammar school, William Payne announced in the *Boston Evening Post*, that he

> ...begs leave hereby to assure all such as shall please to favor him the important task of educating their children, that he shall exert his utmost endeavors by a constant and careful Attention to their Interest to merit their Approbation and deserve their Encouragment. Besides the English Grammar, Reading, Writing, and Arithmetic will be taught as usual; also the Rudiments of Latin to such as chuse to be instructed therein.[32]

This included girls – Eloise Payne, William and Sarah Isaacs Payne's daughter, was famed within and beyond her family circle for her facility with Latin.[33] Though it is not known how many other girls at the school were taught Latin, the example of Eloise Payne demonstrates that Latin scholarship was available to young women at Berry Street. The Latin text included on the frame of Williams's embroidered picture may indicate that, Williams, like Eloise Payne, learned "the Rudiments of Latin." Visually and textually, Williams's *Hector and Andromache* shows that young women were attempting to achieve what historically was only available to their male peers: a classical education.

Lucy C. Huntington, *Hector Taking Leave of Andromache*, 1810

The embroidered picture of *Hector Taking Leave of Andromache* made by Lucy Coit Huntington (1794-1818) in 1810 (Fig. 3.3) is stylistically unconventional but nevertheless relies on Kauffman's painting as a model.

Huntington created her version of *Hector and Andromache* when she was fifteen or sixteen years old. She was likely educated by her relative Lucy Perkins Carew (1758-1832) who described her curriculum in her advertisement in the *Norwich Packet* on April 3, 1798, which included "English grammar, history, etc.," as well as "Drawing, Painting, Tambour, Embroidery, and all kinds of Needle Work."[34] Huntington married Stephen Blythe Cleveland of Newark, New Jersey, in 1817. In 1818, she died after giving birth to their only child, Joseph Huntington Cleveland, ten months after she was married. Her elaborate example of an embroidered silk picture reveals a complicated lineage to Kauffman. The sole threads that link this work to Kauffman's original painting are the four figures in the composition: Hector, Andromache, the nurse, and the baby. Their identities, gestures, and positions bear a strong resemblance to those of Kauffman's *Hector Taking Leave of Andromache.*

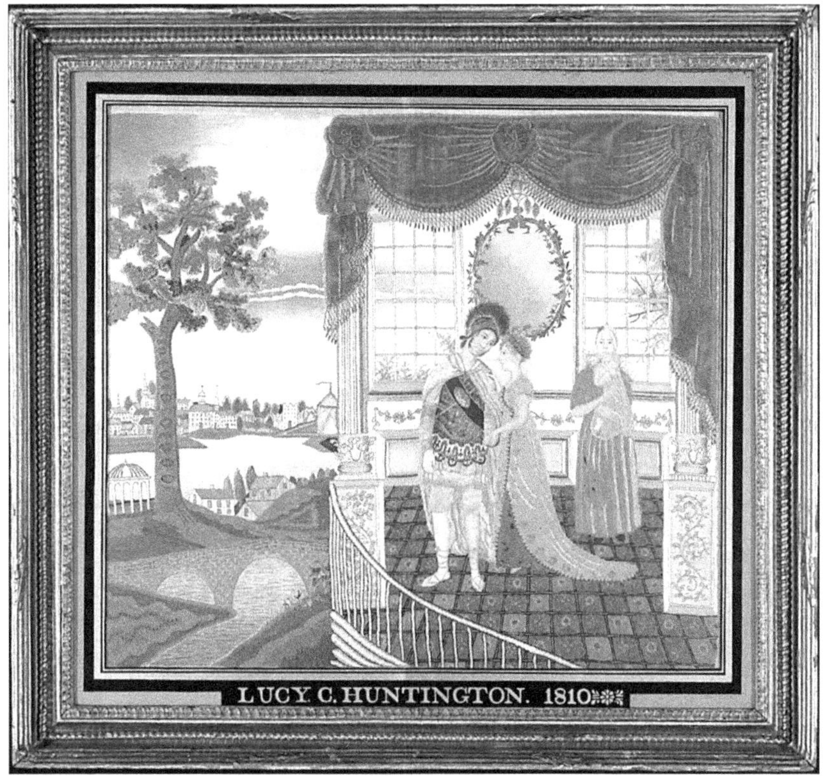

Figure 3.3: Lucy C. Huntington, *Hector Taking Leave of His Family,* 1810.
The Metropolitan Museum of Art, New York

One of the most striking differences between Huntington's and Williams's versions is the extent to which Huntington alters the context of Hector and Andromache's parting. While Williams's picture adheres to Kauffman's composition, Huntington changes their location from the city gate to the interior of their house. As with Williams's embroidery, the nurse and baby are the most altered of the figures, relegated here to the background. While Williams preserves the orientation of Hector and Andromache as depicted in the print, Huntington reverses them, perhaps revealing tracing as part of her process of creation. She creates more separation between mother and child, focusing on Hector and Andromache. Behind the two pairs of figures, a pier glass appears in the center of Huntington's lavishly embellished interior. Velvety curtains with an intricate fringe theatrically open on a richly decorated space. High windows, ornate tiles, serpentine lines, and organic foliate forms adorn the interior. Andromache's dress seems to have been updated to conform more with popular fashion, departing from her appearance in the print after Kauffman. While Andromache has been refurbished, Hector remains very much the same: he appears in his military garb, wearing his helmet. In this inventive interpretation of Kauffman's original iconography, Huntington depicts an elaborate cityscape instead of a battlefield. The triangular tent-like structure can be seen in the background; however, it is accompanied by what looks like a gazebo, along with churches with steeples, buildings anachronistic within the original setting.

Beyond its surface splendor, Huntington's composition focuses on the two main figures of Hector and Andromache and their relationship, a feature in common with Williams's embroidered picture. The focus above all is on the moment of affectionate exchange between husband and wife. Motherhood has been relegated to the background, if only temporarily, in these embroideries and in Kauffman's original painting. We see this as a moment of tenderness before the main characters resign themselves to the gender-based duties assigned to them by society that ultimately result in their tragic deaths. In Williams's and Huntington's embroidered versions, the scene becomes more domestic in context, relocating Andromache within the private interior. In her embroidered picture, Huntington lavishly embellishes and recontextualizes Kauffman's *Hector and Andromache*. She departs in almost every way possible from the print while maintaining a legible resemblance. What began as a scene staged in the liminal space of the city gates now takes place in a more obviously interior, domestic setting. The opulence of materials is part of the point of this picture: the interior walls and the tiles on the floor are all highly ornamented and an ornate mirror hangs between two large windows. Surface decoration extends to the costumes of the couple. Hector's garb includes a plumed helmet, tunic, cape, and laced sandals similar to his previous depictions in painting and print. Huntington considerably revises Andromache's dress. Her garment and hairstyle belong far more to the Neoclassical era than to classical antiquity, refashioning Andromache as a richly dressed woman of 1810.

Huntington's visual overlapping of chronologies renders the scene more immediate and contemporary. She evokes the material world of the Atlantic through her inclusion of furniture, decoration, and the view of the harbor. Her family had strong connections to trade: her father, Joseph Coit Huntington, is described as "a prominent man and merchant in Norwich Town."[35] In Huntington's rendering, this embroidered picture may be more expressive of early nineteenth-century Connecticut than it is of a scene from *The Iliad*. One way this can be seen is in the marginalization of the servant figure. The nurse and baby in this embroidered picture have been placed visually in the background. Instead of interacting lovingly with the nurse, the baby directs his attention toward his parents. The nurse stands expressionless, removed from the scene at hand, appearing distant and reserved. As a result, she seems less a member of the family, isolated based on her social class. Her marginal presence in Huntington's version serves to elevate the social standing of the couple in the foreground, a typical dynamic recurrent in European art including servants.[36] Exceptions where artists have instead emphasized the individuality or humanity of the domestic servant underscore that the pictorial marginalization of these figures is a conscious choice.[37]

Another issue that can be touched on in Huntington's embroidery is that of whiteness: while all the figures in Kauffman's original painting are depicted as such and the embroidery ostensibly functions as an extension of the original, in early nineteenth-century Connecticut members of the servant class were not white by default. According to the 1790 census, more than five thousand people of color lived in Connecticut, approximately half of whom were enslaved (2,648).[38] Connecticut held the largest proportion of enslaved people in New England and did not abolish slavery completely until 1848.[39] Other embroidered pictures made by upper-class white women in Connecticut directly depict enslaved domestic workers, such as in Prudence Punderson's representation of the African-American nursemaid, Jenny Punderson, who was enslaved by her family in *The First, Second, and Last Scene of Mortality*, 1780.[40] The Huntingtons are not recorded as enslavers, but many of their peers in the merchant class were. In the 1820 census, an adult free woman of color is recorded as a member of the Joseph Coit Huntington household but is not named.[41] Huntington's depersonalized characterization of the nurse reflects an isolating picture of domestic servitude and reveals social tensions centering on class and, through its elision, race. Embroidered pictures expressed more than erudition; they reveal the limitations of who was permitted to access an "Enlightened" education.

Huntington's significant departures from the original in her *Hector and Andromache* make one wonder why she used Kauffman's design as the foundation of the composition, if she was going to depart from it so radically. Despite all its visual differences, many of the core elements and message of the subject are maintained: the focus on the husband and wife and their tender moment of affection before they submit to their duty remains. These elements seem to speak to the idea of marriage for affection as well as family alliance. Huntington's embroidered picture operated on multiple levels beyond the simply pictorial: it was demonstration of her skillful needlework, signaling her readiness for marriage, and the classical, morally uplifting subject showed her erudition. The rich materials and techniques involved bespeak the wealth and social status of her family as well as convey her aspirations for a future partner. It is a fantastical vision of Norwich, Connecticut, in 1810, but one that reveals socially stratified dynamics underpinning its creation. While Huntington's imaginative reinterpretation of Kauffman's composition departs from its source, it shows her inventiveness as well as her absorption of the scene's moral lesson, which placed importance on women's roles in the domestic sphere.

Williams and Huntington's embroidered pictures treating the subject of *Hector and Andromache* register changes in education for women and reconcile traditional and progressive attitudes toward the place of needlework in women's education. They achieve this balance by including the traditional features of needlework as an expression of feminine virtue and industry, tied to morality and chastity, but also take for their subject the genre of Neoclassical history painting as represented by an acclaimed woman artist. They employ characteristics of history painting—multi-figural compositions, active heroic narrative, and didactic classical subject matter— as part of their project of enlightened, educated self-fashioning. Kauffman's work was especially appealing because it frequently empathized with the female figure and advanced the cause of the heroine in history painting. Embroidered pictures after Kauffman show which of her works resonated with a female audience, on both sides of the Atlantic. Additionally, they call attention to the ways in which Kauffman's strategy of decorum and virtue within her work constitutes a performance of her gender. Embroidered pictures such as these engage with Enlightenment discourse surrounding the education of women and what an ideal education ought to constitute.

Beauty governed by Reason, rewarded by Merit

The embroidered pictures I have examined in this chapter both confront and seek to accommodate the contradictory advice offered in debates over women's education. Williams and Huntington's embroidered pictures after Kauffman denote the seriousness of their makers' endeavors through their use of the elevated subject of history. Their use of Kauffman's iconography in pictorial embroidery is often not a matter of exact replication, but rather one of selection and adaptation, a feature of academic practice in art. Sir Joshua Reynolds claimed in his *Discourses*, "Invention is one of the great marks of genius, but if we consult experience, we shall find that it is by being conversant with the inventions of others that we learn to invent, as by reading the thoughts of others we learn to think."[42] Using academic history paintings as a resource for the creation of embroidered pictures enabled young women to contribute to debates on female education by demonstrating that their makers' work was no empty accomplishment, but an encapsulation of their talents and education as they sought to negotiate expectations of gender. By creating embroidered pictures after Neoclassical history paintings by Kauffman and other artists, young women sought to combine the graces with the heroic virtues.

While young women may not have directly encountered Wollstonecraft's advice on education due to Godwin's *Memoirs*, published 1798, which contained posthumous revelations about her as an unwed mother, Hannah More's educational theories remained well-known in the nineteenth century. This is evident in an embroidered picture made by Maria Crowninshield (1789-1870) in Dorchester, Massachusetts, at Mrs. Saunders's and Beaches's Academy in 1804 (Fig. 3.4).

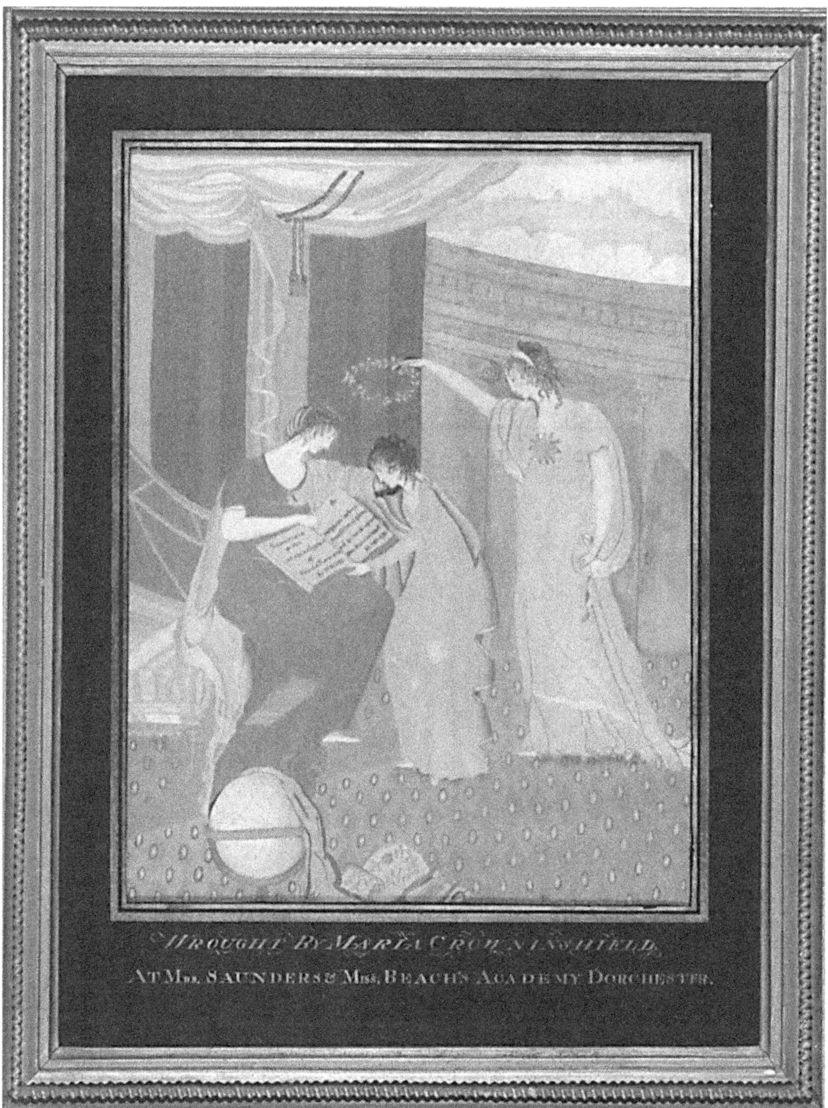

Figure 3.4: Maria Crowninshield, *Painted and embroidered allegorical picture*, 1804. Peabody Essex Museum, Salem, MA

The three female figures in the composition bear a strong resemblance the allegorical figures in Jean-Marie Delattre's print after Kauffman, *Beauty governed by Reason, rewarded by Merit*, 1784 (Fig. 3.5).

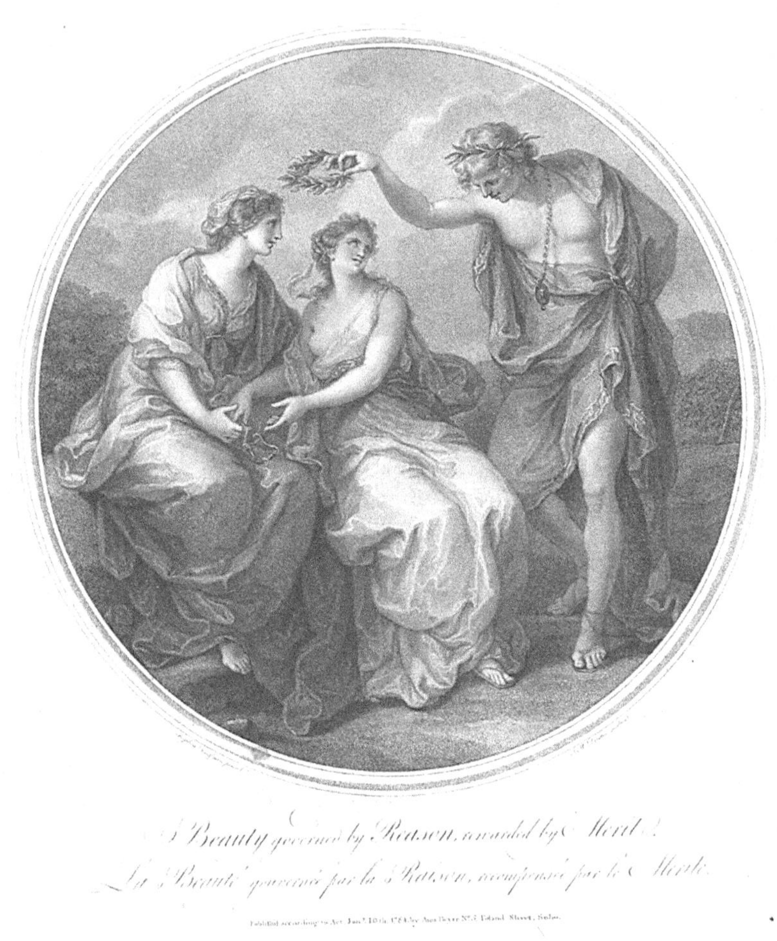

Figure 3.5: Jean-Marie Delattre after Angelica Kauffman, *Beauty governed by Reason, rewarded by Merit*, 1784, National Trust

In Kauffman's design, Reason is represented by the older woman on the left, and Beauty the younger woman in the center, who is about to be crowned with a wreath of flowers by Merit. In Crowninshield's embroidery, rather than looking up at Merit, the young woman attends to the large book held in the lap of the woman on the left, whose right arm encircles her in a compassionate gesture.

The left-hand page is clearly inscribed: "Strictures on the Modern System of Female Education by H. More." A quotation from More's *Strictures* appears on the right-hand side: "By religious instruction God is pleased to work upon the human heart." With her left hand, the teacher points emphatically at the quotation, directing the gaze of young woman. While the textual emphasis is placed on religious instruction by citing More, the use of Kauffman's allegorical composition adds another layer of meaning, pointing to familiarity with the conventions of Neoclassical art. Together, these cues indicate that the making of this embroidery is no empty task, but a reliable index of the maker's merit as a young woman of substance. By becoming conversant with the visual language and subjects of history painting through imitation and invention, the makers of embroidered pictures sought to elevate their needlework above the false accomplishment.

Notes

[1] Mary Wollstonecraft, *A Vindication of the Rights of Woman: With Strictures on Political and Moral Subjects* (London: J. Johnson, 1796) 68.

[2] Betty Ring, *Girlhood Embroidery: American Samplers & Pictorial Needlework 1650-1850, Volume II* (New York: Alfred A. Knopf, 1993).

[3] "Anyone turning over the pages of the catalogues of the Society of Artists, 1761-1791, and of the rival Free Society of Artists, 1761-1783… cannot fail to be struck with the remarkable number of 'freak' pictures… The most popular of all 'freak' pictures were those done in needlework." "'Freak' Pictures," *Times* (London) Aug. 20, 1919, 13.

[4] Heidi Strobel, *The Art of Mary Linwood: Embroidery, Installation, and the Popular Picturesque* (London: Bloomsbury, 2021); Paris Spies-Gans, "Exceptional but not Exceptions: Public Exhibitions and the Rise of the Woman Artist in London and Paris, 1760-1830," *Eighteenth-Century Studies* (Summer 2018): 393-416.

[5] Spies-Gans, "Exceptional but not Exceptions," 398.

[6] Judith A. Tyner, *Stitching the World: Embroidered Maps and Women's Geographical Education* (Burlington, VT: Ashgate, 2015).

[7] Catharine Macaulay Graham, *Letters on Education; with observations on religious and metaphysical subjects* (London: C. Dilly, 1790) 65.

[8] Ibid.

[9] Mary Wollstonecraft, *Thoughts on the education of daughters: with reflections on female conduct, in the more important duties of life* (London: J. Johnson, 1787) 25.

[10] Ibid., 25-26.

[11] Mary Wollstonecraft, *Vindication of the Rights of Woman*, 43.

[12] Ibid., 22.

[13] Ibid.

[14] Hannah More, *The Works of Hannah More. In Eight Volumes* (London: A. Strahan, 1801) 68.

[15] Ibid, 69-70.

[16] Ring, *Girlhood Embroidery*, 20.

[17] Ibid.

[18] Ibid.

[19] Jane Austen, *Sense and Sensibility: A Novel. In Three Volumes, Vol. 2* (London: Charles Roworth, Thomas Egerton, 1811), 54.

[20] Lydia Pearson (born 1791), *Embroidered sampler*, 1802, Made in Newburyport, Massachusetts, United States, Embroidered silk on linen, Metropolitan Museum of Art, Accession Number: 2002.129.

[21] Ring, *Girlhood Embroidery*, 20.

[22] Ibid.

[23] Heidi Strobel, *The Art of Mary Linwood: Embroidery, Installation, and the Popular Picturesque* (London: Bloomsbury, 2021).

[24] Ibid.

[25] Lea C. Lane, "Freak Pictures? The Needlework Paintings of Margaret Ansell," *Antiques & Fine Art* (Winter 2017): 125.

[26] Wendy Wassyng Roworth and David Alexander. *Angelica Kauffman: A Continental Artist in Georgian England* (London: Reaktion Books, 1992) 44.

[27] *The Iliad of Homer, Book VI.* Translated by Alexander Pope (London: Henry Lintot, 1743) 109.

[28] Ibid., 200.

[29] Ibid., 204.

[30] Roworth and Alexander, *Angelica Kauffman*, 46.

[31] Ibid.

[32] O. B. Stebbing, "John Howard Payne. A Memoir," *The Musical Record and Review*, (United States: O. Ditson & Company, 1882) 462.

[33] Ibid.

[34] Carol Huber, "This Way or That Way?: The Carew-Way Connection," *Antiques & Fine Art* (Autumn 2014): 140.

[35] Frederick William Chapman, *The Coit Family: Or, The Descendants of John Coit, who Appears Among the Settlers of Salem, Mass., in 1638, at Gloucester in 1644, and at New London, Conn., in 1650* (United States: Press of the Case, Lockwood & Brainard Company, 1874) 104.

[36] Diane Wolfthal, "Household Help: Early Modern Portraits of Female Servants," *Early Modern Women* 8 (2013): 6-7.

[37] Ibid.

[38] Joseph Adna Hill, Cummings, John, *Negro Population 1790-1915* (United States: Ross, 2005) 56.

[39] Joanne Pope Melish, *Disowning Slavery: Gradual Emancipation and "Race" in New England, 1780–1860* (New York: Cornell University Press, 1998) 1-10.

[40] Jonathan Michael Square, "Prudence Punderson," *Fashioning the Self in Slavery and Freedom*, April 20, 2022.

[41] 1820 U.S. Census; Census Place: *Norwich City, New London, Connecticut*; Page: *631*; NARA Roll: *M33_2*; Image: *623.*

[42] Joshua Reynolds, *Discourses* (London: Cadell, 1797) 109.

Bibliography

Austen, Jane. *Sense and Sensibility: A Novel. In Three Volumes.* London: Charles Roworth, Thomas Egerton, 1811.

Chapman, Frederick William. *The Coit Family: Or, The Descendants of John Coit, who Appears Among the Settlers of Salem, Mass., in 1638, at Gloucester in 1644, and at New London, Conn., in 1650,* United States: Press of the Case, Lockwood & Brainard Company, 1874.

Graham, Catharine Macaulay. *Letters on Education; with observations on religious and metaphysical subjects,* Ireland: C. Dilly, 1790.

Hill, Joseph Adna, and John Cummings. *Negro Population 1790-1915.* United States: Ross, 2005.

Huber, Carol. "This Way or That Way?: The Carew-Way Connection," *Antiques & Fine Art.* (Autumn 2014): 140-143.

Lane, Lea C. "Freak Pictures? The Needlework Paintings of Margaret Ansell," *Antiques & Fine Art.* (Winter 2017): 125-127.

Melish, Joanne Pope. *Disowning Slavery: Gradual Emancipation and "Race" in New England, 1780-1860.* New York: Cornell University Press, 1998.

More, Hannah. *The Works of Hannah More. In Eight Volumes.* London: A. Strahan, 1801.

Reynolds, Joshua. *Discourses.* London: Cadell, 1797.

Ring, Betty. *Girlhood Embroidery: American Samplers & Pictorial Needlework 1650-1850.* New York: Alfred A. Knopf, 1993.

Roworth, Wendy Wassyng and David Alexander. *Angelica Kauffman: A Continental Artist in Georgian England.* London: Reaktion Books, 1992.

Spies-Gans, Paris. "Exceptional but not Exceptions: Public Exhibitions and the Rise of the Woman Artist in London and Paris, 1760-1830," *Eighteenth-Century Studies.* (Vol. 51, no. 4, Summer 2018): 393-416.

Square, Jonathan Michael. "Prudence Punderson." *Fashioning the Self in Slavery and Freedom.* April 20, 2022, https://www.fashioningtheself.com.

Stebbing, O. B. "John Howard Payne. A Memoir." *The Musical Record and Review,* United States: O. Ditson & Company, 1882.

Strobel, Heidi. *The Art of Mary Linwood: Embroidery, Installation, and the Popular Picturesque,* London: Bloomsbury, 2021.

The Iliad of Homer, Vol. I-VI. Translated by Alexander Pope, Esq. London: Henry Lintot, 1743.

Tyner, Judith A. *Stitching the World: Embroidered Maps and Women's Geographical Education.* Burlington, VT: Ashgate, 2015.

U.S. Census Bureau, 1820; Census Place: *Norwich City, New London, Connecticut;* Page: *631;* NARA Roll: *M33_2;* Image: *623*

Wolfthal, Diane. "Household Help: Early Modern Portraits of Female Servants." *Early Modern Women* 8 (2013): 5–52. http://www.jstor.org/stable/23617845.

Wollstonecraft, Mary. *A Vindication of the Rights of Woman: With Strictures on Political and Moral Subjects,* London: J. Johnson, 1796.

———. *Thoughts on the Education of Daughters.* London: J. Johnson, 1787.

Chapter 4

Madame de Genlis's *New Method* and Teaching Drawing to Children in Eighteenth-Century France

Franny Brock

University of North Carolina at Chapel Hill

Abstract

This essay examines drawing pedagogy produced for children in eighteenth-century France and what it can tell us more broadly about childhood education in this period. The central focus is Stéphanie-Félicité, Comtesse de Genlis's treatise, *A New Method of Instruction for Children from Five to Ten Years Old,* which offers moral dialogues, models of composition in writing, and a new process for teaching children to draw. In analyzing Genlis's text, this essay explores how her methods are in conversation with theoretical writing on education, other pedagogical tools for children, and shifting conceptions of childhood. It argues that treatises like *A New Method* played a significant role in the development of pedagogy for children, also reflected in visual representations of children drawing. Finally, this essay examines to what extent texts like Genlis's encouraged girls to access art training, but also reinforced ideas about what they could hope to achieve with their art.

Keywords: drawing, childhood, eighteenth century, girls, pedagogy

***

Introduction

French artist, Jean Antoine Théodore Giroust, exhibited *The Harp Lesson,* a conversation piece *à l'anglaise,* at the Paris Salon in September of 1791 (Fig. 4.1).[1] The large-scale portrait of the daughter of the Duc d'Orléans, taking a music lesson from her governess, Madame de Genlis, and accompanied by her companion and English tutor, Mademoiselle Pamela, caused quite a stir at the Salon when all three sitters visited the painting wearing Phrygian caps, the new symbol of support for the French Revolution.[2] The excitement caused by the appearance of Madame de Genlis and the two young ladies in front of their own portrait added to the already turbulent mood at the Salon. Control of the official exhibition had just been wrested from the Académie royale de peinture et de sculpture by the National Assembly, which ordered the Salon open to all artists. This upheaval within the microcosm of the art world reflected the politically-charged atmosphere of Paris in general at the time. In fact, just two months before the 1791 Salon exhibition, King Louis XVI and his family were caught trying to flee the country and were forcibly returned to Paris.

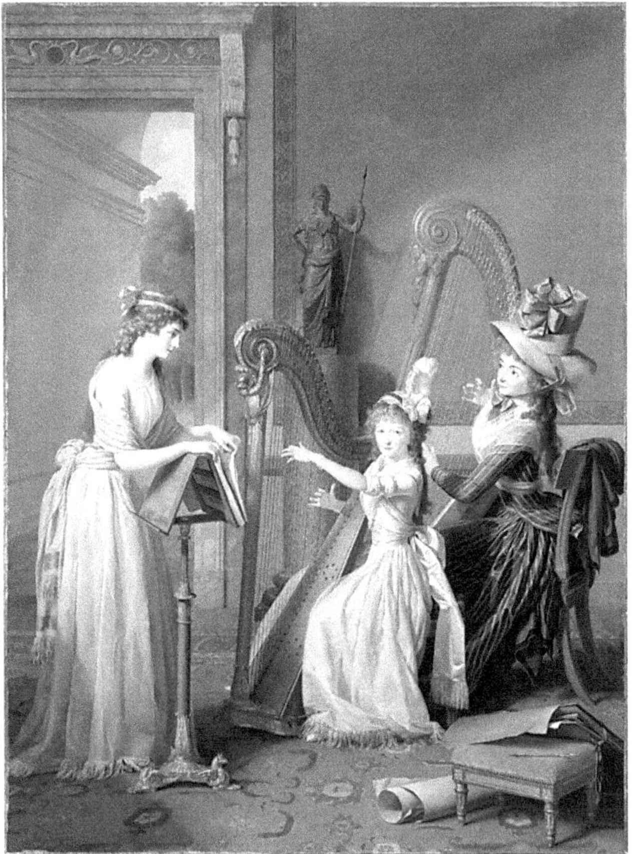

Figure 4.1: Jean Antoine Théodore Giroust, *The Harp Lesson*, 1791. Oil on canvas. Dallas Museum of Art

It was in this environment that Giroust presented *The Harp Lesson* at the Salon. In the painting, the fourteen-year-old Louise Marie Adelaïde Eugénie de Bourbon d'Orléans and Madame de Genlis, seated behind her, play the harp, while Pamela stands and turns the pages of their sheet music. All three figures are elegantly attired and presided over by a bronze statue of Minerva, the Roman goddess of Wisdom and Art, in the background of the scene. The presence of Minerva suits the fashionable, neoclassical interior of the Duc d'Orléans' home. In the lower right-hand corner of the painting, Giroust has carefully depicted drawing paper, a portfolio, and a porte-crayon. As the objects closest to the viewer, one's eyes are drawn to the meticulous rendering of these tools. The blue drawing paper, slightly rough at the edges, is juxtaposed by the rich, red velvet of the footstool. The silver porte-crayon, with its sharpened chalk points, balances on the very corner of the stool; and the portfolio, stuffed with drawings, its ribbon ties hanging loose, is propped up, threatening to slide onto the floor. A drawing lesson for Madame de Genlis's young pupil is either imminent or has just occurred. Giroust's focus in this painting on the accomplishments and education of Mademoiselle Adelaïde helped project an image of the Duc d'Orléans and his family as supporters of Enlightenment values.[3] It also highlighted the newly important agenda of educating and training the future French citizen.

Stéphanie-Félicité, Comtesse de Genlis, was not primarily a drawing teacher, but she wrote about instructing children in the art of drawing. Genlis was a prolific writer and her novels and treatises circulated widely throughout France and enjoyed particular success in Britain, as Gillian Dow has argued.[4] In this essay, I will focus on Genlis's educational treatise, *A New Method of Instruction for Children from Five to Ten Years Old.* First published in 1800, it became popular and was quickly translated into English. *A New Method* offers moral dialogues, stories, models of composition in writing, and a new process for teaching children to draw. Differing from older manuals in its focus on amusement, entertainment, and childhood development, it argues that the "common" method for teaching drawing was ineffective because children considered it tedious and frustrating. Throughout the text, Genlis engages with contemporary theoretical writing on drawing and argues that practicing drawing creates a refined sense of judgment in her pupils. In analyzing Genlis's writing, I explore how her methods are in conversation with theoretical writing on education, other pedagogical tools for children, and shifting conceptions of childhood in the eighteenth century. I argue that treatises like *A New Method* played a significant role in the development of pedagogy for children, also reflected in visual representations of children in the act of drawing in this period. Finally, this essay will examine to what extent texts like Genlis's allowed and sometimes explicitly encouraged girls to access art training, but also reinforced ideas about what they could hope to achieve with their art.

Drawing did not only become an integral part of pedagogical treatises, but images of both boys and girls in the act of drawing became more common over the course of the eighteenth century as a result of new ideas surrounding childhood, education, and the role drawing played in their young lives. As is well-studied, in the eighteenth century, childhood came to be seen as a distinct stage of development, separate from adulthood,[5] and was often characterized by innocence, creativity, emotion, and malleability. Central to these shifting conceptions of childhood were the writings of Jean-Jacques Rousseau and John Locke on education and how best to mold children into adults. After the publication of Rousseau's *Emile, or On Education* in 1762, educational treatises for children proliferated in Britain and France,[6] many of which prescribed drawing as an important skill for the cultivation of taste, judgment, and understanding. Of course, these prescriptions and access to the texts themselves were divided along the lines of class, gender, and race.[7] As exemplified by Mademoiselle Adelaïde in Giroust's painting, many of the images of children engaging in drawing represent the elite higher classes or the burgeoning middle classes who could afford to purchase manuals similar to *A New Method* or pay for training with a tutor or drawing master.

Madame de Genlis and *A New Method*

Madame de Genlis's educational writing grew out of her role as a teacher to royal children. She entered the Palais Royale as a lady-in-waiting to the Duchesse de Chartres (later Duchesse d'Orléans), the wife of Louis Philippe Joseph d'Orléans and mother of several children including Louis-Philippe, King of the French from 1830-1848. Genlis was made governess of the infant daughters of the family in 1777 and became the first woman appointed 'gouverneur' of royal children in 1782.[8] Her coterie of pupils included the sons of the Chartres family, who up until that point would have certainly been under the tutelage of a man.[9] In this role, Genlis developed a detailed system of education for her charges and wrote several works to complement her teaching. She often lamented the lack of suitable teaching tools for children and written plans for education, in particular, she believed that the existing literature on the education of girls was deficient.[10] The best known of her works are *The Theater of Education*, published in 1780 and *Tales of the Castle*, published in 1785. Not only did Genlis publish educational tracts, she wrote novels and plays, and her memoires and many of her letters also survive. The breadth of genres in which she wrote gives the reader a strong sense of her voice and teaching style, which can be at turns practical, contradictory, humorous, or defensive and often filled with personal interjections.

A New Method is no exception. Addressed to tutors, Genlis opens the section on drawing by writing that "to children, drawing is the most irksome and for a long time, the most perfectly useless of all employments."[11] However, she goes on to suggest that this is the fault of the old method for teaching drawing. Teaching drawing to children was not a novel practice in the early nineteenth century when this text was published,[12] but Genlis argues that the "common" method for teaching drawing was unsuccessful because children considered it tedious, boring, and frustrating. In contrast, her focus on amusement, excitement, and holding the child's interest in the process of learning to draw is in dialogue with theories on the importance of educative play proposed by thinkers going back to Locke and Fénelon. In further critique of older methods, Genlis writes that children are usually taught to make bad copies that necessitate heavy retouching by their drawing masters. Genlis calls this "a very common case, and hence it is that so many young ladies, who are said to have drawn and painted so well during their education, can scarcely handle a pencil after they are married, merely because they are deprived of the assistance of a too officious master."[13] Making the claim that under old teaching methods, children, particularly girls, never truly learned to master the skill, she proposes to solve this problem by employing a new method for teaching drawing. One that she says has *five* principal benefits.[14] First, that this method does not tolerate the retouching of students' work. Second, that instead of being tiresome and irksome, it is extremely amusing. Third, that it helps to form understanding, taste, and judgment, as well as giving the student a stock of useful knowledge. Fourth, that if students have natural talents for the arts, their talents will be discovered early in life. And finally, it is quicker and more efficient than the old method.[15]

Throughout her text, Genlis assures the reader that this new method is preferable to the old way of teaching drawing, but in practice how did it differ? Genlis was not an artist, though she saw drawing masters at work and may have read drawing treatises circulating at the time. Similar to the publication of educational treatises, the number and diversity of drawing manuals proliferated in the eighteenth century.[16] Drawing manuals were aimed, above all, at amateurs, although they closely followed the principals taught at the official Académie royale de peinture et de sculpture.[17] Students at the Académie were taught to draw in discrete stages, beginning with copying prints and drawings and culminating with the life class where students drew in front of a live nude model. Learning to draw at the Académie was a hierarchical process in terms of rank, seniority, and gender; for example, advanced students were allowed to sit closer to the live model and work under better light, while novice students were relegated to standing in the back of the room and sketching. Only after students had mastered drawing would they be taught to paint, sculpt, or design architecture. And although a small number of women were officially admitted to the Académie, they were not allowed to attend drawing classes because drawing in front of a nude male model was deemed inappropriate. Since most people did not have access to the Académie's training, they used alternative modes of instruction, such as drawing manuals, private drawing classes, or free drawing schools.

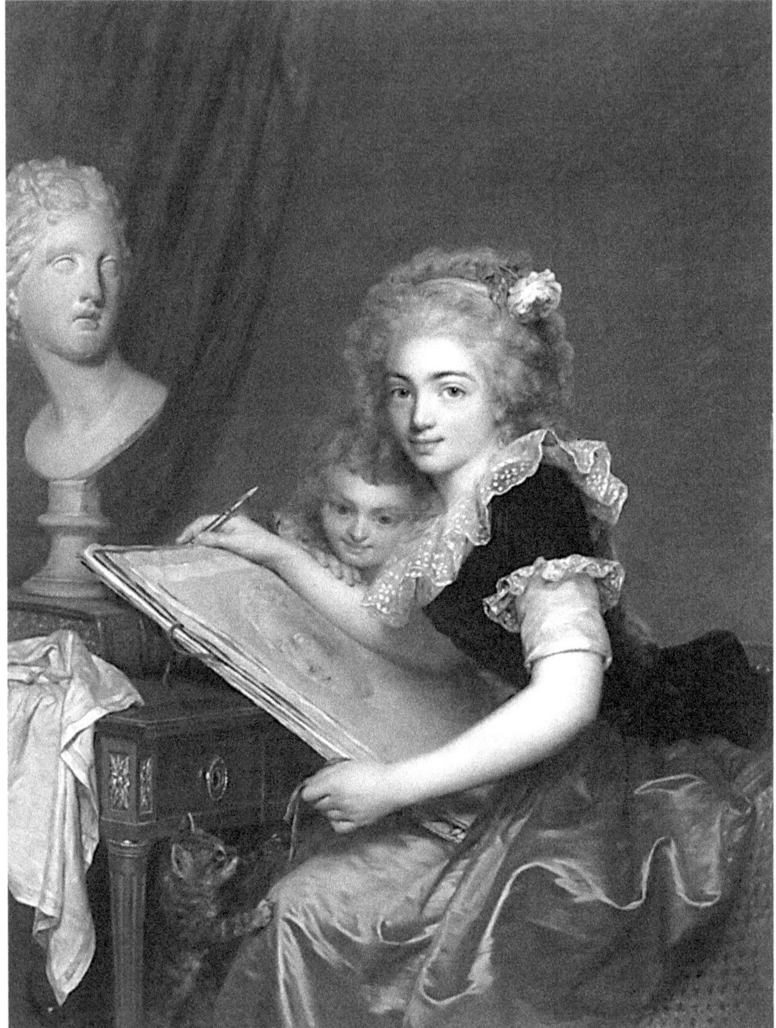

Figure 4.2: Antoine Vestier, *Allegory of the Arts*, 1788. Oil on canvas. The Horvitz Collection

One of the most widely circulated and celebrated of these treatises was Charles-Antoine Jombert's *New Method to Learn Drawing*, published in Paris in 1740. Jombert's manual is more technical than Genlis's; he describes the practical concerns of drawing, what instruments to use, how to effectively copy from the included plates, and what type of paper is best suited for which subject matter.[18] His focus is on mastering the principles of geometry and proportions of the human body. Genlis's approach to teaching drawing to children is similar to both Jombert and the traditional academic model in that it is broken down into stages, which are each assigned a length of time required to master that skill.

She writes that students should start by drawing faces.[19] Each facial feature must be studied separately before drawing the whole face and, only then, are students allowed to move on to the figure.[20] After this, they must understand the principal bones and muscles in the body. Genlis suggests buying a cast representing an anatomical figure for the pupil to study.[21] After the student has mastered the two most important branches of anatomy, osteology and myology, they venture out to study from antique sculpture, architecture, and paintings. One can see such study in Antoine Vestier's 1788 painting, *Allegory of the Arts,* in which he depicts his daughter, Marie-Nicole, drawing an antique bust on a piece of blue paper (Fig. 4.2). Though Marie-Nicole looks out at the viewer, she has just been making a careful study of the bust sitting on the table in front of her. Even the oblique view of her sheet shows Marie-Nicole's practice with dimensionality, light and shadow, and volume. While Genlis's *A New Method* followed a familiar process for teaching drawing in discrete stages, it departs from other drawing treatises in its central emphasis. Genlis is less concerned with the technical aspects of the art, presumably because a drawing master would teach these practical matters, and is more concerned with enthusiasm for drawing and the cultivation of taste and judgment in her students.

Drawing, Observation, and The Cultivation of Judgment

At the beginning of the section on teaching drawing, Genlis observes her students and their drawing:

> ...from thirteen to sixteen they made a real progress, which became daily more and more rapid. I remarked however, that from this period their improvement did not so much depend on the increasing practice of the hand, as on the greater judgment and accuracy of the eye, which was daily improving by our constant excursions to visit monuments, churches, galleries, engravings, sales of pictures, etc. These proved their best lessons in drawing and painting: for thus they accustomed themselves to compare and judge with justice and accuracy, which in fact is the whole secret of the art.[22]

After completing lessons from *A New Method,* Genlis claims that the pupil of fourteen will be "a complete amateur, who to the greatest possible experience, unites a cultivated taste for criticism, and the most perfect theory of the science."[23] She elevates drawing by arguing that it creates a refined sense of judgment in her pupils. It is also clear from this excerpt that she is engaging with contemporary theoretical writing on drawing, taste, and the role of the amateur artist. In his late seventeenth-century practical guide to painting, Roger de Piles writes that practicing drawing had three purposes for the practitioner: "To accustom his eye to correctness; to acquire ease of execution and to break in his hand to working; and to form his taste in good things."[24] In this period, correct judgment was considered one of the most important skills of the amateur artist, a skill that was continually refined by training the eye and by studying works of art.

In addition to producing drawings, some amateurs of the period were amassing huge collections of works on paper. Though there had been interest in collecting drawings since the Renaissance, the eighteenth century saw a considerable increase in the number and size of drawings collections.[25] Collectors such as Pierre-Jean Mariette and the Comte de Caylus sought to acquire a broad range of drawings, from Italian and Dutch old masterworks to drawings by seventeenth-century French artists. Instead of being solely regarded as a step in the process of making a painting, many drawings were collected as finished works of art in their own right. As Kristal Smentek has argued, a connoisseurial appreciation for drawings emerged during this period.[26] Drawings came to be seen as the origin of an artist's style because they were thought to truly reveal the hand of the artist and were subsequently used by connoisseurs and amateurs as empirical evidence to make attributions.[27] The cultivation of judgment and the practice of the eye was key for these activities.

The skill of correct judgment was based on careful observation, one of the major tenants of Genlis's pedagogical approach for children, and before her, in the works of Fénelon and Locke. The importance of observation and its role in both pedagogical literature and the visual arts of the period, especially in works by Chardin, has been explored by Dorothy Johnson.[28] Madame de Genlis engages with these ideas by arguing that the most effective way to learn is through observation – by looking, comparing and contrasting, and making connections in the mind.[29] These practices and skills were also key in theoretical writings on aesthetics and in artistic pedagogy of the late seventeenth and eighteenth centuries.

Learning for the Purpose of Leisure

While it is tempting to see Genlis's *A New Method* as more equalitarian than educational treatises that came before because it suggests drawing training for both girls and boys, it is important not to push her work too far. She was certainly concerned with the education of girls and lamented the limited opportunities for women writers, but her writing was not always radical in terms of expanding opportunities for women and girls in society. For example, *A New Method* sometimes reinforces the domestic and polite associations of drawing for women. Drawing was widely seen as a desirable leisure activity, along with flower painting, miniatures, and ornamental painting. As Ann Bermingham argues, amateur art practices were often social; a woman's desire to draw was thought to show her gentility and refinement, not creativity, and it was a beneficial practice for women trying to find husbands.[30] In a moral dialogue found earlier in Genlis's text, a girl asks her mother why drawing, music, and dancing are useful. About drawing, her mother responds, "drawing is also very useful in a great many kinds of needlework and especially in embroidery."[31] The mother goes on to say that drawing provides entertainment both for the practitioner and her family, and further, that skills in drawing can be used to make money if one becomes destitute.[32] Genlis's advice about draftsmanship seems to be divided along gender lines. This dialogue between a mother and daughter centers around the usefulness of drawing as entertainment; as preparatory for other gendered activities, such as needlework; or as a source of income. In contrast, her writing on teaching drawing in the later sections of the text often uses male pronouns and offers taste and judgment as the outcome. For example, "…if *he* is formed by nature to become a great artist, *his* talents will not fail to be discovered and unfolded at an early period of life, and even should *he* not have a genius for the arts, *he* will still retain a useful talent and much ornamental knowledge."[33]

This association of learning drawing with domestic pastimes for women and girls is also present in earlier texts written by Rousseau and Fénelon. Writing about girls' "natural" inclinations in *Emile*, Rousseau suggests that they are drawn primarily to adornment—dressing and undressing their dolls, making tiny trimmings—and that sewing and embroidery are a natural extension of these interests.[34] He includes drawing as well, but only in so much as it serves her domestic occupations. He writes:

> This voluntary course [embroidery and lacemaking] is easily extended to include drawing, an art which is closely connected with taste in dress; but I would not have them taught landscape and still less figure painting. Leaves, fruit, flowers, draperies, anything that will make an elegant trimming for the accessories of the toilet, and enable the girl to design her own embroidery if she cannot find a pattern to her taste; that will be quite enough.[35]

These limitations on the usefulness of drawing for women reflect societal norms of the eighteenth century. While ideas of childhood were changing, it was still customary for girls to be married by fourteen or fifteen years old, and groomed from childhood to become wives and mothers. This was Rousseau's stated goal for the education of all women.[36] He writes, "A woman's education must therefore be planned in relation to man. To be pleasing in his sight, to win his respect and love, to train him in childhood, to tend him in manhood, to council and console, to make his life pleasant and happy, these are the duties of woman for all time, and this is what she should be taught while she is young."[37] The confinement of women to the domestic sphere is present in many of the images of girls and young women drawing, such as in the case of Jacques-André Portail's *Lady*

Sketching at a Table (Fig. 4.3). This chalk drawing depicts a refined woman in a Rococo interior, sketching in front of a window. Her small dog is curled up on a cushion next to her. In contrast with Vestier's painting of Marie-Nicole, the viewer cannot see what this lady is drawing, and her gaze is directed down at the paper in front of her. Much of the detail in the drawing is dedicated to the woman's elegant dress, her delicate features, and the decoration of the interior space. This type of depiction has much in common with Portail's other drawings of women embroidering, reading, and playing music. In these images, women drawing are associated with a gendered form of leisure activity.

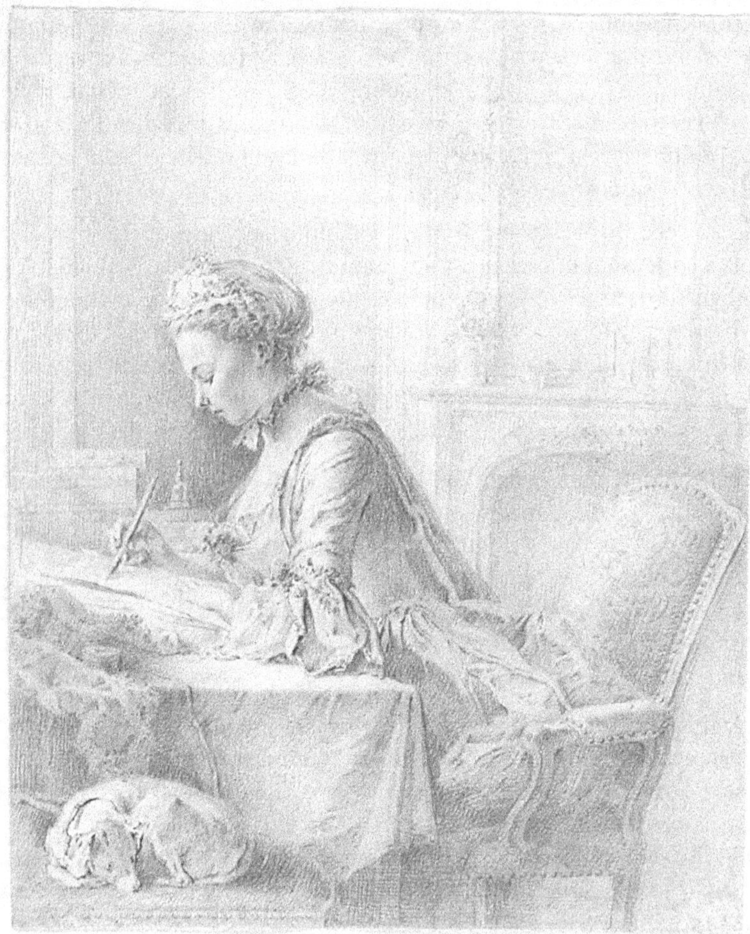

Figure 4.3: Jacques-Andre Portail, *Lady Sketching at a Table*, first half of the 18th century. Black and red chalk, brush and gray wash, with touches of pink and blue watercolor, on paper. The Morgan Library & Museum, New York

However, limitations around the societal expectations of girls existed in parallel with increased access to training, partially as a result of widely circulating educational treatises, such as *A New Method*. This tension also mirrored the multilayered, and sometimes contradictory, status of drawing in the same period. I have argued that while drawing could be seen as a desirable leisure activity for women and girls, it was also closely linked to the foundation of all artistic production and the predominately masculine space of the Académie. Over the course of the century, drawing also became more connected with the performance of artistic individuality and a marker of original genius. These diverse associations need to be taken into account when one considers images of young girls drawing. For example, in two works, one by Louis-François Aubry (Fig. 4.4) and another attributed to Joseph Siffred Duplessis (Fig. 4.5), young women are depicted drawing.

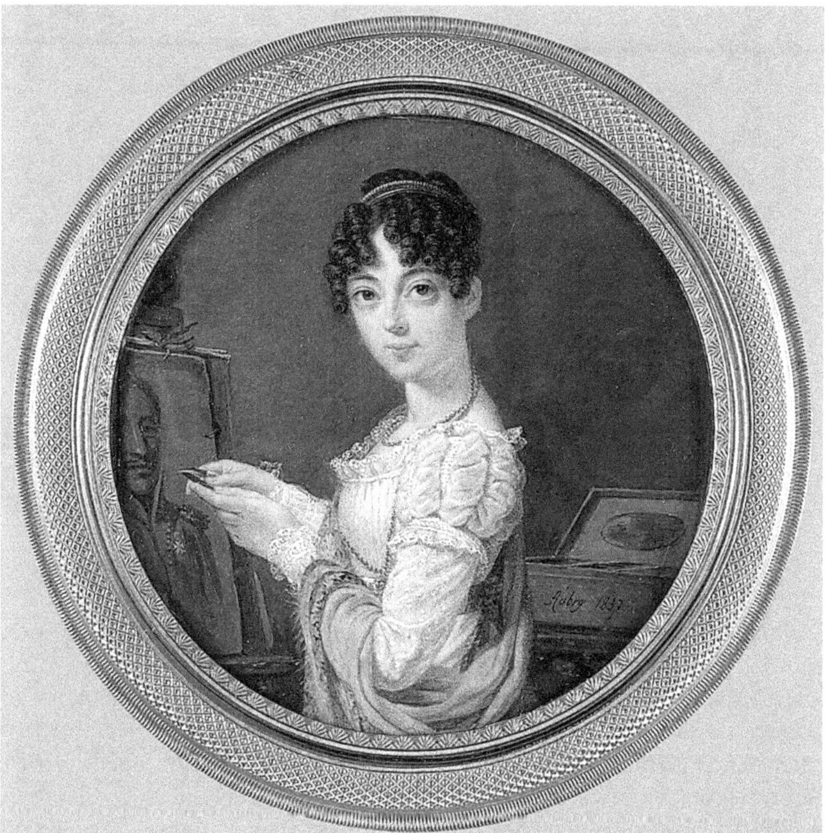

Figure 4.4: Louis-François Aubry, *Young Woman at an Easel*, 1837. Watercolor on Ivory. Cincinnati Art Museum

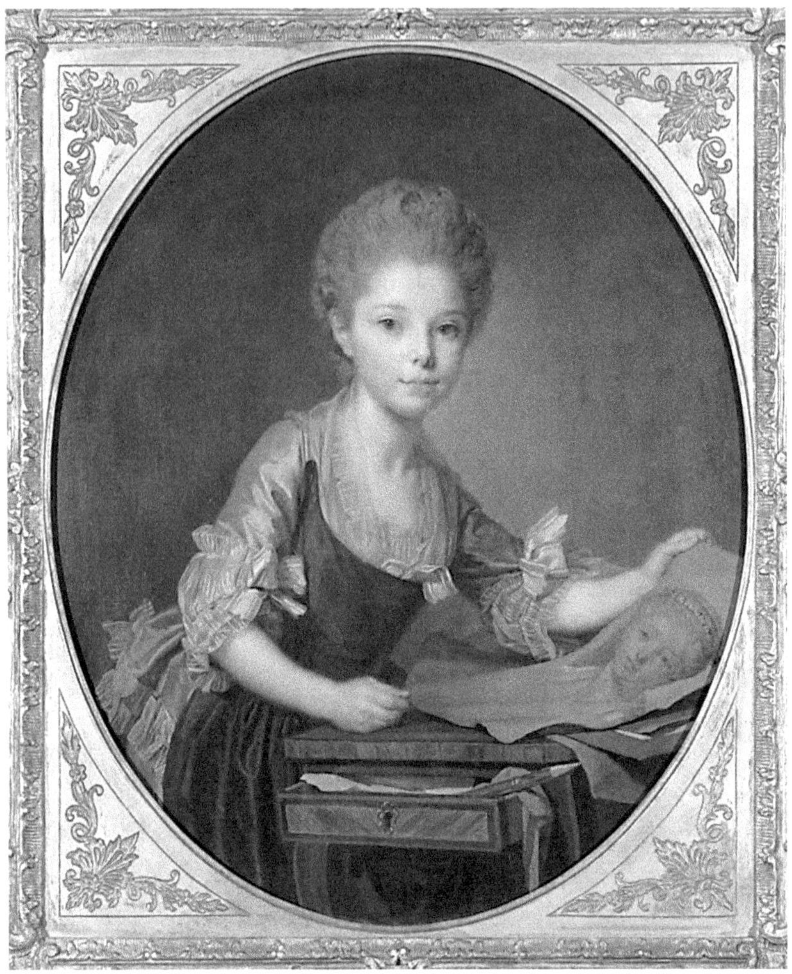

Figure 4.5: Attributed to Joseph Siffred Duplessis, *The Young Artist*, after c. 1775. Oil on canvas. Virginia Museum of Fine Arts

While both of these sitters are elegantly dressed and coiffed, the domestic interior present in Vestier and Portail's works has been stripped away. The viewer is left with a dark background, the subject, and their drawing tools and paper. The girls' works-in-progress are clearly visible to the viewer, and they seem to take no heed of Rousseau's prescription of flowers, fruit, and draperies. Aubry's sitter in the miniature *Young Woman at an Easel* draws a half-length portrait of a man in a military costume, while Duplessis' young artist has copied a work by Jean-Baptiste Greuze. Both girls look directly out at the viewer, showing off their respective drawings. These works engage with references to drawing beyond the domestic, marriage-in-training practice seen in Portail's image. In reality, many girls went on to become professionals working in both the fine and applied arts. Scholars like Melissa Hyde and Paris Spies-Gans have shown that women were omnipresent in the public, professional art world of the later eighteenth century, operating far beyond the domestic confines prescribed by Rousseau.[38] Not only did girls practice drawing in their homes, but they went on to become painters, printmakers, and designers, among other artistic professions. Broadening access to artistic training and education was in part responsible for this shift.

Little Laborers

For girls and boys of lower-class status, educational treatises suggest that skills in drawing can be used to make an income.[39] This is only briefly mentioned by Madame de Genlis in *A New Method*, as it is clear that her treatise is aimed at families who could afford to employ both tutors and drawing masters. However, learning to draw as part of a profession bears exploration as it relates to and diverges from the pedagogical methods I have already discussed. As a practical skill, drawing was an instrument of the trades, seen as essential in design, topography, watchmaking, manufacturing of mathematical tools, woodworking, engraving, and jewelry-making, among other professions. Starting in the mid-1730s in France, there was a push for children to learn to draw so that they could enter the trades well-trained.[40] Jean-Jacques Bachelier, the painter and director of the Sèvres porcelain manufactory, took up the call for more access to training in the 1760s by establishing a free drawing school in Paris. Other regional drawing schools had flourished, but there was no equivalent in Paris because the Académie maintained such control over artistic education. However, as Ulrich Leben argues, people started to become aware that teaching drawing and design to children of the lower classes had a positive economic impact in France and contributed to the increased production of luxury items for the market.[41]

Some similarities existed between the type of education proposed by Madame de Genlis and the one that students at Bachelier's school would receive. For instance, students would copy from prints and would be instructed by drawing masters. However, at the free drawing school, there was always an emphasis on the future profession, and it catered to hundreds of students at a time. Students studied subjects depending on their career choice, though everyone was expected to take courses in geometry and perspective.[42] Students were taught how to translate and copy in two dimensions. They learned to draw from prints alone, not from three-dimensional models or casts.[43] In Bachelier's school, children were not taught to draw for leisure or in refinement of their taste, but for practical ends. They would emerge from the free drawing school ready to enter a profession, make needed income for their families and, in Bachelier's eyes, support the quality of French production.

Design-related vocations also made space for women practitioners. To that end, Bachelier tried to establish a free drawing school for girls like the one he had successfully founded for boys.[44] He intended to educate girls in order to prepare them for these design professions and wrote:

> why leave in ignorance…the sex that equals us in courage and intelligence and that surpasses us in steadfastness in work? There is nothing simpler and easier than the means of bringing about this felicitous revolution; it is but a matter of enlightening the sex that we have estranged from the sciences and arts.[45]

He wanted to educate two hundred girls in a variety of subjects, including geometry, religion, and geography, in addition to drawing practice. Bachelier claimed that skills in drawing were essential for occupations such as silk embroidery, the working of metal or other materials, weaving, sewing, knitting, and painting on porcelain, all acceptably "feminine" occupations.[46] Interestingly, he also considered carving, optics, watchmaking, lathing and its derivatives, engraving, and jewelry-making to be occupations for which girls must be able to draw, extending the range of professions one might have expected women to specialize in.[47] Bachelier's well-laid plans for a girls drawing school ground to a halt at the start of the French Revolution, but others opened in the early nineteenth century, such as the École Gratuite de Dessin pour les Jeunes Filles, founded by Madame Thérèse Justine Frère de Montizon and Madame Fanny Beauharnais.[48]

Conclusion

The Revolution brings to mind the painting with which I began this essay – Giroust's *The Harp Lesson*, produced at the very beginning of the revolutionary period (Fig. 4.1). Despite the fact that Giroust's work depicts Madame de Genlis in the act of giving a music lesson rather than a drawing lesson, draftsmanship and its importance loom large in the painting. Giroust's careful attention to the drawing tools in the corner of the composition and the way the color of the blue paper rhymes with Genlis's dress and the large ribbon in her hat, visually link the tutor with drawing practice. Genlis was not a visual artist, but her advice to tutors in *A New Method* was in direct dialogue with both artistic pedagogy and educational theory of the period. Not only does this text reveal important information about the status of drawing and the multilayered associations connected with the practice, but it also helps illuminate shifting conceptions of childhood and the differences in education based on gender. While Genlis upholds and reifies certain societal norms that limited the possible achievements of women and girls, access to manuals and instruction like *A New Method* was wide-reaching, especially in the case of Genlis's work. Once they were produced and sold, the information and knowledge was only controlled by these norms, rather than the walls of an institution. Mothers and daughters consulting these manuals would have the same access to information as sons. Though not always intended to serve this purpose, printed drawing manuals were sometimes the only teaching tools that women had access to, especially at a young age.

Notes

[1] Listed in the Salon livret as number 16. *Ouvrages de peinture, sculpture, et architecture, gravures, dessins, modeles, &. Exposés au Louvre par ordre de l'Assemblée nationale; Au mois de Septembre 1791; L'an III.e de la liberté* (Paris: de l'Imprimerie des Batimens du Roi, 1791), 5-6.

[2] Joseph Baillio, "Mademoiselle d'Orléans Taking a Harp Lesson: Lot Essay," Christie's, last modified January 27, 2015, https://www.christies.com/en/lot/lot-5868340.

[3] Laura Sevelis, "The Harp Lesson," Dallas Museum of Art, last modified 2015, https://collections.dma.org/artwork/5340929.

[4] Gillian Dow, "The British Reception of Madame de Genlis's Writings for Children: Plays and Tales of Instruction and Delight," *British Journal for Eighteenth Century Studies* 29 (2006): 367-381.

[5] Philippe Ariès, *Centuries of Childhood: A Social History of Family Life*, trans. Robert Baldick (New York: Vintage Books, 1965).

[6] Jennifer J. Popiel, *Rousseau's Daughters: Domesticity, Education, and Autonomy in Modern France* (Durham, New Hampshire: University of New Hampshire Press, 2008), 21.

[7] Andrew O'Malley, *The Making of the Modern Child: Children's Literature in the Late Eighteenth Century* (New York and London: Routledge, 2003), 6.

[8] Dow, "The British Reception of Madame de Genlis's Writings for Children," 367.

[9] Ibid.

[10] Ibid.

[11] Madam de Genlis, *A new method of instruction for children from five to ten years old : including moral dialogues, the children's island, a tale, thoughts and maxims, models of composition in writing for children ten or twelve years old, and a new method of teaching children to draw* (Dublin: Printed by William Porter, 1800), 225.

[12] As Ulrich Leben writes, there was a drive in the 1730s to teach children drawing and design in order to maintain the quality and supremacy of French artistic production. Ulrich Leben, *Object Design in the Age of Enlightenment: The History of the Royal Free Drawing School in Paris* (Los Angeles: Getty Publications, 2004), 18.

[13] Madam de Genlis, *A new method of instruction for children from five to ten years old,* 227-228.

[14] Ibid., 220.

[15] Ibid.

[16] Charlotte Guichard, "Les 'livres à dessiner' à l'usage des amateurs à Paris au XVIIIe siècle," *Revue de l'Art* 143 (2004-1): 49.

[17] The term "amateur" had a different connotation in this period than it does now. In the long eighteenth century, amateurs made art in a non-professional capacity but also participated in a variety of activities, such as commissioning works of art, socializing with professional artists, and writing texts on art or art production. They played a significant role in the art world and their opinions were often sought after.

[18] Charles-Antoine Jombert, *Nouvelle méthode pour apprendre a dessiner sans maître où l'on explique par de nouvelles démonstrations les premiers élémens & les regles generales de ce grand art, avec la manière de l'étudier pour s'y perfectionner en peu de tems* (Paris: Chez Charles-Antoine Jombert, 1740).

[19] Madam de Genlis, *A new method of instruction for children from five to ten years old,* 229.

[20] Ibid.

[21] Ibid., 232.

[22] Ibid., 224-225.

[23] Ibid., 237.

[24] Roger de Piles, *Principals of Painting…Written originally in French by Mons. Du Piles…and now first translated into English by a Painter* (London: J. Osborn, 1743), 45.

[25] Genevieve Warwick, 'Introduction', in *Collecting Prints and Drawings in Europe c. 1500-1750*, eds. Christopher Baker, Caroline Elam, and Genevieve Warwick (Aldershot: Ashgate Publishing Limited, 2003), 2.

[26] Ibid., 1.

[27] Kristel Smentek, "The Collector's Cut: Why Pierre-Jean Mariette Tore up His Drawings and Put Them Back Together Again," *Master Drawings* 47, no. 4 (Fall 2009): 36.

[28] Dorothy Johnson, "Picturing Pedagogy: Education and the Child in the Paintings of Chardin," *Eighteenth-Century Studies* 24, no. 1 (Autumn 1990): 56-57.

[29] Madam de Genlis, *A new method of instruction for children from five to ten years old,* 230.

[30] Ann Bermingham, *Learning to Draw: Studies in the Cultural History of a Polite and Useful Art* (New Haven: Yale University Press, 2000).

[31] Madam de Genlis, *A new method of instruction for children from five to ten years old,* 99.

[32] Ibid., 100.

[33] Ibid., 228.

[34] Jean-Jacques Rousseau, *Emile,* trans. Barbara Foxley (London: Dent, 1966), 331.

[35] Ibid.

[36] Melissa Hyde and Mary D. Sheriff, *Becoming a Woman in the Age of Enlightenment: French Art From the Horvitz Collection* (Boston: The Horvitz Collection, 2017).

[37] Rousseau, *Emile,* 328.

[38] Relevant sources include Melissa Hyde and Jennifer Milam, eds., *Women, Art and the Politics of Identity in Eighteenth-Century Europe* (Ashgate, 2003); Hyde and Sheriff, *Becoming a Woman in the Age of Enlightenment*; Paris Spies-Gans, "Exceptional, but not Exceptions: Public Exhibitions and the Rise of the Woman Artist in London and Paris, 1760-1830," *Eighteenth-Century Studies* 51, no. 4 (Summer 2018): 393-416; and Spies-Gans' forthcoming book, *A Revolution on Canvas: The Rise of Women Artists in Britain and France, 1760-1830.*

[39] Madam de Genlis, *A new method of instruction for children from five to ten years old*, 100-101.

[40] Leben, *Object Design in the Age of Enlightenment*, 18.

[41] Ibid., 19.

[42] Ibid., 77.

[43] As Leben argues, this was because Bachelier wanted to protect his school from the dominance of the Académie. Studying from sculpture, casts, and eventually from the live model was seen as the purview of the Académie.

[44] Ibid., 57-61.

[45] A.N. F/17/1318, Do.7. Undated manuscript by Bachelier as cited and translated by Leben in *Object Design in the Age of Enlightenment*, 60.

[46] Leben, *Object Design in the Age of Enlightenment*, 60.

[47] Ibid.

[48] For a discussion of this drawing school and its founding principles see Delanie Linden, "'The Future of Women Is the Future of the Nation': Marie-Élisabeth Cavé's Drawing Manuals and Art Education in Nineteenth-Century France," *Getty Research Journal*, no. 15 (2022): 102-3.

Bibliography

Ariès, Philippe. *Centuries of Childhood: A Social History of Family Life.* Translated by Robert Baldick. New York: Vintage Books, 1965.

Baillio, Joseph. "Mademoiselle d'Orléans Taking a Harp Lesson: Lot Essay." Christie's. Last modified January 27, 2015. https://www.christies.com/en/lot/lot-5868340.

Bermingham, Ann. *Learning to Draw: Studies in the Cultural History of a Polite and Useful Art.* New Haven: Yale University Press, 2000.

Dow, Gillian. "The British Reception of Madame de Genlis's Writings for Children: Plays and Tales of Instruction and Delight." *British Journal for Eighteenth Century Studies* 29 (2006): 367-381.

de Genlis, Madam. *A new method of instruction for children from five to ten years old: including moral dialogues, the children's island, a tale, thoughts and maxims, models of composition in writing for children ten or twelve years old, and a new method of teaching children to draw.* Dublin: Printed by William Porter, 1800.

Guichard, Charlotte. "Les 'livres à dessiner' à l'usage des amateurs à Paris au XVIIIe siècle." *Revue de l'Art* 143 (2004-1): 49-58.

Hyde, Melissa and Jennifer Milam, eds. *Women, Art and the Politics of Identity in Eighteenth-Century Europe.* Ashgate, 2003.

Hyde, Melissa, and Mary D. Sheriff. *Becoming a Woman in the Age of Enlightenment: French Art From the Horvitz Collection.* Boston: The Horvitz Collection, 2017.

Johnson, Dorothy. "Picturing Pedagogy: Education and the Child in the Paintings of Chardin." *Eighteenth-Century Studies* 24, no. 1 (Autumn 1990): 47-68.

Jombert, Charles-Antoine. *Nouvelle méthode pour apprendre a dessiner sans maître où l'on explique par de nouvelles démonstrations les premiers élémens & les regles generales de ce grand art, avec la manière de l'étudier pour s'y perfectionner en peu de tems.* Paris: Chez Charles-Antoine Jombert, 1740.

Leben, Ulrich. *Object Design in the Age of Enlightenment: The History of the Royal Free Drawing School in Paris.* Los Angeles: Getty Publications, 2004.

Linden, Delanie. "'The Future of Women Is the Future of the Nation': Marie-Élisabeth Cavé's Drawing Manuals and Art Education in Nineteenth-Century France." *Getty Research Journal*, no. 15 (2022): 87-112.

O'Malley, Andrew. *The Making of the Modern Child: Children's Literature in the Late Eighteenth Century.* New York and London: Routledge, 2003.

Ouvrages de peinture, sculpture, et architecture, gravures, dessins, modeles, &. Exposés au Louvre par ordre de l'Assemblée nationale; Au mois de Septembre 1791; L'an III.e de la liberté. Paris: de l'Imprimerie des Batimens du Roi, 1791.

de Piles, Roger. *Principals of Painting…Written originally in French by Mons. Du Piles…and now first translated into English by a Painter.* London: J. Osborn, 1743.

Popiel, Jennifer J. *Rousseau's Daughters: Domesticity, Education, and Autonomy in Modern France.* Durham, New Hampshire: University of New Hampshire Press, 2008.

Rousseau, Jean-Jacques. *Emile.* Translated by Barbara Foxley. London: Dent, 1966.

Sevelis, Laura. "The Harp Lesson." Dallas Museum of Art. Last modified 2015. https://collections.dma.org/artwork/5340929.

Smentek, Kristel. "The Collector's Cut: Why Pierre-Jean Mariette Tore up His Drawings and Put Them Back Together Again." *Master Drawings* 47, No. 4 (Fall 2009): 36-60.

Spies-Gans, Paris. "Exceptional, but not Exceptions: Public Exhibitions and the Rise of the Woman Artist in London and Paris, 1760-1830." *Eighteenth-Century Studies* 51, no. 4 (Summer 2018): 393-416.

Warwick, Genevieve. "Introduction". In *Collecting Prints and Drawings in Europe c. 1500-1750.* Edited by Christopher Baker, Caroline Elam, and Genevieve Warwick. Aldershot: Ashgate Publishing Limited, 2003.

Chapter 5

Outside for Girls in Madame d'Epinay's *Conversations d'Emilie*

Brigitte Weltman-Aron

The University of Florida

Abstract

Louise d'Epinay (1726-83) wrote a pedagogical treatise, *Conversations d'Emilie* (1774), expanded in 1781. The second edition comprises twenty conversations between Emilie and her mother, who supervises her education and her recreational activities. Each conversation addresses various scenes experienced or witnessed by Emilie in her interactions with others, and covers material ranging from discussions of readings adapted to the child's understanding to responses to social or moral dilemmas.

This chapter draws parallels between Rousseau's *Emile ou de l'Education* (1762) and Epinay's treatise, especially regarding recommended outdoors activities for girls. Epinay's views are not neatly opposed to Rousseau's. In particular, the pastimes and physical exercises enjoyed by Emilie demonstrate Epinay's careful handling of pedagogical innovations in female education. She accepts some conventional gendered principles, while modifying or rejecting others. Beyond exposing the merit of being outdoors, *Conversations* reveals what "outside" could encompass and signify for French upper-class girls at the time.

Keywords: Epinay, Rousseau, Exercise, Female Education, Outdoors

***

Louise Florence Tardieu d'Esclavelles, marquise d'Epinay (1726-83), is well known for having been Jean-Jacques Rousseau's host for a few eventful months, and as a friend of Encyclopedists, among them Grimm, Galiani, and Diderot. Studies have shown that her exchanges with contemporary authors included active participation in collective and anonymous undertakings such as the *Correspondance littéraire*, a cultural and political gazette addressed to European elites.[1] She is mostly known today for her pseudo-memoirs or *roman à clé, Histoire de Madame de Montbrillant*, left unpublished during her lifetime, to which Diderot and others contributed, a book that has long been interpreted as a preemptive response to Rousseau's *Confessions*. However, critics increasingly dwell on her works in the field of education, especially her pedagogical treatise, *Conversations d'Emilie* (1774), revised and expanded in a second edition in 1781, for which she received a prize, prix Montyon.[2] Drawing on material based on the author's granddaughter's education, the second edition comprises twenty pedagogical conversations between Emilie and her mother, who supervises her education and her recreational activities. The *Conversations* cover traditional subjects of instruction, such as writing, and reading adapted to the child's understanding.[3] They also address and elucidate for the child various situations experienced or witnessed by Emilie in her interactions with others, the mother providing her with responses to social or moral dilemmas. Instruction is both planned and improvised, since it stems from concrete daily occurrences and incorporates the little girl's reactions and questions, evincing progress in her abilities and her judgment. Madame d'Epinay's contemporaries were struck by the ingenuity with which the mother skillfully took advantage of the immediate circumstances the child found herself in to impart a lesson that did not seem contrived.

The advantages of dialogue in education had long been underscored (for example, by Locke and Fénelon), and the development of common sense and judgment through tangible experiences that was to replace learning by rote is expounded in Rousseau's famous treatise, *Emile ou de l'Education* (1762), as well as in *Conversations*.[4] In the eighteenth century, French pedagogical treatises published after *Emile* often positioned themselves with regard to Rousseau's theses, whether they explicitly acknowledged it or not, and I will draw parallels between the two authors' positions, in particular on recommended outdoor activities for children. Moreover, prominent women writers such as Madame de Lambert preceded Rousseau's endeavor, especially insofar as the methods and objectives of female education were concerned, and Madame d'Epinay also contended with such models, as Rosena Davison rightly recalls in her introduction to her edition of *Conversations*.[5] In *Ancien Régime* France, access to instruction at home or in schools for all children across the board was inequitable. The influence of the Church on education through its teaching orders was felt to be so pervasive that it led some to advocate private over public education. In principle, Madame d'Epinay asserts that public education, or instruction away from home, unlike the one she proposes in the treatise, would be a better form of instruction but declares that it still remains to be instituted to her satisfaction. Her book compares the task of public school teachers to that of gardeners caring for plants: an excess of attention to one plant might prove harmful, whereas the risk of overindulgence is lessened when the gardener must tend to several.[6] Furthermore, several authors emphasized the damaging effects of scant female instruction, or of what Martine Sonnet calls "modest enlightenment," on girls and society in general, the most progressive of them identifying mediocre education as one of the founding causes of inequality between men and women.[7] Madame d'Epinay points out in the tenth Conversation that the lack of training for girls impairs their ability to educate others when they become adults. She opposes in that respect the practices of foreign countries, where governesses are both high-born and well bred, thus competent to teach, to the French custom of entrusting girls to maids, whose own education has generally been deficient.[8] With a mixture of candor and defiance, the mother admits she is (relatively) ignorant in several passages of *Conversations*, and explains that she has mostly been self-taught.

Detractors of Book V of Rousseau's *Emile*, which deals with the upbringing of girls, have pointed out then as now the retrograde elements of his program and contested his evaluation of women's faculties and social roles. Conversely, some of our own contemporaries often concentrate on the feminist arguments of eighteenth-century women writers, so that the assertion of woman's dependent status in *Emile* and of empowerment in women's treatises can be neatly opposed. For example, Sissela Bok isolates Rousseau's most egregious pronouncements about girls and women in Book V which is called "one of the least inspiring ideals of femininity ever put on paper," before contrasting them to Madame d'Epinay's belief that young girls can "explore all the varieties of knowledge and thinking."[9] All the quotations marshaled by this critic are accurate, and yet the difference posited between the two authors needs to be nuanced, in matters belonging to the physical as well as the intellectual and social development of girls, as I will show. As Davison notes, Madame d'Epinay and other pedagogues do not so much reject as sample Rousseau, selecting from his oeuvre what suits their purposes.[10] P.D. Jimack recalls in that respect that the heroine of Rousseau's novel *La Nouvelle Héloïse* was immensely popular among women of his time, who found in Julie "the ideal mother-educator who represents at the same time the ideal human being education seeks to realize."[11] With such an inspiring model at their disposal, Jimack and other critics argue that female writers and readers could disregard what they disliked in Sophie's education. Even then, there is much that they could agree with in *Emile*, starting with the notion that mothers should play a fundamental role in their children's lives from their infancy. Madame d'Epinay's treatise endorses that claim and aims to demonstrate that mothers are best qualified to supervise their daughters' education.

Rousseau goes further than a great number of predecessors aiming like him to "rehabilitate women provided that they restrict themselves to roles assigned to them," in Aurélie Chatenet's words, when he asserts that "the moral regeneration of a corrupt nation" essentially depends on women and mothers, a view that had a far-ranging impact in the years following the publication of Emile.[12] Rousseau claims that women have a prominence in France that is inappropriate as well as ill-conceived, and all his essays depict disastrous consequences for the public good when men become like women at their contact.[13] Conversely, he argues that women's natural ascendancy over men could be channeled properly so as to improve society. Critics have shown the mixture of coaxing and threats in his entreaties that women willingly give up their public pretensions. Yet, that plea, which it is worth reiterating was not Rousseau's only, seems to have persuaded not only men but several influential women of his time, in itself, or because some women saw in it an opportunity for their own happiness or for women's increased status. Elisabeth Badinter argues that while privileged women enjoyed a certain intellectual autonomy at the time, they kept being barred in principle from a number of careers commensurate to their abilities and achievements.[14] Thus, the increased value placed on motherhood by Rousseau and others and the anticipated impact of its heightened relevance in the public sphere could be felt to be a welcome catalyst for change, and perhaps the only one. In that respect, it is striking to note that whereas Rousseau laments gender-bending characteristics among his contemporaries, and argues that women strive to usurp men's prerogatives while neglecting their own singular roles, *Conversations d'Emilie* takes it for granted on the contrary that men and women, at least in the mother's upper class, have entirely separate occupations, and does not foresee any forthcoming change in that situation. According to the mother, "one cannot count on men who belong to the public before belonging to their family," while conversely, "the weakness of our sex and the narrow sphere of our small talents confine us to exercising domestic duties; we have satisfied all that society expects of us by fulfilling them."[15] The latter comment may testify to Madame d'Epinay's prudent wish not to rock the boat or, as Isabelle Brouard-Arends explains, to her "bitter lucidity, without revolt however" when reflecting on the fate of women.[16] Evoking the pressure women have had to endure then and now regarding motherhood, Badinter consistently credits them nevertheless with strategies intended to further their own interests and self-realization: for example, she interprets middle-class women's changing attitudes to motherhood in the last decades of the eighteenth century as endeavors to claim the moral high ground on a terrain no one denies they have the right to occupy, with the goal of being recognized as the ultimate authorities on children within and beyond the family.[17] This helps explain why, in Jean Bloch's words, "Rousseau owed much of the initial success [of *Emile*] to women," some of them agreeing with Rousseau "that woman's role was to inspire men to virtue," and investing in that position.[18]

Furthermore, the rhetoric of *Emile*'s Book V is particularly convoluted, with effects that are often ignored by readers today. For example, Rousseau outrageously asserts that women need to learn to be docile early on "since they never cease to be subjected to a man, or to the judgments of men and they are never permitted to put themselves above these judgments."[19] But several mitigating passages follow that pronouncement, so as to make it utterly inapplicable. To mention just a few, girls are said to be endowed with reason and a conscience that must be cultivated.[20] The amount of culture and knowledge Rousseau finds appropriate for girls and reflective of their abilities undeniably leaves much to be desired. This is clearly the area where female pedagogues like Madame d'Epinay were most likely to ignore his recommendations. Yet, remarkably, Rousseau anticipates at this juncture an objection from reactionary readers wondering whether girls and women have reason at all, or are "capable of solid reasoning" if they have some.[21] While he disagrees with the objection, he accepts that it points to a valid difficulty, which is the perceived necessity to adjust the cultivation of reason in girls to their future "functions."[22] This vocation noticeably hampers girls in a way boys' future fatherhood does not in *Emile*. But this stated difficulty, whereby girls can only become what they will need to be when they are adults is one that Madame d'Epinay constantly struggles with as well, as we shall see when we examine Emilie's physical activities. The point is that having developed her reason and conscience in her upbringing, woman is then said in *Emile* to be in a position to compare what her conscience tells her with the opinions of others and, consequently, "She becomes the judge of her judges; she decides when she ought to subject herself to them and when she ought to take exception to them."[23] It is evident that this statement considerably modifies the first requirement that a woman submit to her husband's and other men's opinions in all circumstances. Admittedly, the position woman is asked to adopt in *Emile* is inordinately complex, and often untenable, as in the example above, in that it demands deferring to contradictory principles. It is never clear why comportment should be so complicated for women and so straightforward for men, and ascribing the difference to nature fails to convince, especially because Rousseau discusses levels of (social) cultivation of (natural) faculties. At one point, the character Sophie remarkably denounces the aporia of her instruction, providing a fascinating instance of the power of fiction against theoretical certitudes, and admirable, too, in that lucidity as to the madness of Sophie's double bind is not sufficient for the author to reconsider the validity of his educational principles.[24] At all events, such byzantine rhetoric is another explanation why women could subscribe to Rousseau's views on women in *Emile*, which were, and *because* they were by no means unified. They extracted Rousseau's recommendations about the education of boys when they wrote about girls, to be sure. But there was enough that was invigorating in what Rousseau wrote about girls that they could adopt, too.

Madame d'Epinay belonged to the upper classes: whether it entirely influenced her outlook or not, the fact is that her treatise does not on the whole contest the social order of her country and of her period. Criticism is reserved in the book for those who do not live up to the expectations of their rank in society, whether high or low. However, the mother is confident that merit ends up being recognized and that the rewards brought by persistent work ethics followed by personal achievements amply make up for the obscurity of low birth. As a rich lady, the mother's responsibilities within her household are quite extensive; the reader understands that the administration of family properties requiring various competences is included in her purview. Thus, in the eighth Conversation, after the mother explains the patriarchal system structuring public and domestic affairs through the well-worn image of a benevolent father, Emilie is puzzled by the contradiction she perceives between the description of the theoretical authority of the King/husband/father and the actual power displayed daily in practice by the mother. In response, the mother recognizes that she holds authority by proxy.[25] Woman's activity is merely said to stop short of the sort of public position held by her husband, whose time-consuming business is divided from hers, with the caveat that his wife had to show herself deserving of his trust through "her prudence and her vigilance."[26] The structure of delegation exposed by the mother seems demeaning, but the book also shows that upper-class women had several compensations and could pragmatically enjoy the authority conferred to them within limits. While the treatise does not contest the socially prescribed system whereby men are destined to hold public positions, the mother ponders in a variant to Conversation 20 "what remains to women," and argues that because they are necessarily sedentary, they "have more time and less distractions than men to dedicate themselves to reflection."[27] This argument might be a brave suggestion for dealing with enforced domesticity, if it were not immediately followed by the remark that "Reflection is the antidote to natural flaws in women," namely, "thoughtlessness, frivolity, laziness, inconsistency, weakness, mental exaltation." These flaws are natural because they are said to stem from women's "delicacy and the mobility of their organs," although the mother concedes that they come above all from "the frivolity with which girls are raised," recognizing in that second position that women's so-called "natural" frivolity is at the very least reinforced, if not entirely produced by social stimuli. Such a sample of Madame d'Epinay's remarks in that vein demonstrates how difficult it is to oppose her thinking to Rousseau's assessment of women's potentialities in absolute terms.

Rousseau writes in *Emile* that a young girl should not be expected to "live like her grandmother": "she ought to be lively, playful, and frolicsome, to sing and dance as much as she likes, and to taste all the innocent pleasures of her age."[28] If he devotes less space to the first years of the girl's childhood than he did in earlier parts of his book to the upbringing of boys, it is partly because in early years recommendations rely for both sexes on similar patterns of "negative" instruction, with some gendered differences. Sophie appears in Book V shortly before she is about to meet Emile and get married, a stage that is never reached in *Conversations d'Emilie*, starting when the child is five years old and ending on the eve of her tenth birthday, which is said to bring childhood to a close on the onset of adolescence.[29] The book does not end with Emilie's marriage, but the eighteenth and nineteenth Conversations revolve instead around the wedding of the daughter of one of the mother's employees that Emilie attended in the country, which gives rise to serious considerations on married women's obligations. Because the book focuses on Emilie's first ten years, however, Madame d'Epinay, who agrees with Rousseau that a young girl should spend time outside exercising and strengthening her body, can afford to be much less austere. The first Conversation indicates that playing and exercising should be Emilie's main purpose at her young age, and this is a leitmotif throughout the book. The sixth Conversation proposes alternating moderate study with time dedicated to "jumping, dancing, working in the vegetable garden, watering the parterre," so as to prevent boredom and instill steady habits.[30] Beyond exposing the physical advantage of being outdoors, *Conversations d'Emilie* reveals what "outside" could encompass and signify for French upper-class girls at the time. When Emilie is not playing in her garden, she is driven to the city center to shop with her mother, walks in the Tuileries gardens where she meets her friends, or spends the summer and warm autumn days in her country house, with outings to the neighboring farm or hiking excursions in its vicinity.

Going outside provides Emilie with an array of experiences, consisting first in discovering what her body can do and the consequences of her movements. Conversation 9 depicts a walk in the country, at the end of which Emilie sees some children from the neighboring house running ahead on the path. In a scene that may echo another in which Rousseau's Emile competes to win a cake in a race with other boys in Book II, the mother suggests she run after the other children, with an extra incentive: "If you catch up to them before they realize it, I will give you [a] little sheep" that Emilie covets, and that she is sure she will get, proving that she is confident in her proficiency— "Ah, Placide, my friend, I will have you at last!"[31] In Conversation 7, Emilie returns from the garden with a "face bruised to a pulp" [*en compote*], a limp, and skinned knees, because she fell from a tall ladder on wheels she had felt like climbing.[32] The mother plays down her injury, congratulates her for being brave and not crying, which would "not help," and especially argues that falling is not a bad experience in that it teaches how to avoid doing so in the future.[33] Thus, outdoors activities are positive because they increase the young girl's physical vigor, and provide opportunities to train her judgment. Emilie first wonders why the maid did not forbid her to climb the ladder since the outcome was harmful, before formulating herself that it is better for her acts to coincide with rational decisions arrived at on her own: "when I tell myself I do not want to do that, my will is very firm, and I am not tempted to fail it."[34] Lessons about her capacities that are drawn from personal experience are more valuable in that they also teach self-reliance and autonomous judgment.

However, as we have mentioned before, Madame d'Epinay does not consistently swerve from conventional positions about what is appropriate for girls to do. Whether she privately agreed with them or not, the fact is that the mother in her book concurs with several normative social expectations, with no ensuing protest from Emilie. About the incident with the ladder, for example, the mother remarks that it would have been "honorable" to have fallen if Emilie had been running or doing another appropriate exercise with her friends, but falling from a ladder seems a little extravagant to her: Emilie should not quite do "the same exercises as her brothers" and "the modesty of her sex demands a decency, a restraint that must be noticed in the midst of the petulance and the effervescence of the first age."[35] The discussion in Conversation 7 seamlessly shifts from recommending self-preservation and avoidance of bodily harm to urging Emilie to control her behavior. The mother reminds her that while it is the "privilege" of her age to be noisy when they are together on their own, excessive racket (*tintamarre*) is not acceptable when there are visitors. On a recent visit, instead of leaving the room to play, Emilie and her brothers chose to remain, and she "made almost as much noise as they did."[36] Yet, only the little girl is to blame, not her brothers. If the visitor disrespected Emilie and treated her like a "puppet," the fault is not his either, but is entirely due to her lack of decorum: "If he had found in your countenance this modesty, this reserve that must never abandon a young person of our sex, he would never have dared to allow himself this small moment of familiarity."[37] The girl is led to conclude that she must be responsible for her behavior and also be "in charge of censuring it" retrospectively, in anticipation of future similar interactions.[38] Several other passages in the book demonstrate this concern over girls' unchecked exuberance, which the mother does not punish, but that she would like the girl to address because her "reputation" is at stake.[39]

Rousseau favored walks in the country over public promenades, such as the Tuileries, which he found "pernicious for children of both sexes" because they encourage vanity and the wish to be looked at.[40] Madame d'Epinay somewhat agrees, and after her regular visits to the Tuileries, Emilie often reports the unwelcome gazes and caustic remarks of others intent on denigrating passersby. Conversation 13 describes her annoyance after her return from the promenade, and her disgust at its uniform and crowded alleys. However, her professed preference for the countryside at this juncture mainly stems from her resentment at disparaging remarks she overheard about her appearance: "She would be quite pretty if she were not so black."[41] She owes her suntanned complexion to the fact that she lately came back from the country where she was outside every day. The mother uses this occurrence to relativize the importance of fashionable criteria for beauty such as fair skin, and to praise healthy looks instead, pointing out that health has its own beauty.[42] Several other Conversations evoke fashion and finery as traps for vanity, which moralists are always prone to detect in girls and women. However, Conservation 15 more profoundly shows that being stylish may not be understood simply as an asset contributing to one's personal beauty but as a means to conform to others' expectations of what is proper in a young woman's appearance. The Conversation starts with a discussion Emilie holds with her doll, in which she deplores the miserable outfits the doll is forced to keep wearing because of her current lack of funds. Emilie promises that she will visit the famous *modiste* Mademoiselle Bertin as soon as she has six francs at her disposal, after which "one will ecstatically talk of our taste and our elegance."[43] Rousseau ascribes girls' love of adornment to their desire to be deemed pretty by others, whereas Emilie has a different interpretation: she has noticed that adults, and even her own mother at times, pay close attention to and pass judgment on others' external appearance, including when they disparage hers. She derives from that focus the notion that being pleasing and attractive to others is a form of social virtue. In that sense, being stylish is being polite. The next step of the lesson will be that such a proper appearance, while entirely expected by and due to others and to herself, does not warrant being uppermost in her mind. It must become effortless, because excessive attention to one's looks is in bad taste. After her mishap in the Tuileries, Emilie is asked whether she would prefer to be deprived of her favorite activities outside in the country, and worry about the sun, the rain and the wind in consideration of her complexion. In reply, she prefers enjoying herself and fully dedicating her days to playing without second thoughts, and when the mother offers her to wear a protective veil in her future promenades out of compassion for her predicament, Emilie refuses. She resolves to set less stock in physical beauty, since she is told it is fugitive and that no happiness can be enduringly derived from a temporary condition, not unlike the doll's accessories that "resemble a little last year's almanac" without affecting the permanence of good taste.[44] Even more remarkably, the mother touches lightly on the futility of fashionable ornaments before reflecting with her daughter on the effect of fashionable words and the current trend of using exaggerated terms, or "big words": Emilie agrees that when she talked to her doll with grand words such as "ecstatically," she "wanted to be trendy," by which she means that she wished "to speak like a high society lady."[45] The lesson for Emilie is that the simplicity of apparel does not exclude the evidence of taste *and* that unadorned speech testifies to refined thinking. The inflation of words devoid of veracity attests to bad taste, and the distorted relationship between expressions and the ideas they are intended to convey has the contrary effect to what was intended: "reasonable persons pay no attention" to these sounds without sense.[46] Throughout the book, the mother frequently asks Emilie to explain the meaning of the words she utters, explaining that it is very difficult to eradicate a false notion, once it is entertained.[47]

At the end of Conversation 2, mother and daughter are about to step out in their garden, and Conversation 3 entirely takes place outside. The conversation revolves around animals and plants. Emilie is prevented by the mother from pulling a fly's wings off, which she wanted to do so it could not escape. This leads the mother to discuss animal and vegetal suffering, and the necessity to respect the sensitivity of sentient beings down to "the smallest productions of nature. A fly, a beetle, a dog, a tree, all are her productions. –Emilie: And so am I."[48] Building on that immediate example, the mother introduces the notion of good and evil, the moral dependence of the weak on the moderation of the strong, with a detour through Roman history and the example of cruel emperor Domitian. Emilie learns that she can already accomplish good things at her young age, by being reasonable and gentle with her maid and her family, and by being friendly and respectful to people in the lower classes. The garden provides other examples of unruly behavior worrisome to those who love her, such as her overeating "all the fruit ripe or not that you [find] within your range."[49] Likewise, the place allows the mother to convey rudiments of natural science and to explain the difference between plants and animals by showing her the seeds of plants in the vegetable garden.[50] Conversation 3 is an astute compendium of practical and moral lessons seemingly spontaneously arising from the child's acts and questions.

Mother and child playfully assert in Conversation 20 that their habit of conversing while walking is reminiscent of the Peripatetic school, whose members never philosophized "except when walking in the Lyceum, which was something like the Tuileries of Athens." More precisely, Emilie says that they are "half-peripatetic: half of our conversations took place while walking."[51] Indeed, throughout the book, nature is their *salon* and outside provides food for thought. Inside activities are occasioned by and often merge with those outdoors, and thinking never is at rest. Yet, on several occasions, the mother blames herself for not having sufficiently discouraged Emilie's sedentary tastes. Rousseau claims that reading is the "plague of childhood," but in a variant of Conversation 20, Emilie, who may have found it difficult at first, recalls her delight when she realized she could read on her own.[52] In her educational approach consisting in developing a healthy body so it can eventually host a healthy mind, the mother accepts in principle the validity of Rousseau's recommendation to defer the time of acquiring that knowledge as long as possible, but when it comes to the point, she is reluctant to apply it in practice.[53] Fearing to "contradict nature in her operations by subjecting [Emilie] to sedentary life too early," the mother first contemplated banishing long-lasting study of any kind: "Let's see what will happen with our little savage girl."[54] But the fear of being extravagant, of "calling attention to herself" (*se singulariser*), changed the mother's mind and her plan: "One may run great risks by going out of the beaten path".[55] Even though she approves of it, the lack of demonstrated success of this novel method fosters caution in the pedagogue, who also feels the scrutiny of others in judgment of her attempt, just as Emilie felt unpleasantly looked at in the

Tuileries: "Boldness does not suit our sex in any genre. This reflection may have preserved you, my dear friend, of the danger of being a freak. It has been said that a perfect woman is the one who is never talked about whether for good or ill; thus, I hope that you will never be mentioned in any way."[56] Such remarks attest to Madame d'Epinay's careful handling of pedagogical innovations, so as not to rehearse trite advice while not offending her readers.

Conversation 20 proposes a metaphor to show the challenge of putting oneself in the child's place when planning her education: not being able to remain at that level at all times, the pedagogue may be tempted to raise the child too soon to the adult's range of information, as if she were a plant grown in a hothouse instead of outside, where it would imperceptibly ripen over time and through natural means.[57] Yet, Emilie may be absolved from the fate of artificially ostentatious hothouse plants. Her utterly charming character largely prevents the treatise from pedantic seriousness. Emilie is a playful recipient of knowledge, whose sincerity serves to unmask what the social fabric conceals, with the help, of course, of "the best" mother. In our time of lockdown and confinement, she demonstrates that being an upper-class girl in the eighteenth century did not mean being housebound, but being encouraged to draw connections between inside and outside.

Notes

[1] Adrien Legros, "Un Complément de Mme d'Epinay à l'article 'Genève'" dans le Tome VII de l'*Encyclopédie*," *Revue du Nord* 16, no. 64 (1930): 261.

[2] The prize was awarded by the Académie française for "the most useful" work in competition (Francis Marcoin, "L'effet Montyon," *Romantisme* 93 [1996]: 65).

[3] In the Second Conversation, the mother points out that learning to write correctly cannot be acquired "in one day," and that good handwriting depends on the adequate posture of the body and the right handling of the pen (Madame d'Epinay, *Les Conversations d'Emilie* [Oxford: Voltaire Foundation, 1996], 64). On writing in upper-class girls' upbringing, see Dena Goodman's study of epistolary practice in eighteenth-century France, *Becoming a Woman in the Age of Letters* (Ithaca: Cornell University Press, 2009).

[4] Laurence Vanoflen, "La Conversation, une pédagogie pour les femmes?" in *Femmes éducatrices au siècle des Lumières*, ed. Isabelle Brouard-Arends and Marie-Emmanuelle Plagnol-Diéval (Rennes: Presses Universitaires de Rennes, 2007), 183.

[5] Rosena Davison, "Introduction," in D'Epinay, *Conversations*, 15-16.

[6] D'Epinay, *Conversations*, Conversation 20, 404.

[7] Martine Sonnet, *L'Education des filles au temps des Lumières* (Paris: Les Editions du Cerf, 1987), 18. In her study, Sonnet does not focus on pedagogical treatises but on public schools for girls in Paris in the eighteenth century, showing that parents with various financial means could actually rely on a "female educational market" in the capital (19). The situation could differ greatly in the provinces.

[8] D'Epinay, *Conversations*, Conversation 10, 188. On several occasions, Madame d'Epinay referred to the flaws of her own education, just as the mother in Conversation 12, who deplores being taught as a girl a superficial veneer of subjects and skills without any attempt to form her reason, and who notes the absence of all scientific instruction (239). The mother adds that she had to teach herself so as to educate Emilie properly, and that it is an open-ended process (239).

[9] Sissela Bok, "The Contested Self-Portrait of Madame d'Epinay," *Ploughshares* 10.2/3 (1984): 176, 177.

[10] Davison, in D'Epinay, *Conversations*, 13.

[11] P.D. Jimack, "The Paradox of Sophie and Julie: Contemporary Response to Rousseau's Ideal Wife and Ideal Mother," in *Woman and Society in Eighteenth-Century France: Essays in honour of John Stephenson Spink*, ed. Eva Jacobs *et al.* (London: The Athlone Press, 1979), 163.

[12] Aurélie Chatenet, "La femme, maîtresse de maison? Rôle et place des femmes dans les ouvrages d'économie domestique au XVIIIe siècle," *Histoire, Economie et Société* (2009/4): 21; Jean Bloch, "Women and the Reform of the Nation," in *Woman and society in eighteenth-century France*, 6.

[13] In other writings, Rousseau is much more likely to recognize the benefits of women's influence, including in education. For example, it would be impossible to find in *Emile* what he says in the *Confessions* about Mademoiselle du Châtelet, who "had that taste for observational morality that leads to studying men; and it is from her that this same taste came to me in its first origin," or, a little later, "it is certain that interesting and sensible conversations with a woman of merit are more fit for forming a young man than all the pedantic philosophy of books" (The *Confessions*, Christopher Kelly, tr., London and Hanover: University Press of New England, 1995), 143.

[14] Elisabeth Badinter, *L'Amour en plus* (Paris: Flammarion, 1980), 105.

[15] D'Epinay, *Conversations*, Conversation 20, 393, 394.

[16] Isabelle Brouard-Arends, "Trajectoires de femmes, éthique et projet auctorial, Mme de Lambert, Mme d'Epinay, Mme de Genlis." *Dix-huitième siècle*, n° 36 (2004): 193. Other celebrated women writers of her time, such as Madame de Genlis and Madame de Staël, echo Madame d'Epinay's analysis. The same mixture of rejection of restrictions placed on women's intellectual abilities, and recommendation that girls be trained to accept their future lot is found in Madame de Genlis (Jimack, "Paradox," 159), and Madame de Staël disagrees that women's submission to men is caused by their weakness, but argues that they must deliberately limit themselves through love and from a position of strength (Jean Bloch, *Rousseauism and education in eighteenth-century France* [Oxford: Voltaire Foundation, 1995], 218). Madame d'Epinay affirms that moral strength is all the more precious and indispensable to those who are deprived of physical strength (*Conversations*, Conversation 16, 339).

[17] Badinter, *L'Amour en plus*, 289. Badinter's book, published in 1980, traces the legal evolution in France from paternal authority in the seventeenth century to shared parental authority at the time she writes.

[18] Bloch, *Rousseauism and Education*, 215-16. Bloch adds that at first, "What criticism there were against Rousseau tended to come from men," not women (216).

[19] Jean-Jacques Rousseau, *Emile*, Allan Bloom tr. (New York: Basic Books, 1979), 370.

[20] Ibid., 382. See Madame d'Epinay: "when you carefully cultivate your reason, and adorn it with useful and solid knowledge, you open for yourself many new sources of pleasure and satisfaction" (*Conversations,* Conversation 12, 249).

[21] Rousseau, *Emile,* 382.

[22] Ibid.

[23] Ibid., 383. This may be compared with the mother's statement: "The approbation of our conscience makes us happy on its own and independently of the approbation of others; the latter, on the contrary, does not flatter us at all if our conscience contradicts it" (D'Epinay, *Conversations,* Conversation 6, 127).

[24] In that respect, I take the liberty of referring to my "Educating Girls: Rousseau's Sophi(e)stry," *Studies on Voltaire and on the Eighteenth Century* 362 (1998): 41-53. Another instance of contradiction: Rousseau claims that unlike boys, girls do not aspire to be free, yet he gives in Book II as an illustration of his argument that children misread La Fontaine's fables, the example of a little girl of his acquaintance who burst into tears when she heard the fable of the lean wolf and the fat dog: instead of a lesson in moderation and docility, she "was irritated by being chained [...] She was crying at not being a wolf" (*Emile,* 116).

[25] D'Epinay, *Conversations,* Conversation 8, 151-52.

[26] Ibid., 152.

[27] D'Epinay, *Conversations,* Appendice III, 512.

[28] Rousseau, *Emile,* 374.

[29] D'Epinay, *Conversations,* Conversation 20, 391.

[30] D'Epinay, *Conversations,* Conversation 6, 119. Interrupting one's activities "ceaselessly and without reason" is a disorderly habit and can lead to unsteadiness and lack of methodical goals (Conversation 8, 153).

[31] D'Epinay, *Conversations,* Conversation 9, 180.

[32] D'Epinay, *Conversations,* Conversation 7, 129. This episode may be contrasted with Rousseau's opinion that "it is not contusions that [women's] faces await" (*Emile,* 147). Earlier, Emilie had learnt not to be dramatic about bad weather: to the desire to go inside because "rain falls on my nose," the mother answers that "Since it can do you no harm, I advise you to get used to this small annoyance" (Conversation 3, 71).

[33] D'Epinay, *Conversations,* Conversation 7, 137, 132.

[34] Ibid., 132.

[35] Ibid.

[36] Ibid., 134.

[37] Ibid., 135.

[38] Ibid., 138.

[39] "The good reputation of a young person is her most precious possession, that is what she must cherish all her life; and when one is once set against her, it is so difficult to establish it again that I am careful not to tell your flaws, as long as I keep the hope to see you have corrected them" (D'Epinay, *Conversations,* Conversation 6, 111-12).

[40] Rousseau, *Emile,* 141. Criticism of the immorality of public promenades of cities is frequent in the eighteenth century. See Louis-Sébastien Mercier's discussion of the alleys

of Palais Royal also discussed by Rousseau (*Emile,* 141) just before the French Revolution, *Tableau de Paris,* Paris: Mercure de France 1994, T II, 939.

[41] D'Epinay, *Conversations,* Conversation 13, 253.

[42] Ibid., 261.

[43] D'Epinay, *Conversations,* Conversation 15, 303. Several scenes show Emilie playing with her doll. Rousseau's take on a girl's absorption in her games with dolls is that "She awaits the moment when she will be her own doll" (*Emile,* 367). With his habit of drawing the ultimate conclusions of his position, Rousseau asserts, unlike strict moralists, that girls' delight in ornaments and prettiness should be encouraged within reason since the aim is for women to be pleasing to their husbands.

[44] D'Epinay, *Conversations,* Conversation 15, 259, 406.

[45] Ibid., 307.

[46] Ibid., 309.

[47] D'Epinay, *Conversations,* Conversation 5, 96.

[48] D'Epinay, *Conversations,* Conversation 3, 69.

[49] Ibid., 71.

[50] Ibid., 75.

[51] D'Epinay, *Conversations,* Conversation 20, 401.

[52] Rousseau, *Emile,* 116; D'Epinay, *Conversations,* Appendice III, 507.

[53] See Sandrine Aragon, "Des Révolutions dans les représentations de lectrices," *Dix-huitième siècle* 36 (2004): 241.

[54] D'Epinay, *Conversations,* Conversation 12, 241.

[55] Ibid., 242.

[56] Ibid.

[57] D'Epinay, *Conversations,* Conversation 20, 402.

Bibliography

Aragon, Sandrine. "Des Révolutions dans les représentations de lectrices," *Dix-huitième siècle* no. 36 (2004): 237-48.

Badinter, Elisabeth. *L'Amour en plus : histoire de l'amour maternel (XVIIe-XXe siècle).* Paris: Flammarion, 1980.

Bloch, Jean. *Rousseauism and education in eighteenth-century France.* Oxford: Voltaire Foundation, 1995.

———. "Women and the Reform of the Nation." *Woman and society in eighteenth-century France: Essays in honour of John Stephenson Spink.* Eva Jacobs, W.H.

Barber, F.W. Leakey, Eileen Le Breton, eds. London: The Athlone Press, 1979.

Bok, Sissela. "The Contested Self-Portrait of Madame d'Epinay." *Ploughshares* 10.2/3 (1984): 166-78.

Brouard-Arends, Isabelle. "Trajectoires de femmes, éthique et projet auctorial, Mme de Lambert, Mme d'Epinay, Mme de Genlis." *Dix-huitième siècle* no. 36 (2004): 189-96.

Chatenet, Aurélie. "La femme, maîtresse de maison? Rôle et place des femmes dans les ouvrages d'économie domestique au XVIIIe siècle." *Histoire, Economie et Société* (2009/4): 21-34.

D'Epinay, Louise. *Les Conversations d'Emilie. Studies on Voltaire and on the Eighteenth Century* 342. Rosena Davison, ed. Oxford: Voltaire Foundation, 1996.

Goodman, Dena. *Becoming a Woman in the Age of Letters.* Ithaca: Cornell University Press, 2009.

Jimack, P.D. "The Paradox of Sophie and Julie: Contemporary Response to Rousseau's Ideal Wife and Ideal Mother." *Woman and society in eighteenth-century France: Essays in honour of John Stephenson Spink.* Eva Jacobs, W.H. Barber, F.W. Leakey, Eileen Le Breton, eds. London: The Athlone Press, 1979.

Legros, Adrien. "Un Complément de Mme d'Epinay à l'article 'Genève' dans le tome VII de l'*Encyclopédie.*" *Revue du Nord* 16, no. 64 (1930): 257-66.

Marcoin, Francis. "L'effet Montyon." *Romantisme* 93 (1996): 65-82.

Mercier, Louis-Sébastien. *Tableau de Paris.* Paris: Mercure de France, 1994.

Rousseau, Jean-Jacques. The *Confessions.* Christopher Kelly, Roger D. Masters, and Peter G. Stillman, eds. Christopher Kelly, tr. Hanover and London: University Press of New England, 1995.

Rousseau, Jean-Jacques. *Emile, or On Education.* Allan Bloom, tr. New York: Basic Books, 1979.

Sonnet, Martine. *L'Education des filles au temps des Lumières.* Paris: Les Editions du Cerf, 1987.

Vanoflen, Laurence. "La conversation, une pédagogie pour les femmes?" In *Femmes éducatrices au siècle des Lumières,* edited by Isabelle Brouard-Arends, Marie-Emmanuelle Plagnol-Diéval, 183-195. Rennes: Presses Universitaires de Rennes, 2007.

Weltman-Aron, Brigitte. "Educating girls: Rousseau's Sophi(e)stry." *Studies on Voltaire and on the Eighteenth Century* 362 (1998): 41-53.

Chapter 6

Reforming Education in Eighteenth-Century Spain: Padre Sarmiento's Reflections on Teaching Young Children

Madeline Sutherland-Meier
The University of Texas at Austin

Abstract

The focus of this chapter is an essay on educational reform written by the Benedictine monk Martín Sarmiento (1695-1772). Written in 1768, the full title of the work is "Discurso sobre el método que debe guardarse en la primera educación de la juventud, para que sin tanto estudiar de memoria y a la letra tuviesen mayores adelantamientos."* Topics Sarmiento addresses include the role of parents in a child's education, class size, who should teach, what should be taught, how, in what order, and in what language. For Sarmiento, education takes place both in and outside of the classroom. One issue that is unclear in the *Discurso* is if the expression *la juventud,* which means youth and is used in the title, includes girls as well as boys. Finally, I discuss Sarmiento's concerns about the health of children and remedies he proposes for combatting the most common illnesses they suffer from.

*"Reflection on the method that should be used in the early education of young children, so that without so much rote memorization, they might make greater advancements"

Keywords: Sarmiento, Martín; Education and native language; Education – 18th century Spain; Children's health – 18th century Spain; Medicine – 18th century Spain

***

This chapter focuses on an essay about education written by an important Spanish Enlightenment figure, the Benedictine monk Martín Sarmiento (1695-1772). The full title of the work is "Discurso sobre el método que debe guardarse en la primera educación de la juventud, para que sin tanto estudiar de memoria y a la letra tuviesen mayores adelantamientos."[1] Written in 1768, the *Discurso* circulated in manuscript form for many years before it was published in 1789, 17 years after Sarmiento's death in 1772. The intrepid and tireless editor Antonio Valladares de Sotomayor included it in Volume 19 of his periodical the *Semanario Erudito*.[2]

In my discussion of the *Discurso*, I will concentrate primarily on the ideas Sarmiento sets forth regarding reforms in teaching, which should aid students in their learning. I will next look at what his *Discurso* reveals with regard to his ideas about education and gender. The health of children is also a topic of concern to Sarmiento and he brings it up at a couple of points in the *Discurso*. Since sickly children are not always up to learning, it is important to know how best to care for them when they are babies and later on when they are ill. To begin, I offer a brief discussion of his life and writings. Like many of his enlightened contemporaries, Sarmiento was a man of wide-ranging interests with firm opinions on many subjects.

The Life and Works of Martín Sarmiento

The figure we know as Martín Sarmiento was named neither Martín nor Sarmiento.[3] He was born Pedro Joseph García Balboa in Villafranca del Bierzo (León) in 1695. The following year, the family moved to Pontevedra (Galicia), where young Pedro attended a school run by the Jesuits. In 1711, when he professed in the Benedictine Convento de San Martín in Madrid, he took the name Martín García Sarmiento, choosing the new name Martín in honor of the patron saint of the convent. García was his father's first last name and Sarmiento was his mother's second last name.[4]

He left Madrid in 1711 to study Arts and Philosophy at the Benedictine monastery in Irache (Navarra). In 1714, he moved to a Benedictine monastery in Salamanca to study Theology. Around 1717, while still in Salamanca, he dropped the García and became, simply, Martín Sarmiento.

Once he had completed his studies, Sarmiento taught at various Benedictine monasteries in Spain. From 1717 until 1720 he was at the Monasterio de San Pedro in Eslonza (León). In 1720, he moved to Asturias, first to Llanes and then, in 1723, to the Monasterio de San Vicente in Oviedo. It was here that he met a fellow Galician intellectual and writer, Benito Jerónimo Feijóo, who was the abbot. This encounter proved to be decisive in Sarmiento's development as a thinker and scholar. He became part of an intellectual circle around Feijóo and remained in regular contact with him for the rest of his (Feijóo's) life.[5]

Sarmiento would later write two defenses of the *Theatro Crítico Universal*, his mentor's multi-volume collection of essays. In 1726, Sarmiento replied to criticisms of Feijóo's ideas about medicine that were made by a doctor named

Juan de Lesaca. Since Lesaca wrote under the pseudonym Martín Pascual de la Roca, Sarmiento entitled his piece *Martinus contra Martinum* and signed it Martín de la Peñabaylon. This document circulated in manuscripts. In 1732, Sarmiento published a much longer defense of Feijóo's work, which extended over two volumes, *Demonstración crítico-apologética del Theatro Crítico Universal que dió a luz el R. P. M. Fr. Benito Geronymo Feijoo.* This was the only work that Sarmiento published during his lifetime.[6]

In 1725, Sarmiento came back to Madrid and the Convento de San Martín, which was to be his home for the rest of his life. He left for a little over a year between February 1726 and May 1727 to help catalog books in the library of the Cathedral of Toledo. He also made two extended visits to Galicia. The first of these trips was from June of 1745 until January of 1746. The second, of longer duration, extended from May of 1754 until November of 1755. He recorded his observations on the botany, natural history, and archaeology of the region. He also documented how the Galician language was spoken, something that has been of great value to historians of the language.

Following his return to Madrid in 1755, he plunged back into writing.[7] In the years that followed, Sarmiento wrote on numerous subjects including science, natural history, botany, medicine, linguistics, and geography. In his letters, reflections and other writings, he expressed his concern over problems that vexed other enlightened Spaniards, such as the economic decline of Spain, the depopulation of the countryside, and the fact that Spain had fallen behind other European countries in areas such as science, medicine, and education. He encouraged the construction of libraries and botanical gardens in cities and in small towns. He was also tapped to create an iconographic plan for decorating the Royal Palace in Madrid. Some of his writings were in response to requests or queries. For example, he reflected on the construction of new roads and the advantages that would accrue from it following a request he received in the summer of 1757 from the Conde de Aranda.[8] In other writings, he focused on topics that interested him.

When reading Sarmiento's works, it is important to remember that he was not writing with an eye to being published. He only ever published one of his works, his 1732 defense of Feijóo, and it has been suggested that the harsh criticisms he received following its appearance put him off publishing permanently. Another theory is that he did not publish his works as a result of his excessive modesty. Whatever the reason, he explained his decision not to publish in a concise fashion in a 1758 piece entitled "El porque sí y el porque no," which Valladares published in the sixth volume of the *Semanario Erudito.* Explaining how he responds to the two questions he is most frequently asked, he writes, "To the first question: *Why do I live in such seclusion?* I reply: Because I do. And to the second: *Why don't I become a writer?* I reply: Because I don't." [9]

Sarmiento's style at times is meandering, mentioning one thing leads him to another and the discussion easily veers away from the original topic, so corralling his ideas can be a challenge. Addressing this issue, Santamarina Fernández writes, "His writings do not obey a strict plan; the main theme is often interrupted by digressions that can at times definitively break the chain of thought [literally, the thread of the discourse]."[10]

Let us now consider Sarmiento's ideas about education.

The Education of Young Children

In the eighteenth century, having an educated population was an essential part of the Enlightenment project. So the proper education and formation of young children was especially important. From the beginning, Sarmiento writes, their education should be based on science and truth, not on superstitions and falsehoods. "Childhood is the most propitious time to receive the most pure seeds of truth and science."[11] Unfortunately, nursemaids, parents, and even teachers fill the impressionable young children's heads with all kinds of superstitions and falsehoods, terrifying them with ghosts and boogeymen, and teaching them old-fashioned ideas, as well as histories and genealogies that simply are not true. They then take this false knowledge with them into adulthood. In addition to eradicating superstition, a cause he shared with his mentor Feijóo, Sarmiento sought to modernize the way students were taught by eliminating the traditional modes of education, which included rote memorization and instruction in Latin. Ángeles Galino writes, "Sarmiento wants to implant modern scientific and pedagogical methods conserving the sense and character of Spanish culture." [12]

Sarmiento covers a number of topics in his *Discurso*: who should teach, what should be taught, how it should be taught and in what order, and in what language instruction should take place. His goals are to make learning accessible and enjoyable for children rather than difficult and punitive, to stimulate children's curiosity and encourage them to take on new and more difficult subjects and to enable them to learn how to teach and to learn from themselves. In addition to explaining the method Sarmiento advocates, in the sections that follow, I will also consider what the essay reveals regarding Sarmiento's ideas about education and gender. Does the expression *la juventud* [youth], which is used in the title, include girls as well as boys? And what role do parents, that is mothers as well as fathers, play in the education of their children? Finally, I will look at what he says about the health of children, another topic he devotes time to discussing and expresses strong opinions on.

Before explaining his educational method, Sarmiento writes about who should teach young children and, perhaps more importantly, who should not. So we will begin there.

Who Should Teach and Who Should Not

For Sarmiento, parents should be their children's first teachers, and the first lesson they must teach their offspring is the fear of God. Sarmiento writes, "There is not a father or a mother who does not understand this divine maxim, which in the common tongue means *the fear of God is the beginning of all wisdom*: the fear of God means the Catechism and its practice, good manners and the veneration of fathers, mothers, and older people."[13] Basic religious instruction should be in the hands of parents, who will teach their children the Catechism and, through their example, will teach them morality, respect, and good manners far more effectively than anyone else could. "What children learn from their father is almost indelible and what they hear from tutors and pedagogues is all useless."[14]

In Sarmiento's view, it would be ideal if parents also took charge of their children's early academic instruction as well. He is strongly opposed to hiring tutors and bringing them into the home to instruct young children, as he regards most of these individuals as totally unfit for the job. And the fashion of employing foreigners, whom he calls swindlers and idiots, is an even worse idea. Sarmiento is opposed to foreign teachers on various grounds: first, they are incapable of teaching a Spanish child his/her native language because even those who have lived in Spain for many years do not know it. The other problems with foreign teachers are that they are incapable of teaching children anything of value and they set bad examples: "No foreign adventurer is capable of teaching children the Castilian language since they never know it, even those who have lived in Spain for many years. . . . [T]hey cannot teach anything good and with their example can lead then into much that is bad."[15]

Sarmiento also expresses doubts about taking young children to school where, in a typical class, the student-teacher ratio is far too high for any meaningful learning to take place. "Let's be clear, what can a teacher who has to teach 500 boys at once teach about grammar?"[16] Later in the essay, he explains that the ideal student-teacher ratio is one to one, but he is willing to consider three to one, when the children are from the same household, and at most, nine to one.[17]

The fashion of sending students abroad to study is also undesirable, although for religious rather than strictly academic reasons. "The Catholic faith is so pure in Spain that it would be an intolerable abuse to send students to study in foreign countries where Catholicism is drowned by so many impious libels by libertines. The same can be said of moral customs, which are entirely relaxed."[18] And so, it is far preferable to have the youngest children begin their studies at home, where their father or a member of the extended family, such as an uncle who is a cleric, will teach them their earliest lessons. If the family has books, then it is all the better that the youngsters learn at home.

Having ruled out a number of possible instructors, who would Sarmiento have teach young children? He believes the established practice of entrusting the instruction of older students to the most educated, most experienced teachers, the *doctores*, is completely wrong as it inevitably means leaving the instruction of the youngest students to the least experienced, least qualified teachers. Sarmiento uses a number of unflattering expressions to refer to these individuals. The youngest children should be put in the hands of the most experienced and the most learned. He expresses this idea through a botanical metaphor: "Doctors in Agriculture, Doctors in Botany should be the ones who begin a new planting of trees; it matters little whether it is Doctors or those who know nothing who care for them after they are established."[19]

The ideal teacher is "a wise, erudite, learned, calm, prudent man who knows how to adapt himself to the tender age of the children not with punishments and severity . . . but rather with flattery, love, prizes, and emulation . . . ."[20] There is also an age requirement; they should be at least 50 years old.[21]

Now that we know who should teach children, how should those children be taught?

Sarmiento's Method

Sarmiento's method consists, first, of educating children in their native language rather than in Latin or, in the case of Galician children, Spanish. In Galicia, instruction should be in *Gallego*: "I have not read about a similar cruelty, making children study one dead language, which is Latin, in another, which for them is even more dead, which is Castilian, and forget the language they learned with their mother's milk, which is native to them, which is the Galician language."[22]

Mastering one's native language is the key to learning, to thinking, and to expressing oneself. If a student has a language in which to learn, to understand, to explain things, and to communicate their knowledge to others, then memorization is unnecessary. The importance of a thorough knowledge of one's language is also at the root of Sarmiento's objections to foreigners teaching Spanish (or Galician) children and his insistence that regardless of how well they may speak the language, it is not native to them.[23]

The first step in Sarmiento's educational method is the acquisition and development of vocabulary beginning with nouns. It should begin early on, with the wet nurse telling the child the names of the objects around them. This process should continue once a teacher takes over.

The teaching of vocabulary should follow a plan. Children should first be taught "the names of the visible things that God has created" followed by "the names of the visible things that men have made."[24]

The vocabulary to name the visible world God created is the vocabulary of natural history. While teaching this subject matter, the instructor should employ only words the students already know, steering clear of the invisible, the spiritual, and the metaphysical as these are topics for later. At this early point in their formal education, Sarmiento would have children learn about all of the natural kingdoms; he mentions land animals, birds, fish, insects, plants, fruit trees, vegetables, herbs, grasses, rocks, minerals, planets, and stars. He goes on to say that the microscope and the telescope have vastly augmented the number of natural things we know about and so the vocabulary necessary to talk about them has grown as well.

The second group of visible objects the child should learn to name are artificial objects made by humans. Here Sarmiento gives quite deliberate instructions as to how this vocabulary, as well as the vocabulary relative to the natural world, is to be taught: "Briefly, the way the child learns these things is that the teacher . . . points to each thing with his finger, be it natural or artificial, and says the name loudly and clearly three times."[25] Farther on in the essay, he suggests that children should learn five or six new words each day.

Once the child has learned about the visible world, the teacher should begin to teach about things that are invisible and spiritual. In this discussion, Sarmiento presents another argument in favor of older teachers, which is that they are more capable of explaining the spiritual and incorporeal to young students. Sarmiento also advises teaching this material through visual representations: "At this tender age, instruction should be through paintings of the spiritual and the mysteries of the Catholic faith; in this way, the child will become accustomed to it without confusion . . . and will become familiarized with the names and spiritual things and with the sacred sciences."[26]

Not all instruction needs to take place in the classroom. Sarmiento advocates taking children on walks to different places—among the places he suggests are a garden, a field, a riverbank, a factory—in order to learn different classes of words. It is also of note that he finds great value in the games children play and the songs they sing. The teacher should allow for playtime as it is another opportunity to learn. "It is up to the well trained teacher . . . from time to time to allow the child to go out into the street to play, tangle, and romp with other children, and there, without memorizing anything, they learn the games, and their names, and even old verses; everything can be of benefit and of use to them."[27] In this same discussion, we see Sarmiento the historical linguist, evince a great appreciation for popular culture or folklore. "The oldest spoken language [language that is not Latin] that we have is that in which the old sayings and the verses that go with children's games are preserved."[28]

Sarmiento next outlines his method for teaching spelling and reading. To learn these skills the child needs a *cartilla de leer,* or primer, which has the letters of the alphabet printed on one side and a syllabary on the other. The *cartilla* should follow the established custom of placing a simple cross at the beginning. "The children's primer begins + A B C D E F G H &c. and should be read *Christus* A B C D &c. This primer should be printed and affixed to a clipboard . . . ."[29] The teacher should teach the letters the same way he taught his students the names of objects, by pointing at them and saying their names clearly. The children will then repeat what they have heard. The *cartilla* should show three alphabets: capital letters, printed letters, and letters in cursive. The syllabary on the back should be simple in the beginning, showing the consonants with each of the five vowels.

In this section of the *Discurso,* Sarmiento digresses into a consideration of alphabets, first bemoaning their arbitrary nature, which makes it difficult for children to learn them, as well as discussing the many different alphabets that exist and have existed to represent the world's many languages. Teachers should know at least a major portion of these alphabets and be able to show children the similarities and the differences between them. The kind of knowledge the teacher must have in order to do this means that he cannot be "a snot-nosed idiot," by which Sarmiento means young and inexperienced, but, rather, mature and seasoned, "an erudite teacher of 50."[30]

Once children have a certain grasp of their native language, Sarmiento proposes using his method to teach them Latin. He labels as completely backwards the practice of making students memorize rules about the language in Latin rather than by teaching them vocabulary. They should master vocabulary first with the teacher pointing to a word in Latin and then to its meaning in the children's native language. There will be plenty of time later to introduce the rules of Latin syntax.[31]

Sarmiento's opposition to rote learning and memorization is a thread that runs throughout the *Discurso.* So it is notable that he carves out one space in which memorization should take place and that is in religious instruction. "So as not to delay the learning of Christian doctrine, I am of the feeling and of the opinion that at the corresponding age, a child should be made to study and memorize Astete's *Catechism* and the prayers of the Church."[32] The text Sarmiento specifies here, the *Catecismo de la Doctrina Cristiana*, was written by the Spanish Jesuit Gaspar Astete in 1576, and is still in use today.

Education and Gender

Who were the youngsters whose education Sarmiento was striving to reform? Or, to pose the question another way, is Sarmiento writing about the education of girls as well as boys? It is difficult to be certain about the gender of the students that he is referring to in the *Discurso* because he uses terms such as *la juventud*, which means youth, and so would include girls as well as boys, and *los niños*, which translates either as boys or as boys and girls. In their article on Sarmiento and scientific education, Uxío Pérez Rodríguez, María Álvarez Lires, y José Lillo Beviá, make the same observation: "An explicit approach to the education of women is not found in his writings. In his texts about the education of youth he almost always uses the masculine form of nouns and it is not clear that he includes girls in education in the sciences and the technical arts."[33] Antón Costa Rico takes a different point of view and states unequivocally that in the *Discurso*, Sarmiento is "attending to the education of boys – never girls – from birth to approximately twelve years of age . . . ."[34]

Parents, as we know, play a special role in the formation and education of children as they too are teachers. It is notable that near the beginning of the text, when explaining that the fear of God is the beginning of all wisdom, Sarmiento mentions both parents twice: "There will not be a father or a mother," and "the veneration of fathers and mothers and older people." [35] Later on the same page, he casts the father as the teacher of lessons the children will not forget, writing, "What children learn from their father is almost indelible."[36] A few pages farther along, he divides the roles of the two parents clearly along gender lines, the father is once again given the role of educator while the mother is the nurturer: "The natural balance requires that since the mother is the appropriate one to nurse the child, the father should be the one to educate him."[37] So, while Sarmiento makes both parents responsible for a child's religious and moral education, instruction in the more academic subjects falls to a father, an uncle who is a member of the clergy, or a teacher who is also male.

There are other important areas of knowledge, however, that are particular to women, especially traditional medicine. As we will see in the next section, Sarmiento has great respect for the home remedies women in the villages have used over the years to cure their children.

The Health of Children

As I noted earlier in this chapter, Sarmiento believes that great care must be taken with the health of children since some illnesses can leave them weak, sickly and not up to going to school. And whether or not they receive an education, their health will affect the profession they eventually pursue.

His concern with how children are raised and cared for begins at their birth. He is strenuously opposed to the use of *amas de leche* or wet nurses. He begins his attack on this custom, which he says originated with wealthy women, early in the *Discurso* suggesting that his readers reflect upon the words of the Roman author Aulus Gellius (125 AD – 180 AD), who not only called mothers who had others nurse their children "half mothers," but also pronounced the practice to be against nature.[38] Sarmiento argues that not only is it the normal course of nature for mothers to nurse their infants – "This is the general rule in all viviparous females"– it is also what God intended: "It isn't believable that God would have deposited an abundance of milk in the breasts of a woman who has recently given birth were it not to nourish her baby outside her body, just as before she fed the fetus with her blood in her body or womb."[39]

In support of his belief that it is beneficial for both parties if mothers nurse their own babies, Sarmiento develops what we would today call a theory of attachment. He begins by explaining that a much more loving relationship develops between mother and child if a wet nurse does not come in between them and thus become the first object of the child's attention and affection: "The poor village women who have nursed their children love them much more and the children reciprocate this love; it is not this way when wet nurses come in between them, because the children love them and hardly know their mothers."[40] With this established, he then describes the mutual recognition of mother and child. Remembering Adam's description of Eve in *Genesis* 2:23 as "bone of my bones and flesh of my flesh," Sarmiento continues, "When a mother sees her child, the one she has nursed, she will be able to say something similar, but not the mother who because it is fashionable abandoned her child to an unknown wet nurse. . . . When the child placed in the arms and between the breasts of his legitimate mother, looks at her with attention or instinct, and laughs for the first time, Virgil says that then he begins to know her as the mother who gave birth to him."[41]

In addition to explaining the benefits of nursing to the emotional well-being of mother and child, Sarmiento raises important questions about the health of the wet nurse as the quality of her milk will affect the health, intelligence, and development of the child. If she is ill or sickly, her milk will not be good. What is more, such women generally come from the lower classes, and thus, he suggests, may be infected physically or morally.

Sarmiento also discusses childhood diseases, which, he says, are up to a child's mother and God (rather than a physician) to cure. He singles out the three most well-known, and deadly: *viruelas, lombrices*, and *alferecía* [smallpox, roundworms, and epilepsy]. Young children must be treated with great care as these illnesses can have a detrimental effect on their health going forward.

The cures Sarmiento recommends are all traditional cures, which would have been passed down from one generation to another. He believes that both roundworms and epilepsy have their origins in breast milk. It may have been different in Sarmiento's time, but today, only in rare cases are roundworms passed on through breast milk. The primary way people become infected is by walking barefoot on soil contaminated with feces. Hookworms, a particular kind of roundworm, can cause anemia and weakness and can negatively affect a child's physical and cognitive development, so eliminating them is important. There does not seem to be any evidence that children contract epilepsy through breast milk, in fact, to the contrary, nursing seems to protect children against seizures.

To cure roundworms, Sarmiento prescribes feeding the child purslane during the waning moon and for the duration of the infection. Epilepsy should be treated by giving the child half a spoonful of powdered valerian root mixed with milk. He also states that parents of children with epilepsy should not bother with amulets as they are nothing but fakery and offer no protection against the disorder.

Sarmiento had a wealth of botanical knowledge, so it is not surprising that the curative properties of both purslane and valerian are well-attested historically. Purslane has long been used in traditional Indian and Chinese medicine as a remedy for hookworms. "Human clinical trials have shown both purslane juice and tablets to be effective against intestinal parasites such as hookworms."[42] In a review of available literature on the use of valerian to treat epilepsy, the neurologist Mervyn J. Eadie writes, "By the late eighteenth and early nineteenth centuries, it was often regarded as the best available treatment for the disorder. . . . In favorable circumstances, high valerian doses can be calculated to have sometimes provided potentially effective amounts of anticonvulsant substance for epilepsy patients."[43]

Sarmiento has considerably more to say about the origins of smallpox and measures to prevent it than he does about either roundworms or epilepsy. He believes that children who were nursed by their mothers are less susceptible to the illness as are children born to mothers in their fifties. Once again, his understanding of the origins of the ailment is not correct, but the way he suggests to prevent it was the best practice medicine at the time had to offer. It is common knowledge, he writes, that smallpox originates in the mother's menstrual blood, by which he means the lining of the uterus that is shed monthly except in the case of pregnancy. How serious a case of smallpox will be depends upon the state of the mother's blood at the time she has intercourse. Related to this idea is the Chinese belief, which he also discusses, that smallpox is caused by the fermentation of the mother's blood that is left in a child's umbilical cord. For this reason, before the midwife ties the cord, she should clean out whatever blood is left so none enters the child's body.

When Sarmiento explains the best way to guard against smallpox, he uses the term *inoculación*. What he is talking about is variolation. In variolation, an uninfected person comes into contact with pustular matter from another who has the disease, contracts a mild form of it, and in this way, achieves immunity. In Asia, dried scabs were blown into the nose of the uninfected person. Sarmiento suggests something similar, dipping tufts of cotton into the pustules and then placing the wet tufts under the nose of the child so that he will breathe in the virus as he sleeps. Nothing more will be necessary.[44] The National Library of Medicine estimates that 1% to 2% of patients who were variolated died, while 30% who contracted smallpox naturally succumbed to it.[45]

Conclusion

Although the focus of his *Discurso* is the education of young children, Sarmiento reflects on far more than what happens in a classroom. While he has very definite ideas about who should teach and how, about class size and language of instruction, he is also concerned with what happens outside of the classroom. Educating young children is the duty of other individuals in addition to the teacher. Parents must instruct their children also, provide them with a proper religious and moral formation, and safeguard their health.

What is most important to Sarmiento is that the process of education create individuals who can continue to educate themselves, to learn outside of the classroom. The phrase he uses is "hacerse *Autodidactus*," to become self-taught. The ultimate goal of all who teach young children should be to set them on this path.[46] As he closes his essay, a suddenly melancholy Sarmiento reflects on the time and effort he wasted as a result of the pedagogical methods used when he was young and expresses the wish that he had been educated in the way he proposes in his *Discurso*, "So I wish I had been taught . . . ."[47]

Notes

[1] The term *discurso* has various meanings. In the context of Sarmiento's writing, a *discurso* contains thoughts and reflections on a certain subject and is written to consider or persuade. Sarmiento's title, roughly translated, is "Reflection on the method that should be used in the early education of young children, so that without so much rote memorization, they might make greater advancements." From this point forward, my translations of Sarmiento's text will appear in the body of the chapter and the original Spanish quotations will

appear in endnotes. My translations of comments by historians and literary critics will also appear in the body of the text with the Spanish originals placed in endnotes. Quotations from Spanish sources appearing only in endnotes will show the English translation followed by the Spanish original in brackets.

2 Valladares (1737-1820) was a prolific and popular playwright who also wrote a nine-part novel and was engaged in a number of editorial ventures. The *Semanario Erudito*, his most successful periodical, was published in Madrid between April of 1787 and February of 1791. All quotations from Sarmiento's *Discurso* are taken from the text that appears in the *Semanario Erudito* 19: 167-256. Since all quotations are from the same volume, the Spanish originals will be followed by page numbers.

3 I borrow this formulation from José Santos Puerto, "Una Bio-Bibliografía actualizada de Martín Sarmiento," 72. Santos Puerto describes our author as, "the monk who signed his name Martín Sarmiento but who was neither named Martín nor was his last name Sarmiento" [el monje que firmaba Martín Sarmiento pero que ni se llamaba Martín ni se apellidaba Sarmiento].

4 Sarmiento's parents were Alonso García Cerage and Clara Balboa Sarmiento de Quiroga. His father was an architect who was involved in the restoration of churches. For more information on the family, see the Proxecto Sarmiento website: http://www.consellodacultura.gal/sarmiento/

See also the study by Antón Santamarina Fernández that appears on the website of the Real Academia de la Historia: http://dbe.rah.es/biografias/7699/pedro-joseph-garcia-balboa and the biography by Antolín López Peláez., *El gran gallego (Fr. Martín Sarmiento).*

5 "In this relationship, first as a disciple and later as correspondent and collaborator, we find the key to understanding Sarmiento's intellectual trajectory." [Nesa relación, primeiro de discípulo e posteriormente de corresponsal e colaborador, áchase a clave principal para entender a traxectoria intelectual de Sarmiento.] Henrique Monteagudo, "Biografía de Martín Sarmiento," accessed June 22, 2021, http://www.consellodacultura.gal/sarmiento/biografia-de-fray-martin-sarmiento/ .

6 The two-volume *Demonstración* was first published in Madrid by the Viuda de Francisco del Hierro. According to Santos Puerto, "Una Bio-Bibliografía actualizada de Martín Sarmiento," 86, no. 24, six editions were published in the eighteenth century but none in the centuries that followed.

7 Santamarina Fernández, "Pedro Joseph García Balboa," writes that at this point, "He secluded himself once again in his cell, which he left no more than three times a year . . . and entered the most productive period of his life . . . ." [se recluyó de nuevo en su celda de la que no salió más que tres veces al año . . . y comenzaba la época de mayor fecundidad de su vida . . ..]

8 Valladares was also the first to publish Sarmiento's reflections on the necessity of good roads, "Apuntamientos para un discurso sobre la necesidad que hay en España de unos buenos Caminos Reales. . . ." It appeared in 1789 in the *Semanario Erudito* 20: 11-225.

9 "Al primero: ¿Por qué vivo tan retirado? Respondo: Porque sí. Y a él segundo: ¿Por qué no me meto a escritor? Respondo: Porque no." *Semanario Erudito* 6: 122.

10 "[S]us escritos no obedecen a un plan estricto; el tema principal es frecuentemente interrumpido por digresiones que pueden a veces romper definitivamente el hilo del discurso."

11 "[L]a edad de la niñez es la mas propia para recibir las mas puras semillas de la verdad y de las ciencias." 169.

12 Ángeles Galino."El espacio del Padre Sarmiento en la historia de la educación," 223. "Sarmiento quiere implantar los métodos científicos y pedagógicos modernos conservando el sentido y carácter de la cultura española."

13 "No habrá padre ni madre que no entienda esta divina máxima, reducida al vulgar el temor de Dios es el principio de toda sabiduría: al temor de Dios se reduce al Catecismo y su práctica, las buenas costumbres, y la veneración a los padres y madres y mayores . . . ." 171.

14 "Es casi indeleble lo que los niños aprenden de su padre, y toda hojarasca lo que oyen á ayos y pedagogos." 171.

15 "Ningun extraño aventurero es capaz de enseñar a los niños la lengua Castellana, pues jamas la saben, aún los que en España han vivido muchos años . . . . [N]o los podrán enseñar nada bueno, y con el exemplo los podrán inducir á mucho de malo." 170.

16 "[H]ablemos claros, ¿qué podrá enseñar de Gramatica el maestro que ha de enseñar de un golpe a quinientos muchachos?" 175.

17 "El verdadero modo de enseñar ha de ser un maestro solo para un solo discipulo, y quando mas á tres niños solos de parentela, y a todo tirar no han de pasar de nueve." 239.

18 "[E]stando tan pura en España la fé Católica, seria intolerable abuso, que los niños Españoles pasasen á estudiar á países estrangeros, en donde el catolicismo está ahogado con tantos libelos impios de libertinos. Lo mismo digo de las costumbres morales, que están relajadas enteramente." 178.

19 "Doctores en Agricultura, Doctores en Botánica deben ser ya los que forman un nuevo plantío de árboles; poco importa que sean Doctores o ignorantes los que cuidan de estos árboles después que ya llegaron a su consistencia." 167-168.

20 "[U]n hombre sabio, erudito, docto, pacífico, prudente, y que sepa acomodarse a la tierna edad de los niños; no con castigos y rigores . . . sino con halagos, cariños, premios, y emulación . . ." 179.

21 "[L]os Maestros no han de baxar de cinqüenta años de edad" 193.

22 "No he leído semejante barbaridad, obligar a los niños a que estudien una lengua muerta, qual es la lengua latina, por otra que para ellos es más muerta, qual es la lengua castellana, y que olviden la lengua que han mamado, que les es nativa, cual es la gallega." 187.

23 For a more detailed discussion of Sarmiento's support of the use of native languages, see María Ángeles Figueira Iglesias, "El gallego en la enseñanza."

24 "los nombres de las cosas visibles que Dios ha creado . . . los nombres de las cosas visibles que han fabricado los hombres." 188.

25 "El modo de saberlas en breve se reduce á que el maestro . . . vaya señalando cada cosa de por si con él dedo, ya natural ya artificial, y pronunciando tres veces en voz alta y clara el nombre." 193.

26 "[S]e le debe instruir en su tierna edad por medio de la pintura de las cosas espirituales, y de los misterios de la fé Católica; de este modo se irá habituando el niño sin confusion . . .

y se ira familiarizando con las voces y nombres, y cosas espirituales, y con las ciencias sagradas." 196.

27 "Tocará al maestro bien instruido . . . permitir de quando en quando salga [el niño] á la calle á jugar, enredar, y retozar con los demás niños, y que alli sin estudiar nada de memoria aprendan los juegos, y sus nombres, y aún las coplillas antiguas; de todo se sacará provecho y utilidad." 209-210.

28 "El lenguaje vulgar mas antiguo que tenemos, es el que se conserva en los refranes viejos, y en las coplitas de los niños para sus juegos . . . ." 210.

29 "La cartilla de los niños comienza así: + A B C D E F G H &c., y se debe leer *Christus* A Be Ce De &c. Esta cartilla suele andar impresa y se pega en una tablita . . . ." 201.

30 The terms used in the Spanish original are "un mocoso idiota" and "un maestro erudito quinquagenario" 204.

31 "[En España] enseñan el latin al revés á los niños; cargándoles de reglas para que las estudien de memoria y á la letra . . . pero jamás se les muestran con el dedo los significados de las cosas y voces que juegan con el texto. Al contrario, yo quiero que primero se les muestren con el dedo esos y otros significados, y que despues ligeramente se les propongan de sentado las reglas de la Sintaxis" 208.

32 "Por no retardar que el niño sepa la doctrina Christiana, soy de sentir y de dictamen, que en la edad correspondiente se le haga estudiar de memoria y á la letra el Catecismo de Astete y las oraciones de la Iglesia." 193.

33 Uxío Pérez Rodríguez, María Álvarez Lires, José Lillo Bevía, "Fray Martín Sarmiento y la educación científica," 88. "[N]o se encuentra en sus escritos un planteamiento explícito sobre la educación de las mujeres. En sus textos sobre la educación de la juventud habla casi siempre en masculino y no está claro que incluya a las chicas en la educación de las ciencias y de las artes-técnicas."

34 Costa Rico, Antón. "A dimensión pedagóxica do Padre Sarmiento," 247. "[Sarmiento está] atendendo á educación dos nenos—nunca nenas—desde o seu nacemento ata a idade aproximada dos 12 anos . . . "

35 "No habrá padre ni madre" and "la veneracion á los padres y madres y mayores . . ." 171.

36 "Es casi indeleble lo que los niños aprenden de su padre . . . ." 171.

37 "Pide la natural equidad, que como la madre es la mas propia para dar leche al hijo, deba darle el padre la enseñanza." 173.

38 "Gelio llama media madre á la que pare el hijo, y despues busca aya ó nutriz para que le dé la leche, *quod est contra naturam* . . ." 171.

39 "Esta es regla general y constante en todas las hembras de los animales viviparous . . . . no es creíble que Dios haya depositado con abundancia en los pechos de una recien parida la leche sino con el fin de que alimente con ella su criatura fuera del cuerpo, como poco antes le alimentaba el feto con su sangre en el cuerpo ó vientre." 172.

40 "Las madres aldeanas y pobres que han dado el pecho á sus hijos, les tienen un cariño muy superior y material, y el amor de los hijos para con sus madres es muy correspondiente: no asi cuando median amas de leche, pues éstas cargan con el amor de los niños, y éstos apenas conocen á sus madres." 172.

41 "Cosa semejante podrá decir la madre cuando ve á su hijo, á quien ha dado leche: no así la madre que por moda abandonó á su hijo á una ama de leche desconocida. . . .

Quando el infante puesto en brazos y entre los pechos de su legítima madre, la mira con alguna atencion ó instinto, y suelta la primera risa donosa: dice Virgilio, que entonces empieza á conocerla por madre que le parió." 172-173.

42 Michael J. Balick, *Rodale's 21st Century Herbal*, 240.

43 Mervyn J. Eadie, "Could Valerian Have Been the First Anticonvulsant?"

44 "[T]omese dos guedeguitas de algodon, mogense en el licor, ó materia de las postillas de las viruelas, y quando el niño esté durmiendo, apliquense a las ventanas de las narices dichas guedeguitas, y no se necesita mas para que se excite el fermento de las viruelas" (182).

45 For more information on smallpox, variolation, vaccination, etc. see "Smallpox. A Great and Terrible Scourge."

46 "[Y] este es el fin que el maestro se ha de proponer para la enseñanza de la juventud." 256.

47 "Asi quisiera yo que me hubiera enseñado a mi . . ." 256.

Bibliography

Primary Sources

Sarmiento, Martín. "Discurso sobre el método que debe guardarse en la primera educación de la juventud, para que sin tanto estudiar de memoria y a la letra tuviesen mayores adelantamientos." *Semanario Erudito* 19: 167-256.

Secondary Sources

Balick, Michael J. *Rodale's 21st Century Herbal. A Practical Guide for Healthy Living Using Nature's Most Powerful Plants.* Rodale, 2014.

Costa Rico, Antón. "A dimensión pedagóxica do Padre Sarmiento," in *O Padre Sarmiento e o seu tempo. Actas do Congreso Internacional do Tricentenario do Fr. Martín Sarmiento (1695-1995), Santiago de Compostela, 19 maio – 3 xuño de 1995. Tomo II. Lingua, Folklore e Educación, Ciencias Naturais e Medicina*, 245-302. Santiago de Compostela: Consello da Cultura Galega, Universidade de Santiago de Compostela, 1997.

Eadie, Mervyn J. "Could Valerian Have Been the First Anticonvulsant?" *Epilepsia* 45, no. 11 (2004): 1338-1343. https://doi.org/10.1111/j.0013-9580.2004.27904.x.

Figueira Iglesias, María Ángeles. "El gallego en la enseñanza." In *O Padre Sarmiento e o seu tempo. Actas do Congreso Internacional do Tricentenario do Fr. Martín Sarmiento (1695-1995), Santiago de Compostela, 19 maio – 3 xuño de 1995. Tomo II. Lingua, Folklore e Educación, Ciencias Naturais e Medicina*, 237-244. Santiago de Compostela: Consello da Cultura Galega, Universidade de Santiago de Compostela, 1997.

Galino, Angeles. "El espacio del Padre Sarmiento en la historia de la educación." In *O Padre Sarmiento e o seu tempo. Actas do Congreso Internacional do Tricentenario do Fr. Martín Sarmiento (1695-1995), Santiago de Compostela, 19 maio – 3 xuño de 1995. Tomo II. Lingua, Folklore e Educación, Ciencias Naturais e Medicina*, 221-236. Santiago de Compostela: Consello da Cultura Galega, Universidade de Santiago de Compostela, 1997.

López Peláez, Antolín. *El gran gallego (Fr. Martín Sarmiento).* La Coruña: Andrés Martínez, 1895.

Monteagudo, Henrique. "Biografía de Martín Sarmiento," Proxecto Sarmiento, accessed June 22, 2021, http://www.consellodacultura.gal/sarmiento/biografia-de-fray-martin-sarmiento/.

Pérez Rodríguez, Uxío, María Álvarez Linares, José Lillo Beviá. "Fray Martín Sarmiento y la educación científica. I. contexto histórico y posiciones pedagógicas sarmentianas," *Revista de Investigación en Educación,* 6 (2009): 79-91.

Proxecto Sarmiento, accessed June 22, 2021, http://www.consellodacultura.gal/sarmiento/.

Santamarina Fernández, Antón. "Pedro Joseph Garcia Balboa," Real Academia de la Historia, accessed June 30, 2021, http://dbe.rah.es/biografias/7699/pedro-joseph-garcia-balboa.

Santos Puerto, José. "Una Bio-Bibliografía actualizada de Martín Sarmiento: Catálogo de los pliegos (. . .) sobre diferentes asuntos," *Sarmiento* 6 (2002): 69-95.

"Smallpox. A Great and Terrible Scourge," National Library of Medicine, National Institutes of Health, accessed July 1, 2021, https://www.nlm.nih.gov/exhibition/smallpox/index.html.

Chapter 7
Religious Education and the Lasting Effect on Goya's Depictions of Saints

Karissa E. Bushman

Quinnipiac University

Abstract

Throughout his career, Francisco de Goya had a complex relationship with the Catholic Church. Some of his images depict anticlerical themes that criticized the corruption within the clergy while his paintings of the saints were faithful to the texts of their lives. One aspect of his religious painting that has been thus far not studied is how his early religious education in childhood may have influenced his paintings of the saints. While Goya was an Enlightenment thinker, he was a devout Catholic and found a way to use his religious education to inform his paintings of the saints by closely examining the history of their lives. This chapter examines the religious education that Goya would have had as a child and its impact on his paintings of the saints.

Keywords: Goya, Painting, Enlightenment, Education, Religion

***

Francisco de Goya once stated that his three inspirations were Rembrandt, Velázquez, and Nature. Velázquez was considered to be one of the greatest painters Spain had produced and Goya idolized him. In his early career, he copied Velázquez's works and Goya's first series of prints were after Velázquez's paintings in the Royal collection. Goya and Velázquez had several similarities in their careers as painters. They both were born outside of Madrid in regions that were not typically known for their artistic achievements; Velázquez was from Andalucía and specifically Sevilla, while Goya was from the kingdom of Aragón. They both trained with artists who were known for their talents as teachers, and both eventually rose to the highest artistic position available in Spain, first court painter. While Goya looked to Velázquez throughout his career as is evinced in his writings and many of his paintings and aspired to become first court painter as the Spanish Baroque master was to Philip IV, one aspect that differed greatly in Goya's career path was his fondness for religious painting. Velázquez, like many other painters who achieved high status, did not focus on religious painting once he was established within the royal court. History painting and portraiture were much more lucrative and prestigious. Goya, however, who had trained as a religious painter, continued to paint religious scenes throughout his entire career.

As Goya achieved the same status of Velázquez, he could have easily stopped accepting religious commissions; however, he consistently chose to accept religious commissions as well as used religious themes in many of his works of art that were not specifically religious scenes. Goya's relationship with religion, as presented in his works, is extremely complicated. Throughout his life, he completed many drawings, prints and paintings with anticlerical themes as I have discussed in my doctoral dissertation. Goya's depictions of anticlericalism were satirical and many times contained harsh and biting criticisms of the corruption and abuse of power of the Catholic clergy in Spain.[1] In contrast, as Goya was a devout Catholic, his depictions of the saints were in line with Catholic doctrine, faithful to the stories of their lives, and reflect the religious education he received from childhood through adolescence.

In examining the religious education and training Goya received as a child in Catholic schools and during his first artistic apprenticeship, it is evident that religion played a crucial role in his development as an artist and a human being. At the same time, Goya lived during the Spanish Enlightenment and fully embraced many of the newer philosophies and ideas. The emphasis on examining things for a deeper understanding of them that Enlightenment figures advocated for dovetails perfectly with Goya's religious education that taught him to pay closer attention to religious doctrine and texts such as the Bible and the lives of the Saints. In this chapter, I explore Goya's religious education, especially the focus on the lives of the saints that shaped his artistic career. This is an aspect that has not yet been given its due in academic scholarship on Goya. I will examine a few select examples of artwork from various stages of his life to explore how Goya paid more attention to the stories of the saints' lives and to Catholic doctrine than his contemporaries and predecessors did which reveals the lasting impact that his religious education had on his art.

Goya was born to a commoner father of Basque ancestry and a mother from a family of petty aristocracy from the kingdom of Aragón. While he was born in the small village of Fuendetodos, he grew up and trained in the capital of Aragón, Zaragoza.[2] In the eighteenth century in Spain, religion played a crucial role in the lives of all citizens. While it is true that the Catholic Church had lost a lot of the power and influence it once had on society and the government of the preceding centuries,[3] Spain was still a country where the Catholic Church had an impact on almost every aspect of life, from government to education. Francisco de Goya attended a Catholic school which was typical of children who received education at this time period, and most of the documents we have concerning his early childhood come from church records.[4] Religion was important to the Goya family as witnessed not only through the many family documents addressing the different sacraments they all received in different churches as well as their enrollments, but also through Goya's letters in which he refers to God and religious subjects many times. The Catholic faith was so important to Goya's family that Francisco's youngest brother became a priest and served as the vicar in a church in the small village of Chinchón.[5]

Growing up, Goya would have been exposed early to religious art as his father was a master gilder and many of his commissions came from churches. It has, in fact, been suggested that the reason why Goya's birth took place in Fuendetodos rather than Zaragoza was due to the possibility that his father was working on the main retable for the parochial church in the small village.[6] We also know that Goya was exposed to his father's work on religious art at an early age due to the mention of his presence in the Calahorra Cathedral, where his father José and the brother of Goya's first painting instructor, Juan Luzán Martinez, worked together on gilding the organ for the cathedral. Goya was ten years old while he was with his father as he worked on this project.[7]

At age fourteen, Goya entered the studio of Luzán, and we know through documentation, including mentions in Goya's letters to his friend Zapater, that he was also attending a religious school in Zaragoza. In his book *Goya Y Aragón,* Arturo Ansón Navarro does an excellent job of examining the letters in which Goya mentions his education as well as investigating the different religious schools in Zaragoza, explaining which were the most likely for him to have attended.[8] While it is not known exactly which school he attended, it is likely that he was enrolled in either one run by the Jesuits or one of the Escuelas Pias.[9] In either of the schools Goya would have received a basic education in which he would have been taught how to read and write, as had been the case with the male members of his family for at least the past three generations. While the curriculum at each of the schools would have had minor variations, both of them would have focused much of their education on religion. At the school, the priest who instructed him "drummed the elementary dogmas of life into him with a cudgel amid invocations of the saints."[10] In further examining the curriculum of the Escuelas Pias in Zaragoza, it becomes evident that religion played a key role in the pedagogy and lessons of clergy who were teaching the children. Joaquín Lecea's book, *Escuelas Pias en Aragón en el siglo XVII,* specifically discusses the curricula of the schools within the region and when focusing on the ones in the city of Zaragoza that Goya would have attended, expressed multiple ways in which religion was key to the education of the students. One of the main examples of this is how it specifically discusses that the last quarter hour of the morning lessons and afternoon lessons were specifically reserved for religious teachings so that both of the major sessions of the day, which had other religious lessons throughout them, would end by emphasizing the importance of the teachings of the Catholic Church.[11]

Goya's religious education left a lasting impression on him throughout his training and career as an artist. Goya's training in Luzán's studio consisted mostly of copying from prints, many of which had religious subject matter. Luzán had spent years in Italy studying in Naples where he adopted a late baroque Neapolitan style for his painting. It was likely due to this time and training in Naples that Luzán developed his techniques and his insistence on gaining inspiration from the masters of art, especially the Italian masters. In studying with Luzán, Goya learned the fundamentals of drawing and the lesson of copying from the prints stayed with him for even in his later religious paintings, the influence of Italian engraving can be found.[12] It was only towards the end of his training in Luzán's studio that he began to paint and his initial commissions were all for religious works.

In what is believed to be one of Goya's earliest works, *Apparition of the Virgin of the Pillar,* painted on the doors of a reliquary for a church in Fuendetodos, the influence of Luzán can be seen. The painting was destroyed in the Spanish Civil War, so the images that remain of this work are black and white photographs.[13] Goya painted two other panel paintings depicting Saint Francis and the Virgin as well as a fresco of a canopy held by angels for the same church which was also destroyed. These four paintings, the first of his commissioned works mentioned to his friend Martín Zapater, have all been lost and it is hard to imagine exactly what they looked like. However, what has been mentioned by previous art historians is how Goya's style in each of the paintings was greatly influenced by the teachings of Luzán, and was possibly also based on Italian prints.[14]

In studying the photographs that remain of the *Apparition of the Virgin of the Pilar* we see that Goya painted the doors of the reliquary with a scene depicting the Virgin appearing to Saint James on the bank of the Ebro River in Zaragoza and presenting him with a column and a statue of herself to place upon it. This vision took place where the cathedral of El Pilar stands and the exact location of the apparition is marked by the Santa Capilla within the cathedral.[15] Goya painted the saint in the lower right-hand corner looking up towards heaven, where the Virgin is seated on a cloud and among angels. She looks down upon him and points to the middle of the left door of the reliquary where the statue of the Virgin and the column are depicted. Both the statue and the column are being carried down from the heavens towards earth and the saint. The diagonal formed by the column points towards the top of the right-hand door, into heaven where the Virgin is seated. There is another diagonal formed when looking at where the column and statue are being carried down to where the saint is on earth. The composition of this painting can be compared to Goya's instructor José Luzán's painting *Armario del Tesoro* from 1757. The way in which Luzán composed the saints and holy trinity seated on clouds and surrounded by angels forming compositional diagonals with each other is similar to how Goya structured his composition. This painting marks an important beginning point in Goya's career as his first commission was one of a religious nature and would be the precedent for many of his early paintings which also focused on religious scenes, emphasizing the importance of Catholicism to the artist. Goya would revisit this same story of the apparition of the Virgin of the Pilar several times throughout his career due to the popularity of the story in the city of Zaragoza.

In October of 1771, Goya was requested to present sketches to the committee overseeing the frescoes in the Cathedral of El Pilar. He was competing for the commission to paint a small barrel vault in a choir. Goya submitted a sketch for the commission in November demonstrating how he was planning to compose the scene if he was selected by the committee. Goya needed to provide for his family and wanted to gain as many prestigious commissions as he could in order to become more well known, which made him more competitive against the other two painters competing for the commission by suggesting he could paint the scene for significantly less money. Goya offered to complete the barrel vault for 15,000 reales and he would pay for his assistants and all of the materials. In comparison, a much more established artist, Antonio González Velázquez, suggested that his fresco would cost 25,000 reales as well as all of the expenses of equipment, assistants, and the expenses of his trips between Madrid and Zaragoza to paint the fresco.[16] The other painter competing for the commission was Juan Andrés Merclein, who was the teacher and father-in-law to Goya's second artistic instructor, Francisco Bayeu.[17]

Goya mostly likely knew the competition he was facing and he painted the preliminary sketch for the competition in a very traditional manner that would have been familiar to the committee. While it is not completely known whether this particular sketch survives, it is highly likely that the earliest sketch for the fresco which was attributed to him in the 1980s, was the initial sketch submitted to the committee. Assuming that this was the first sketch submitted by Goya for *Adoration of the Name of God* (Fig. 7.1)[18] one of the most important things to note is how Goya was mimicking the art of his competition in the sketch to prove his talent and ability.

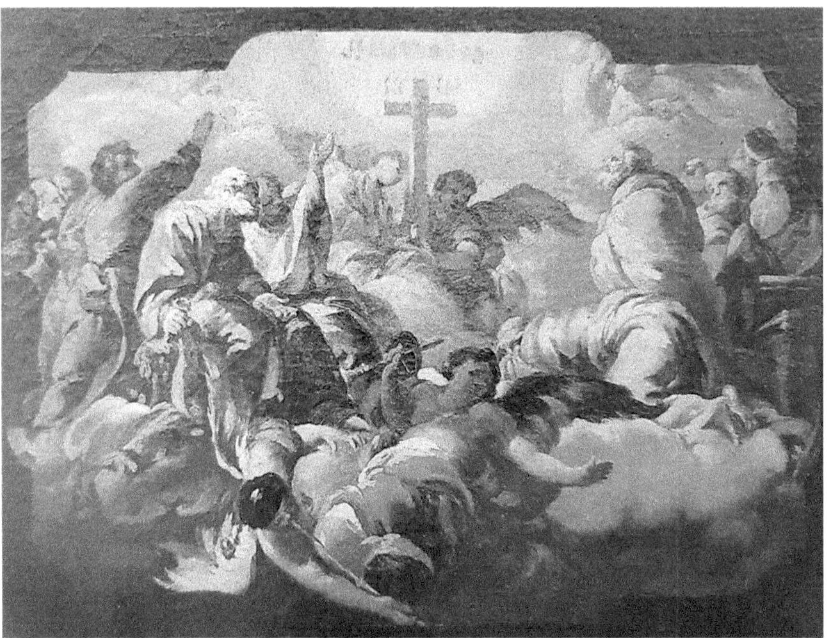

Figure 7.1: Francisco de Goya, First sketch for *Adoration of the Name of God,* 1771. Public Domain

It has been suggested that Goya looked at his competitors' work for inspiration when he painted the sketch as it closely resembles González Velázquez's painting of the same theme in the Santa Capilla in Zaragoza. Due to the style and format in which he painted it, the sketch was even attributed to González Velázquez until the 1980s.[19] It would make sense for Goya to do this as he was a younger, lesser-known artist competing against established artists who were well known in Zaragoza. In completing a sketch in the style of his competitors and offering to complete the fresco at a highly reduced rate, Goya was making a statement to the committee that his work would rival his competitors at a fraction of the cost.

Goya's first sketch for the painting depicts the angels carrying a cross in the upper half of the center of the composition. The cross is set against a yellow background with the upper half of the cross encircled in a lighter yellow, drawing our attention to it. Below the cross and on either side are Christ's apostles looking up towards and paying homage to the cross. Directly below the cross are several angels, one of which is in the center of the composition dressed in red and looking out towards the viewer. Another angel to the left is blowing a trumpet that is cropped at the bottom of the painting. Goya is demonstrating his newly acquired foreshortening techniques that he learned while in Italy in the figures of the two angels. Overall most of the colors of the painting are light and subdued pastel colors with very little bright red which is similar to his painting, *The Victorious Hannibal Seeing Italy from the Alps* of 1771. Goya's painting, therefore, not only mimics the work of his competitor Antonio González Velázquez, but also demonstrates his newly acquired knowledge and training from his Italian sojourn. In doing so, Goya was trying to be competitive with the artists in Spain who had trained and worked in the Italian traditions of painting as he knew this style was sought after by patrons of the time.

Goya received the commission for the vault and was asked to complete a second sketch that would be submitted to the committee as well as the Academia de San Fernando for approval prior to his painting of the vault.[20]

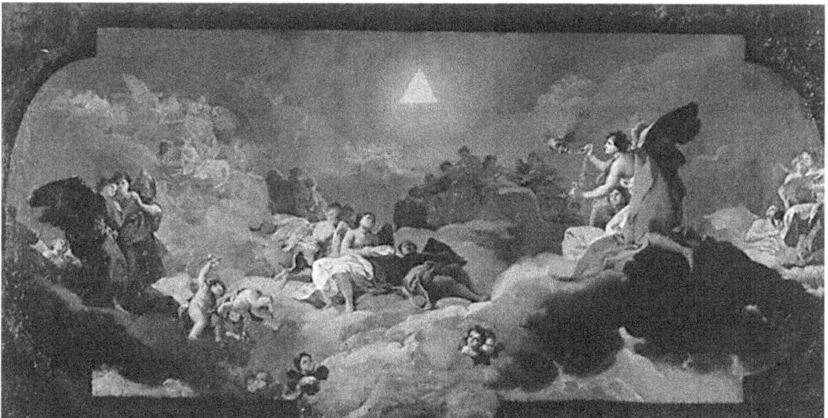

Figure 7.2: Francisco de Goya, Second sketch for *Adoration of the Name of God*, 1771-72. Public Domain

Goya's second sketch (Fig. 7.2) makes significant changes to the design and style of the first. The cross, which had been the main focal point of the original sketch, has been replaced by a triangle in the top center of the composition. The triangle then becomes the main focal point in the composition not just because of its position but also because of how light in color it is compared to the rest of the painting. It is encircled in a slightly darker ring of light, but overall contrasts against the much darker tones of the rest of the painting. Goya has also made significant changes in the second sketch with regard to the figures. While the figures are all still seated on clouds, they are pushed back from the front plane of the painting, making them appear further away from the viewer in the second sketch. Furthermore, many of the figures in the second sketch are also cast in darker light which, combined with the figures' smaller sizes, causes them to be less distinguishable than in the first sketch; this suggests that the figures are now all being depicted as various types of angels rather than having a large portion of the focus be on figures of the apostles, as in the first sketch.

While the figures and scene present us with a style of painting that is similar to that in the first sketch, overall the second sketch has significantly changed the composition and characteristics of the scene.

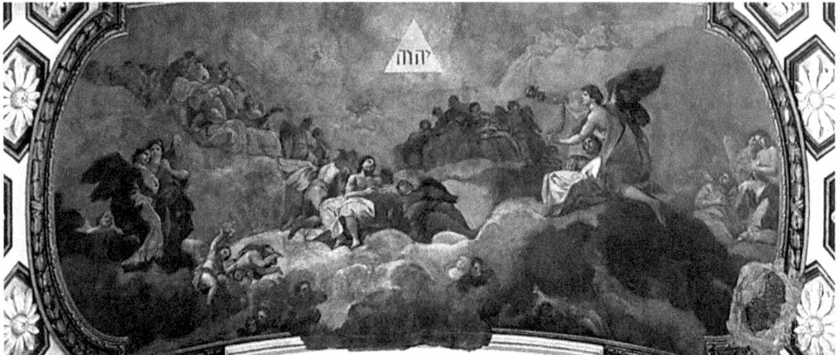

Figure 7.3: Francisco de Goya, *Adoration of the Name of God,* 1772. Public Domain

The fresco of *Adoration of the Name of God* (Fig. 7.3) is similar to the second sketch with only minor changes. The scene ended up being painted overall with lighter yellow tones throughout the composition which differs from the darkness of the second sketch. The rich primary colors that are present in the sketch also become more subdued and painted on a more pastel color palette similar to the first sketch. One of the greatest changes was the addition of Hebrew lettering to spell out the name of God onto the triangle in the top center of the composition causing it to be more distinguishable.[21] The figural compositions of the angels also direct the viewer's attention to the triangle as many of them are looking towards it or pointing to it, which constantly directs the attention back to that focal point in the image. Overall though, the figures and major compositional elements of the painting have not changed position or style from the second sketch to the completed fresco.

Still assuming that the first sketch was the one that Goya presented to the committee for the commission, the second sketch and the final fresco reveal Goya's departure from the compositions of his predecessors and contemporaries in order to add his own artistic interpretation to the scene and to also emphasize his study of religious themes and texts. None of the changes he makes in the second sketch and final painting challenge church doctrine or radically challenge the artistic conventions of his time. However, the compositional and stylistic changes he makes are significant enough to note that in doing so, Goya was making a very bold statement about his painting. With the first sketch being done in the style of his competitor in order to gain the commission and his second sketch making major changes to the composition, Goya effectively cast away the work of his contemporaries in order to promote himself and his artistic style. This second sketch marks one of the first instances in which Goya chooses to paint a religious scene that differs from those of his Spanish contemporaries and predecessors.

In changing the main symbol of God from the image of a cross to that of the Triangle with God written in Hebrew, he seems to have reconsidered how he wanted to represent God within the painting. As the painting was commissioned to be an adoration in the name of God, it makes sense that he chose to change the symbols. The cross, while being a reference to God, is more closely associated with Christ and can be interpreted as part of God or the Son of God. The triangle however represents the Holy Trinity, God the father, Christ, and the Holy Spirit and therefore encompasses all aspects of God rather than just Christ. In adding the Hebrew name of God to the triangle, he fully completes the idea of this being an adoration in his name rather than an adoration with a symbol. The Hebrew lettering seems a little odd for this painting especially considering the troublesome relationship that Spain had with Jewish people. However, as Goya likely attended one of the Pious Schools in Zaragoza, he was likely exposed to more sympathetic viewpoints on Jewish people and their faith. José de Calasanz (who Goya painted later in his career and I discuss this portrait later), the founder of the Pious schools specifically emphasized that everyone should have access to his schools, including Jewish children.[22]

The choice to include the Hebrew lettering was both bold and risky on Goya's part. While the building committee seems to have liked Goya's final fresco, when he bid to complete other vaults in the cathedral, he was turned down in favor of Francisco Bayeau. Bayeau had returned to Zaragoza while also being a court painter in Madrid and effectively took charge of the committee that named painters to work on the different campaigns within the Cathedral. Even though Goya did not receive the next commissions within the Cathedral, his *Adoration of the Name of God*, gave him greater recognition within the city of Zaragoza and he started to receive more commissions, especially for religious paintings. When he was passed up for the new vaults in the Cathedral in favor of Bayeau, this created a rivalry and tension between the two artists that would later and only briefly be tamed by Goya's marriage to Bayeau's sister in 1773.[23] Goya would compete for commissions against Bayeau in both Zaragoza and Madrid for years until the two collaborated on the Cathedral of El Pilar in the early 1780s.

One of the best examples of Goya's use of his religious studies comes from when he was commissioned by the Duke and Duchess of Osuna, two of his most important patrons, to paint two large religious paintings from the life of Saint Francis of Borja to be placed in the family's side chapel in the Valencia Cathedral. The chapel consists of three paintings from the saint's life. The central one was painted by Goya's contemporary, Mariano Salvador Maella and depicted the Saint with the corpse of Saint Isabel, while the two side paintings were completed by Goya. One of these side paintings, discussed a great deal by art historians as one of Goya's most innovative works, is *San Francisco de Borja Asistiendo a un Moribundo Impenitente* (Fig. 7.4), known in English as *Saint Francis Borja at the Deathbed of an Impenitent.* The painting depicts the saint on the right side of the canvas with his hands held up and a crucifix in his right hand, contrasted with a dying man lying on the bed on the left side. San Francisco has a halo of light around his head which is echoed by the window above him, while the dying impenitent is diagonally slanted downward on his bed with demons behind him and his side of the circular window is eclipsed by a curtain. San Francisco's crucifix in his right hand is depicted with blood spurting from Christ's hand in the direction of the impenitent's face.

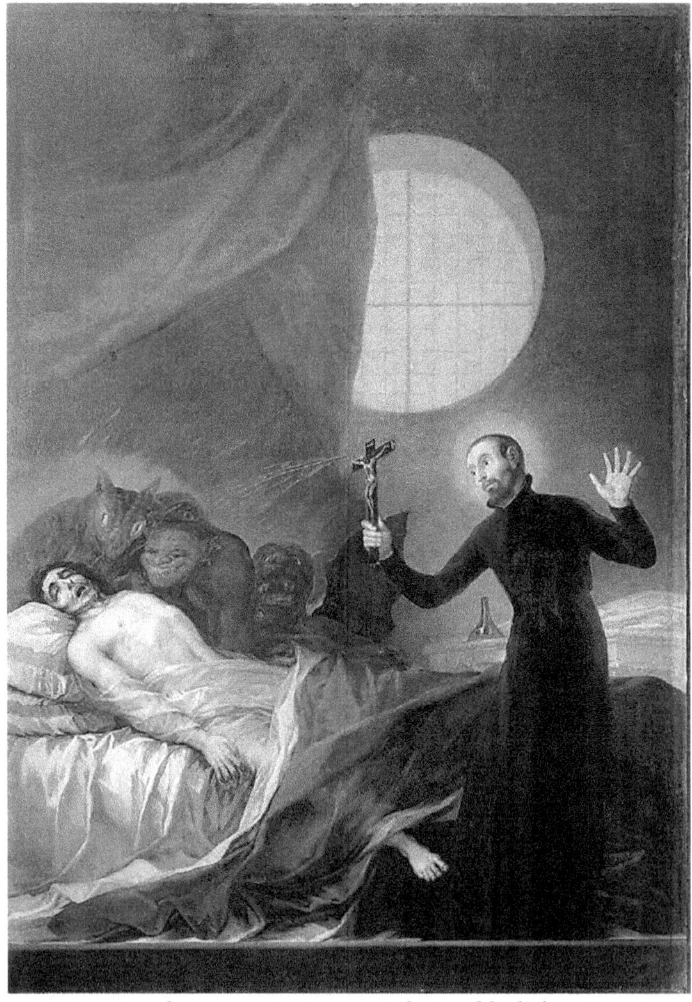

Figure 7.4: Francisco de Goya, *Saint Francis at the Deathbed of an Impenitent*, 1788. Public Domain

The most recent scholarship on this painting focuses on an eighteenth-century account of the saint's life by Álvaro Cienfuegos. As this is the only painting of this subject from the saint's life ever painted, art historians have used this text to explain where Goya may have gained his inspiration to paint this event. Frank Hecks began to discuss the literary example for this painting in his 1985 dissertation thesis, *Supernatural Themes in the Art of Francisco Goya.*[24] Subsequent scholars use his dissertation as the basis for their arguments about the painting as they all quote nearly exactly the same portion of the following passage that Hecks translated:

> "... feeling exasperated, detached its nailed right arm, and placing its hand in that profusely bleeding lacerated wound on its chest, withdrew a fist filled with a lot of blood, and hurled it with indignation at the frowning, denigrated face, saying 'since you scorn this blood, which was shed for your glory, let it serve for your eternal unhappiness.' Then that pitiful man, with an awful, blasphemous shout directed against Jesus Christ, gave up his soul, convulsed by a horrid moan, and it was turned over to the infamous ministers of fire and fright."[25]

In doing so, none of them referred to the original Spanish text and only use what has been translated by Hecks as well as his interpretation of what the text said and how it relates to the painting. Their general argument is that the text from this eighteenth-century account of the life of the saint emphasizes that the scene is one of condemnation as Jesus rips his hand from the crucifix to throw his blood on the dying impenitent, damning him to hell and the demons behind him. However, I believe that the use of the selected passage takes the quote out of context, therefore altering the story and also that the translation is not entirely correct.

Before the part of the story where Christ supposedly condemns the dying man to hell, Cienfuegos writes about how San Francisco de Borja arrives in a town where he is told that a man is dying and will not confess his sins in order to seek eternal salvation. San Francisco wants to help the man and as is the case with much of the rest of the stories from the life of the saint, he looks to his crucifix for guidance. Christ lifts up his head and offers his assistance to San Francisco and says to the saint "Francisco, vè è visitar esse enfermo, que yo assistirè visiblemente contigo en trage de Medico, mientras tu le persuades à que se confiesse luego."[26] Acting upon Christ's advice San Francisco goes to the home of the impenitent to try to save him. When he is there, the impenitent man refuses to confess his sins and instead directs blasphemous comments at the saint.

The saint leaves the home sad and feeling as if he failed. Christ, realizing that the saint was upset about his inability to help the dying man, turns to him in the inn and once again offers his advice by stating that they should return to the house of the impenitent and this time, he would play a larger role in helping to get the man to confess and thus save him from damnation. San Francisco cheers up and rushes back to the home where both of them try to convince the dying man to confess his sins so that they can save him. In an attempt to help cleanse him the crucifix starts spurting blood which then begins to cover the bed with what Christ sacrificed for humanity. The dying man absolutely refuses to confess his sins and we finally come to the part of the story where art historians have interpreted it as a scene of damnation.

However, it is important to examine the original Spanish version of the text in order to better understand exactly what happened according to this account. While the Saint is upset about the impenitent's refusal to confess, Christ states the following before the referenced quote: "Advierte, ò miserable, lo que essa alma rebelde me hà costado! Mira los extremos, que haze mi amor por tu salud eterna, y por recibirle en mis brazos, y en las felicidades de la gloria, si quieres convertirte à penitencia!" [27] This emphasizes that all along in the story, Christ and the saint have been doing all they could to bring about the salvation of the dying man.

This can be further supported by examining the original Spanish text of what all former art historians have quoted as being the condemnation of the impenitent. It reads:

> el qual irritado desclavó el brazo derecho, y metiendo la mano en aquel seno pródigamente roto, sacó cerrado con mucha sangre el puño y se la arrojo con indignación al ceñudo rostro denegrido, diciendo: *Esta sangre, que se derramaba para tu gloria, pues la desprecias, sirva para tu infelicidad eterna.* Entonces aquel desdichado con un clamor pavoroso, y blasfemo contra Jesu Christo, despedió el alma embuelta en un gemido horroroso, y fué entregada á los infames Ministros del fuego, y del espanto. Y Borja entre el horror, la pena, y el susto no acertaba á moverse de aquel infeliz sitio…[28]

In examining the quote, the translation as presented by Hecks says that Jesus says "since you scorn this blood, which was shed for your glory, let it serve for your eternal unhappiness." This however could be an incorrect translation of eighteenth-century Spanish and I propose a better approximation of what Christ said is "This blood which was shed for your glory, because you reject it, may it serve for your eternal unhappiness."

Hecks rearranged the order of the statement which changes the meaning of the quote. Rather than Jesus ripping his hand from the cross pulling out a fist full of blood and throwing it at the impenitent to condemn him, it seems more likely that he is doing so as a last effort to save him while he knows that it will not work. The keyword that emphasizes this is "serve" which Christ uses to emphasize that his blood could either serve one for salvation or in condemnation, but the choice was that of the impenitent as he rejected Christ's shed blood, not that of the saint or Christ himself. When examining the painting, the detail of the blood being thrown onto the impenitent is key to this interpretation that I am proposing. Focusing on the stream of blood from the hand of Christ to the impenitent, it leads directly into the impenitent's gaping mouth. Therefore Christ is throwing his blood into the mouth of the dying perhaps evoking the act of Communion, another sacrament in the Catholic Church that leads to salvation.

Furthermore, it seems unlikely that Goya would want to cast the saint in a negative light considering where the painting was hanging and who the patrons were. The previously mentioned art historians who have written about this painting all argue that Goya has cast the Saint in a negative fashion since he is playing a role in the condemnation of the impenitent. John J. Ciofalo states "In this case Goya is condemning, not mythologizing, the saint. Indeed, Borja, as Goya has depicted him, does not exude saintly or even human, compassion."[29] This, however, seems highly unlikely considering who the patrons were for the painting as well as the fact that it was to be hung in the Valencia Cathedral in the side chapel dedicated to San Francisco de Borja.

The Osunas were among some of Goya's most important patrons and religious painting was and had been one of the most lucrative means by which Goya earned a living. Considering that the Duchess of Osuna had familial ties to San Francisco de Borja and that the Osunas were an Enlightened couple who were highly educated and intelligent, Goya would not have risked offending them by presenting the saint in a negative manner. He also would not have done so in a painting that would hang in a cathedral. Had he done so, this could have had disastrous effects on his career as the Osunas would most likely have never commissioned him to paint for them again, and it would have damaged his reputation as a religious painter.

What is also interesting is that the painting's title in Spanish, as stated by the Cathedral, is completely different than what the English translations have titled it. The title in the Cathedral reads "San Francisco de Borja asistiendo a un moribundo impenitente" which properly translated into English is "San Francisco de Borja assisting a dying impenitent." It therefore seems as if past interpretations of this painting have been quick to jump to conclusions about the intention of the saint and of the crucified Christ and it should be read not as a condemnation but as a failed salvation.

It is believed that this is the only extant painting that portrays this scene from Saint Borja's life. It is not a typical scene that is represented, but rather a very odd one. Therefore, it is obvious that Goya had to have read the life of the saint in order to have come up with this subject for his painting and to be able to do so in a way that was true to the eighteenth-century text on the life of the saint.

This aligns with his early religious education in which he was taught to study the lives of the saints carefully. As in Goya's other paintings of the saints, this painting shows that Goya paid more attention to the textual stories of the lives of the saints, which likely derived from his early religious education, than other artists who typically followed the pictoral conventions of how popular saints were depicted.

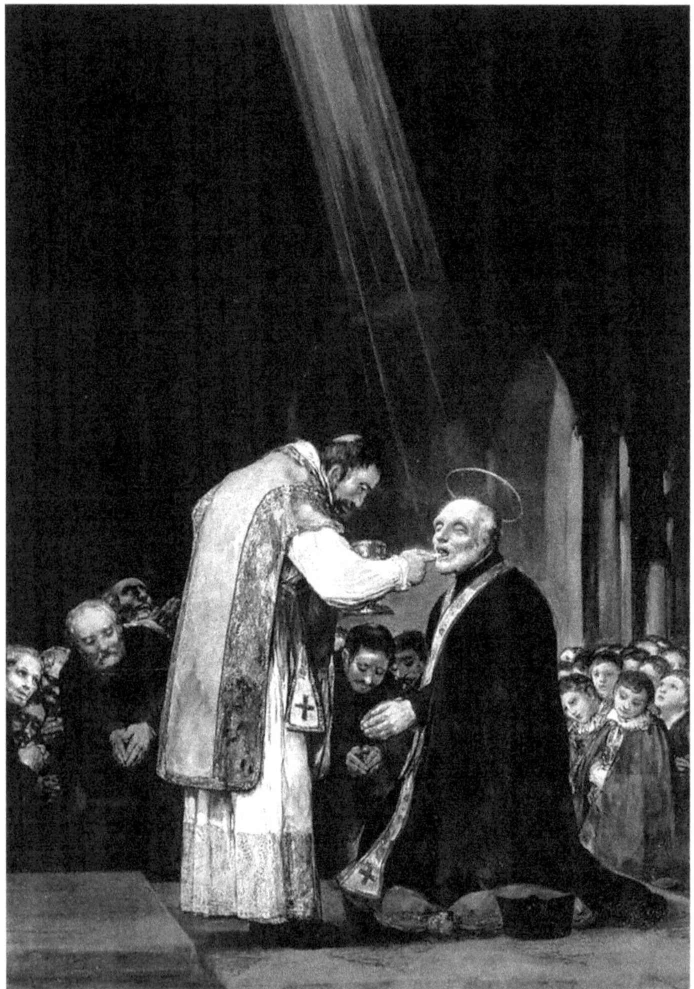

Figure 7.5: Francisco de Goya, *The Last Communion of Saint José de Calasanz,* 1819. Public Domain

As stated earlier, Goya attended a Catholic school as a child and it is likely that it was one of the Pious Schools which had been founded by San José de Calasanz. In one of Goya's late paintings from his final years in Madrid, he was commissioned to paint the *Last Communion of San José de Calasanz* from 1819 (Fig. 7.5) for the church of San Antón del colegio de la Esquelas Pías (the schools that San José de Calasanz founded) in Madrid. The painting was an altarpiece for one of the chapels in which people would receive communion, therefore it has a thematic similarity between the representation and the use of the space in which it was located.[30] Goya's painting, like his *Saint Francis of Borgia at the Deathbed of an Impenitent,* has no precedent in the history of art for this specific scene regarding the saint. Art historians have made comparisons to other last Communion paintings, such as the Domenichino's *Last Communion of Saint Gerome,* but Goya's version is drastically different from those of a similar theme.[31] Goya's painting shows the nearly ninety-one-year-old saint taking his last Communion in the Roman church of Saint Pantaleon surrounded by his pupils and followers.

Goya likely felt a kinship to the saint due to his advanced age at the time, as he was also contemplating his final years. The painting was completed around the same time as Goya's *Self Portrait with Doctor Arrieta* in which Goya depicts himself aged and near death. Goya also has several biographical connections to the saint. San José, like Goya, was from the region of Aragón, and the saint was widely celebrated in the region. Goya would have been exposed to his life story at an early age because of the regional connection. Since he may have attended one of the Escuelas Pias that had been founded by the saint, this would further Goya's knowledge and connection to him. Saint Calasanz was also persecuted by the Inquisition[32] and was a friend to Galileo, just as Goya had been questioned by the Inquisition after the War of Independence for his painting *The Naked Maja.* As there was no precedent for this subject matter for Goya to look to, he likely read one of the texts on the Saint's life as he did with his painting of Saint Francis of Borgia. In doing so, Goya made the work of art more accurately reflect the accounts of the Saint's last communion before his death. This attention to the text again shows the influence of Goya's religious education in which the lives of the saints were studied with vigor.

Throughout this chapter, I have used three main examples of Goya's religious painting to examine how he paid closer attention to the lives of the saints as well as Catholic doctrine which would had been strongly emphasized throughout his religious education as a child. His *Adoration of the Name of God* is from relatively early in his career, his *Saint Francis of Borgia at the Deathbed of an Impenitent* is from the middle of his career, and lastly, *The Last Communion of Saint José Calasanz* came from his late career. He consistently went beyond what was typical of a painter in Spain in studying the subjects of his painting to ensure he was consistent with the textual accounts of the events he painted. Besides being a reflection of the values taught to him in Catholic school, this also reflects well on the ideas of the Enlightenment which emphasize reading and thinking. As many Enlightenment thinkers argued for a better understanding and higher knowledge, Goya, who was influenced by and friends with many of the main Enlightenment thinkers in Spain, embraced these ideas.

Notes

[1] Karissa Bushman, "Anticlericalism in Goya's Works." (PhD diss., University of Iowa, 2013.)

[2] Pierre Gassier and Juliet Wilson, *The Life and Complete Work of Francisco Goya* (New York: Harrison House, 1981), 33.

[3] For more information see Richard Herr, *The Eighteenth Century Revolution in Spain* (Princeton: Princeton University Press, 1969), 3-10.

[4] José Luis Ona González, *Goya y Su Familia en Zaragoza: Nuevas Noticias Biográfica* (Zaragoza: Institución Fernando el Católico, 1997). In this book Ona González has gathered and discusses many of the archival documents pertaining to Goya and his family during the times that they lived in Zaragoza. The first portion of this relates to Goya's parents and when Goya was a small child. Nearly all of the documents listed and written about come from different parishes within Zaragoza announcing events such as Goya's baptism. Documents that were not primarily concerned with religious events were typically ones detailing where the Goya family was living or were partially quoted letters to friends and acquaintances.

[5] Gassier and Wilson, *The Life,* 33.

[6] Ona González, *Goya y Su,* 38.

[7] Janis Tomlinson, *Francisco Goya y Lucientes: 1746-1828* (London: Phaidon Press, 1999), 11.

[8] Arturo Ansón Navarro. *Goya y Aragón: Familia, Amistades y Encargos Artisticos* (Zaragoza: Caja de Ahorros de la Inmaculada de Aragón, 1995), 34-41.

[9] This is discussed at length in *Goya y Aragón* as the author tracked down two priests by the name that Goya mentions in his letter to Zapater who taught children Goya's age at the time. One of the schools was run by the Jesuits before their expulsion from Spain, and the other was from the Order of the Escuelas Pias that was founded by Saint Jose de Calasanz, who Goya painted late in his career. This painting will be discussed towards the end of this chapter.

[10] Otto Bihalji-Merin, *Goya Then and Now: Paintings, Portraits, Frescoes,* Trans. by John E. Woods. (New York: Harcourt Brace Jovanovich, 1981).

[11] For more information on the schools and curriculum that Goya would have been experiencing see Joaquín Lecea, *Escuelas Pias en Aragón en el siglo XVII* (Madrid: Publicaciones ICCE, 1972).

[12] Gassier and Wilson, *The Life,* 35.

[13] This is discussed further in Tomlinson *Francisco Goya,* 11-12.

[14] Ibid., 12.

[15] Ibid.

[16] Arturo Ansón Navarro. *Goya y Aragón Familia,* 88-9.

[17] Ibid. and Tomlinson, *Francisco Goya,* 18.

[18] José Luis Morales y Marín, *Goya, Pintor Religioso* (Zaragoza: Departamento de Cultua y Educación, 1990) 56.

[19] Ibid.

[20] Tomlinson. *Francisco Goya.* 18 and Arturo Ansón Navarro, *Goya y Aragón,* 88.

[21] Arturo Ansón Navarro, *Goya y Aragón,* 88-93 discusses the changes made between the second sketch and the resulting fresco and specifically addresses the triangle with the Hebrew lettering in it.

[22] Josep Domènech i Mira, "Joseph Calasanz" in *PROSPECTS: the quarterly review of comparative education,* vol. XXVII, no. 2, (June 1998): 327-39 discusses the biography and pedagogy of José de Calasanz and how he insisted on the inclusion of Jewish children in the Pious Schools that he founded.

[23] Tomlinson, *Francisco Goya,* 18.

[24] Hecks translates passages of Cardinal Alvaro Cienfuegos, *La heroyca vida, virtudes, y milagros del grande S. Francisco de Borja* (2nd ed., Madrid, 1717). For more information see Frank Irving Hecks, "Supernatural Themes in the Art of Francisco Goya." (Ph.D. thesis, Ann Arbor, 1985.)

[25] This is the exact quote that Janis Tomlinson uses while John J. Ciofalo and Schulz both omit the first two words. For more information see Tomlinson, *Francisco Goya,* 73; John J. Ciofalo, *The Self-portraits of Francisco Goya* (New York: Cambridge University Press, 2001), 99; and Andrew Schulz, "The Expressive Body in Goya's St. Francis Borgia at the Deathbed of an Impenitent," *The Art Bulletin* Vol 80, No. 4 (Dec 1998): 666-8.

[26] Cienfuegos quotes Christ on the crucifix talking to San Francisco de Borja. Cardinal Alvaro Cienfuegos, *La heroyca vida, virtudes, y milagros del grande S. Francisco de Borja* (2nd ed., Madrid, 1717), 266. "Francisco, go visit this sick person, that I will visibly assist with you in a medical suit, while you persuade him to confess later."

[27] Ibid., 267. "I warn you miserable one, of what that rebellious soul has cost me! Look at the extremes my love has done for your eternal health, and for receiving you in my arms, and for your happiness and glory, if you want to convert to penance."

[28] Ibid. "Irritated he unnailed his right arm and putting his hand into his profusely broken breast, removed his closed fist with much blood, and threw it with indignation at the scowling denigrated face saying "This blood which was shed for your glory, because you reject it, may it serve for your eternal unhappiness." Then that wretch with a terrifying cry, and blasphemy against Jesus Christ, the soul left enveloped in a horrible groan, and was delivered to the infamous ministers of fire, and fright. And Borja, amidst horror, sorrow, and shock, could not move from that unhappy place..."

[29] Ciofalo. *Self-Portraits,* 99-100.

[30] Several art history texts have addressed this painting and the commission of it. Most notably information on this painting can be found in Janis Tomlinson, *Francisco Goya,* 250-2.

[31] Ibid., 250.

[32] Josep Domènech i Mira, "Joseph Calasanz," 327-39.

Bibliography

Ansón Navarro, Arturo. *Goya y Aragón: Familia, Amistades y Encargos Artisticos.* Zaragoza: Caja de Ahorros de la Inmaculada de Aragón, 1995.

Bihalji-Merin, Otto. *Goya Then and Now: Paintings, Portraits, Frescoes.* Trans. by John E. Woods. New York: Harcourt Brace Jovanovich, 1981.

Bushman, Karissa. "Anticlericalism in Goya's Works." PhD diss., University of Iowa, 2013.

Cienfuegos, Cardinal Alvaro, *La heroyca vida, virtudes, y milagros del grande S. Francisco de Borja.* 2nd ed., Madrid, 1717.

Ciofalo, John J. *The Self-portraits of Francisco Goya.* New York: Cambridge University Press, 2001.

Domènech i Mira, Josep. "Joseph Calasanz" in *PROSPECTS: the quarterly review of comparative education,* vol. XXVII, no. 2, (June 1998).

Gassier, Pierre and Juliet Wilson. *The Life and Complete Work of Francisco Goya.* New York: Harrison House, 1981.

Hecks, Frank Irving. "Supernatural Themes in the Art of Francisco Goya." Ph.D. thesis, Ann Arbor, 1985.

Herr, Richard. *The Eighteenth Century Revolution in Spain.* Princeton: Princeton University Press, 1969.

Lecea, Joaquín. *Escuelas Pias en Aragón en el siglo XVII.* Madrid: Publicaciones ICCE, 1972.

Ona González, José Luis. *Goya y Su Familia en Zaragoza: Nuevas Noticias Biográfica.* Zaragoza: Institución Fernando el Católico, 1997.

Schulz, Andrew. "The Expressive Body in Goya's St. Francis Borgia at the Deathbed of an Impenitent." *The Art Bulletin* Vol 80, No. 4 (Dec 1998).

Tomlinson, Janis. *Francisco Goya y Lucientes: 1746-1828.* London: Phaidon Press, 1999.

Index

E

F

G

H

Q

R

S

T

U

V

W

www.ingramcontent.com/pod-product-compliance
Lightning Source LLC
LaVergne TN
LVHW050649100826
845148LV00011B/2044

9781648896996